CATALOGING AND MANAGING FILM AND VIDEO COLLECTIONS

ALA Editions purchases fund advocacy, awareness, and accreditation programs for library professionals worldwide.

CATALOGING AND MANAGING FILM AND VIDEO COLLECTIONS

A GUIDE TO USING RDA AND MARC 21

COLIN HIGGINS

An imprint of the American Library Association
CHICAGO 2015

COLIN HIGGINS is Librarian of St Catharine's College, University of Cambridge. He holds a BA in Philosophy from Trinity College Dublin, an MSc in Library Science from the University of Wales, and an MPhil in Philosophy from King's College London, where he is currently completing a PhD. He writes and reviews on libraries for a wide variety of publications. His main research interests are in cataloging and classification, particularly their historical and philosophical aspects. Colin serves on a number of professional committees, and has been chair of the Cambridge College Libraries Forum. He maintains two blogs—*Libraries at the Movies* explores the representation of libraries in film, and *Cutter's Last Stand* addresses contemporary issues in cataloging and classification.

© 2015 by the American Library Association.

Extensive effort has gone into ensuring the reliability of the information in this book; however, the publisher makes no warranty, express or implied, with respect to the material contained herein.

ISBN: 978-0-8389-1299-7 (paper)

Library of Congress Cataloging-in-Publication Data

Higgins, Colin, 1979-
    Cataloging and managing film and video collections : a guide to using RDA and MARC21 / Colin Higgins.
      pages   cm
    Includes bibliographical references and index.
    ISBN 978-0-8389-1299-7
    1. Cataloging of motion pictures. 2. Cataloging of video recordings. 3. Libraries—Special collections—Motion pictures. 4. Libraries—Special collections—Video recordings. I. Title.
    Z695.64.H54 2015
    025.3'473—dc23   2014040988

Cover design by Kirstin Krutsch. Image © Shutterstock, Inc. Composition by Dianne M. Rooney in Minion Pro and Gotham typefaces.

♾ This paper meets the requirements of ANSI/NISO Z39.48-1992 (Permanence of Paper).

Printed in the United States of America

19 18 17 16 15   5 4 3 2 1

CONTENTS

Acknowledgments vii
List of Abbreviations ix

	Introduction	*1*
1	A Brief History of Film and Its Formats	*11*
2	Production and Distribution, Cast and Crew	*29*
3	Content	*57*
4	Technical Features	*95*
5	Television	*123*
6	Older and Unusual Formats	*137*
7	MARC 21 Records and AACR2	*151*
8	Managing the Collection	*159*
9	Streaming Video and the Future of the Optical Disc	*173*

Further Resources 185

APPENDIXES

A   Sample Records   *195*

B   Symbols Found on DVDs, Blu-ray Discs,
      and Their Cases   *205*

  Index   207

ACKNOWLEDGMENTS

THIS VOLUME WOULD NEVER HAVE BEEN COMPLETED HAD I not received consistent support from many people. I'd like to thank my colleagues throughout the libraries of the University of Cambridge, and within the academic and support communities of St Catharine's College, for their inspiration, their conversation, and their patience. In particular, I would like to express my gratitude to Paul Hartle, Simon Summers, and Jean Thomas for granting me time away from the library, enabling me to write. And to Lucy Delap, who challenged my early complacency and doubts, and convinced me for the first time that this book was realizable.

Over the past few years, a number of librarians have suffered under my cataloging tutelage, and tolerated my obsessions with obscure films and MARC fields. Sophie Fisher, Jo Harcus, Carolyn Keim, Victoria Morris, and the indispensable Sarah Fletcher have all been interested, critical, and skeptical about film cataloging in just the right measures. Sarah and Victoria generously gave their time to read draft versions of the text.

Thanks are due to others who read the work in various states of completion, and highlighted an embarrassing number of errors and infelicities: Ros Brown, Céline Carty, Greta de Groat, Bethany Levrault, Lawrence Morris, and Jennifer Snoek-Brown. Muireann Maguire and Jay Weitz read every word and provided invaluable feedback and advice. For the errors that remain, I accept responsibility.

I am immensely grateful to the editors who have overseen this project: Christopher Rhodes, for his initial guidance and enthusiasm, Patrick Hogan and Angela Gwizdala, for overseeing the book's production with amiable efficiency, and Helayne Beavers, who cleansed the manuscript of its grammatical transgressions, and the worst of its contrariness.

My thanks also to Raphael Woolf and Shaul Tor, supervisors of my long-drawn-out doctoral thesis, and Mark Textor, my Director of Postgraduate Studies, who trusted my claim that writing this book wasn't just an excuse for failing to read Plato.

This book is dedicated with love and admiration to Muireann Maguire.

ABBREVIATIONS

The following abbreviations are used throughout this book. Where numbers and letters follow the abbreviations, they refer to text in the published editions listed below.

AACR2—Anglo-American Cataloguing Rules, prepared under the direction of the Joint Steering Committee for Revision of AACR, 2nd edition, 2002 revision, 2005 update (Chicago: American Library Association, 2002–2005). Accessible through Cataloger's Desktop (https://desktop.loc.gov) and the RDA Toolkit.

AMIM—*Archival Moving Image Materials: A Cataloging Manual,* 2nd edition, the AMIM Revision Committee, Motion Picture, Broadcasting, and Recorded Sound Division, Library of Congress (Washington, DC: Library of Congress, Cataloging Distribution Service, 2000). Accessible through Cataloger's Desktop.

CC:DA—Committee on Cataloging: Description and Access (CC:DA), an ALA committee charged with developing policy positions on RDA, and discussing possible revisions and additions to the standard.

FRBR—Functional Requirements for Bibliographic Records, the conceptual model upon which RDA is founded. Written by a study group of the International Federation of Library Associations and Institutions (IFLA), the FRBR Final Report was published in Munich by K. G. Saur Verlag in 1998. Amended and corrected PDF and HTML versions are available

ix

free at www.ifla.org/publications/functional-requirements-for-bibliographic-records.

IMDB—The Internet Movie Database (www.imdb.com). Founded in 1990, and one of the first websites to appreciate the potential of hyperlinking content across different web pages, IMDb remains the most extensive and authoritative source for information about films and television programs, and is indispensable to the film cataloger. It has been owned by Amazon.com since 1998.

LC-PCC PS—Library of Congress-Program for Cooperative Cataloging Policy Statements, accessible through the RDA Toolkit and Cataloger's Desktop. These statements provide guidance on the Library of Congress and Program for Cooperative Cataloging interpretations of RDA rules. They are shorter and less prescriptive than the Library of Congress Rule Interpretations (LCRI) for AACR2.

LCSH—Library of Congress Subject Headings, the most widely used controlled vocabulary of subjects for libraries. LCSH, though still important for film cataloging, is less significant for audiovisual than for monograph materials. Available through Classification Web (https://classificationweb.net).

LCGFT—Library of Congress Genre/Form Terms. Moving image terms were moved to a stand-alone thesaurus in 2011, so are now formally separate from LCSH. LCGFT offers a concise vocabulary of film genres and forms, based on literary warrant, with helpful definitions for the layman. Available through Classification Web and on the OLAC website (http://olacinc.org/drupal/capc_files/GenreFormHeadingsList.pdf).

NAF—Name Authority File, maintained by the Library of Congress and Name Authority Cooperative Program of the Program for Cooperative Cataloging and updated daily; available free at http://authorities.loc.gov.

OLAC—Online Audiovisual Catalogers, "an international organization for catalogers concerned with all types of nonprint materials." Among other activities, OLAC publishes a range of useful and practical guides to assist film cataloging.

PCC—Program for Cooperative Cataloging, a cooperative effort to develop, clarify, and unify interoperable metadata standards worldwide, and increase the quality and availability of bibliographic records and authority files. PCC has over eight hundred active institutional members and a secretariat drawn from LC staff. It has four programs, covering bibliographic standards, serials cataloging, name authorities, and subject authorities.

RDA—Resource Description and Access, a cataloging standard "designed for the digital world and an expanding universe of metadata users." Accessible online by subscription through the RDA Toolkit (http://access.rdatoolkit.org). Annual print update editions are published by the American Library Association, the Canadian Library Association, and the Chartered Institute of Library and Information Professionals. Changes to the text of RDA continue to be made (over 500 updates were implemented in April 2014), so use of the online RDA Toolkit is advised.

INTRODUCTION

Why Collect Film?

A single grainy shot, forty-six seconds long, from a motionless camera.

It is noon. Streaming out of a French factory come women in long white skirts and wide-brimmed sun hats, men in caps and boaters, a dog pouncing at a bicycle, and finally two horses. Some of the workers look nervously across the street where, invisible to us, all too visible to them, sat Louis Lumière, their boss. They'd been warned to act as though nothing extraordinary was happening, and most importantly of all, not to look at the camera, but some still turn towards it as they rush past. It is a sunny spring day, and everyone looks well. Not one knew that they would be remembered that way for eternity, the permanent players in what was later known as *La Sortie de l'Usine Lumière à Lyon* (*Workers Leaving the Lumiere Factory*) (1895), popularly regarded as the first motion picture.

A few months later in Lyon, Louis and his brother Auguste projected a different scene to a curious audience. Their short film showed a train of holidaymakers pulling in to a Provençal station. At first hidden by the crowd awaiting its arrival, the train enters the frame on the right and approaches ever closer until it fills the left of the screen. The first audiences of *l'Arrivée d'un Train en Gare de La Ciotat* (*The Arrival of a Train at La Ciotat Station*) (1895) were (allegedly) so frightened by the oncoming celluloid locomotive that that they rushed to the back of the room to avoid being hit. The Lumières may not have invented film (Louis Le Prince's *Roundhay Garden Scene* predated their first productions by seven years), but the pseudo-historical pack of panicked cinemagoers shows how, by combining technology, entertainment, verisimilitude, and human interest, the brothers forged a new art form. The early history of film is a tangle of uncertain patrimony, yet if anyone deserves to be called the father of cinema, it is Louis Lumière.

Ever since its invention, film has offered valuable descriptions and reflections of society and, for better or worse, it is the means by which many people engage with history, and interact with unfamiliar societies. Film is one of the most engaging, lucrative, and successful forms of popular entertainment. Film can also be great art. As there are good and bad books, so there are good and bad films. As two of the most popular media through which storytelling takes place, there are cultural similarities between books and films, and a symbiotic productive relationship between them. In recent years, between one-half and two-thirds of the films nominated for the Best Picture Academy Award have been based on preexisting literary works.[1] Spin-off publications promote cinematic releases, and are often a source of significant revenue in their own right.

The greatest libraries have always collected books *and* other cultural products. In 1906, Melvil Dewey wrote that

> what we call books have no exclusive rights in a library. The name "library" has lost its etymologic meaning and means not a collection of books, but the central agency for disseminating information, innocent recreation or, best of all, inspiration among the people. Whenever this can be done better, more quickly or cheaply by a picture than a book, the picture is entitled to a place on the shelves and in the catalogue.[2]

Since 1989, the Library of Congress has committed to long-term film preservation through the Library's Audio-Visual Conservation Center, which adds twenty-five "culturally, historically or aesthetically significant" films to the National Film Registry every year.[3] The socioeconomic pressures that have drawn people back to public libraries have implications for the lending of films. A 2006 survey found that "Americans' biggest complaint about going to the movies is the cost."[4] To some of the constituencies that libraries would like to target more effectively, films have greater cultural appeal than books.

And yet many librarians hesitate to embrace film, and develop film collections half-heartedly. This reluctance has a variety of causes, among which are an ever-present (if dilute) bibliophilia, a discomfort with the commercial aspects of the film industry, and unclear collection-development policies. But in their stated preference for books over films, librarians are not being old-fashioned; they are just reflecting a social prejudice that the former are somehow superior to the latter. The two are often compared as though they were in competition, and books usually win. "The movie was good, but the book was better," is said so often that the phrase has lost all meaning. How many times have you heard the reverse? Yet the sentiment doesn't really have any meaning to start with: books are not better than films, just as the Venus de Milo isn't better than Titian's Venus of Urbino. We may prefer one or the other, but there are natural limits to their similarities beyond which any comparison is nonsensical. As the sculpture and the painting both belong in the Louvre, so books and films both belong in libraries. In arguing for the relevance and importance of film, this volume calls for a greater appreciation of its intellectual and artistic capacities.

The film-shy librarian may believe that the physical and informational complexity of DVDs and Blu-ray Discs makes their purchase uneconomical. It is thought that cataloging film is difficult and time-consuming. A cursory glance at some of the bibliographic description out there will show a diversity of inconsistent practice. These concerns, although very real, can be addressed.

AACR2 was developed partly to accommodate non-book materials, but its intellectual forebears can be traced back to at least 1876, when Charles Ammi Cutter published his *Rules for a Printed Dictionary Catalog,* the first "Object" of which was "To enable a person to find a book."[5] RDA is often found wanting when it comes to instructions on describing film, but unlike AACR2 and its precursors, at least it claims to have "the scope needed to support . . . comprehensive coverage of all types of content and media" (RDA 0.3.1), and it proposes to offer catalogers a nominally format-neutral standard.

Excellent rule books for cataloging film using the prevailing bibliographic standards have been available since 1981, when Nancy Olson's volume on audiovisual cataloging was published.[6] This book, and the more specific and comprehensive guidelines published by OLAC in 2002 and 2008, provided clear and accessible perspectives on cataloging films using AACR2.[7] The literature has evolved with the standards. There are a few free online guides to RDA and MARC 21 film cataloging, the most impressive of which is provided online by the Stanford University Libraries.[8] This volume aims to expand upon the instruction found in these guides, and where necessary, reinterpret them. Even more so than with monographic material, when cataloging films issued on disc the standards are open to interpretation, for they are frequently unclear, and unappreciative of the complexity of both form and physical manifestation. The rules of RDA and MARC 21 are never broken here, but at times they are bent by necessity. My guide attempts to be the most comprehensive published to date, while recognizing that RDA is still evolving, and that new cataloging practices have yet to become definitive, standardized, or orthodox.

This book aims to be more than another guide to cataloging and managing collections. It also offers librarians a primer on comprehending film itself—its history, its formats, its vocabularies, and its participants. To catalog films, we must first understand them. Books are simple material objects. The way they encode and embed their content is recognizable and understandable to anyone who can read. Optical discs are more complex. It is no good instructing catalogers to enter the words "anamorphic widescreen" or "dual-layer" into particular MARC 21 fields. Catalogers need to know what these words, and the related alphabet soup of acronyms (PAL, NTSC, EAN, BBFC), mean. Just as you shouldn't catalog a book if you don't know what pages or publishers are, so you shouldn't catalog a DVD or Blu-ray Disc if you don't understand what you are providing a description of, access to, and guidance upon.

This complexity is not solely due to unfamiliar technical vocabulary. Catalogers know what functions authors, editors, and illustrators perform. What about cinematographers? Producers? Art directors? The role of an actor is straightforward, and we understand what it involves because, in the words of Marlon Brando, "acting is the least mysterious of all crafts. . . . Most people do it all day long."[9] We have a sense that the role of the director is important—they somehow make a film by telling everyone else what to do. But what does this mean when it comes to creating a catalog record? Do these individuals belong, in the old-fashioned terms, in a main or added entry? Should we include them in a statement of responsibility appended to the film's title? Where else, if anywhere, should we record these people, and how should we qualify them? And what about, for example, the cinematographer—is his or her work significant enough to warrant inclusion in our catalog records? Is it ever significant enough that it might inform our purchasing decisions? This volume aims to aid your comprehension by answering these kinds of questions.

Despite the prominent place of film in the social, cultural, and economic spheres of contemporary society, training in the cataloging and management of film library collections has always been "rare and inconsistent.... What [has been] surprising (and disconcerting) is the persistence of this gap in professional training."[10] I aim to go some way toward meeting this challenge by intertwining guidance on the technical aspects of cataloging optical discs with, to misquote Woody Allen, everything you always wanted to know about film, but were afraid to ask. The confident application of rules and the use of standard vocabularies and workflows undermines the assumption that collecting optical discs is an inefficient use of monetary resources.

Films are both temporally and physically fragile; this much is true. Demand for most titles drops off quickly. Optical discs are easily damaged. Yet good collection-development policies answer questions about the currency of titles and the physical storage of discs: you just need to apply the same principles as you do to the purchase of books. You need to be well informed. It is also true that the evolution in home video formats and current technological trends are altering the ways viewers consume film. We are moving from DVDs to Blu-ray Discs while puzzling over the fact that it seems like only yesterday that we were replacing VHS. The problem of technological obsolescence is a real one. But the enthusiasm with which librarians have pursued potential ways of delivering e-books despite even more rapid evolution of standards and gadgets, demonstrates how libraries can develop models to provide other digital material, such as streaming media. The ways by which we provide access to, organize, and describe these emerging technologies are not likely to differ greatly from our approaches to managing collections of optical discs.

This book is written for anyone with an interest in the cataloging and/or management of library film collections. I hope it will be useful both to librarians who are cinephiles and those with only a passing interest in film. It presupposes knowledge of the basic precepts of descriptive cataloging using RDA and MARC 21, and where cataloging principles do not differ between optical discs and books, this knowledge will be assumed. My principal aim is to provide a useful reference text for the cataloging of film collections, not a primer on cataloging per se.

However, I don't presume that readers will have an extensive knowledge of the history of filmmaking, or of optical disc formats. The vocabulary of film, like that used to describe optical discs, can frighten people. This book breaks down and explains the language of film. If you already feel comfortable with this, and with the technical aspects of DVDs and Blu-ray Discs, I hope you will find new material to complement your existing knowledge. At the very least, this volume attempts to gather information that has previously been scattered.

The first chapter presents a history of cinema and the formats on which films have been stored and distributed, along with a brief historical overview of audiovisual librarianship. It will explain why DVDs and, increasingly, Blu-ray Discs, have become the preferred medium for sales of films after their theatrical release.

Chapters 2 through 6 discuss instructions on how to catalog DVDs and Blu-ray Discs with a description of the environment in which the production and distribution of film takes place. Avoiding the temptation to organize by means of FRBR categories, or other unhelpful pseudo-philosophical distinctions, I have themed the chapters under broad, practical topics, the better (hopefully) to assist with a holistic understanding. Introductory text provides the context to the content recorded in MARC 21 bibliographic fields. MARC may be unsuited to the age of linked data and cloud computing (and RDA seems to have been consciously developed with the aim of making it obsolete), but any practical cataloging guide is still more usefully organized by MARC fields than by RDA chapters. So chapters 2 to 4 provide three sequential groups of MARC 21 fields, dealing, quite broadly, with people, content, and technical features—or the who, what, and how of films on optical disc.

Chapter 2 covers the individuals and organizations who make film: its producers, cast, and crew. Descriptions of what film people do are presented alongside information about how to acknowledge this input in good cataloging practice. This chapter also outlines film's publication and distribution history, and the MARC fields in which these details are recorded, including the standard numbers assigned for the purposes of identification during distribution and sale.

Chapter 3 deals with film titles and the intellectual and artistic content of optical discs, incorporating subject and genre headings. The main entry in a MARC record for a film on DVD or Blu-ray Disc is normally a title statement. Its recording is complicated by the differing title placements, forms, and statements of responsibility found within the film and the physical object upon which it is stored. This complexity will be unravelled, and guidelines given on the recording of accompanying material (e.g., additional special features) and related titles (e.g., novels from which films are adapted).

Chapter 4 covers the technical features of optical discs. The abbreviations and technical terms found on a DVD or Blu-ray Disc case will be explained, as will the MARC fields in which they should be recorded.

Chapter 5 covers the cataloging of television programs, and chapter 6 the cataloging of older formats, focusing on VHS and photochemical film. Recognizing that AACR2 is still alive, chapter 7 provides a sequential list of the MARC 21 bibliographic fields in which AACR2 practice differs from RDA.

Collection management is the topic of chapter 8, which covers collection development, storage, classification, and censorship, among other issues. The final chapter looks to the slow death of the optical disc, and its inevitable replacement by video streaming; it also explains what streaming is, how it works, how to catalog it, and the ways in which it might be integrated into library services.

A bibliographical afterword advises readers on how to keep up-to-date with contemporary trends in audiovisual librarianship. Useful websites, publications, and blogs are listed. For those interested in film theory and criticism, direction is given to introductory works. Finally, two appendixes: the first provides sample MARC records (in RDA format) for the range of material objects described in the previous chapters, the second provides images of the most common symbols found on optical discs and their accompanying material.

Notwithstanding the widespread use of optical discs for computer software, videogames, education and training, and archival storage, this book focuses almost exclusively on film and television. Throughout this book I give preference to the word *film* over its synonyms. The words *cinema, film, movie,* and *motion picture* are sometimes used interchangeably, sometimes differentiated. But they're also loaded terms—the Urban Dictionary states that *film* is "a word that people who think they are smart use instead of 'motion picture,' 'picture,' or 'movie'" (www.urbandictionary.com/define.php?term=film&defid=5758914). It is the second-most popular definition but not quite fair—in Britain, for example, the word *movie* is rarely used even for the most action-packed blockbuster. Many film theorists maintain a distinction between *filmic,* the relationship between the production and the surrounding world, and *cinematic,* which relates to structure and aesthetics.

The three most commonly used words are distinguished by film critic and historian James Monaco: "'movies,' like popcorn, are to be consumed;

'cinema' . . . is high art, redolent of esthetics; 'film' is the most general term with the fewest connotations."[11] This work agrees with Monaco's suggestion that *film* is the least troublesome word. It is also in keeping with contemporary library practice in assigning subject headings: the Library of Congress (LC) uses the word *film* to refer "to works that are originally recorded and released on motion picture film, on video, or digitally."[12] Unfortunately, as in many aspects of cataloging, we are burdened with the practices associated with superseded formats. LC was not clarifying the use of the word *film* against the perceived confusion with *movie* but with the literary warrant associated with the earlier use of *video*, which is still frequently used in cataloging and classification standards for a variety of purposes. When cataloging, we are sometimes forced to use this word, but in writing about the cultural objects of this book's concern, *film* is favored as more neutral and global, with an older provenance than *movie*.

RDA is still subject to regular amendment, and the MARC 21 bibliographic format continues to evolve to accommodate it. Communities of practice have yet to develop definitive best practices. This volume interprets RDA one way—there are others. However, this book assumes that the implementation of RDA is a done deal, and that catalogers will be using this standard in the records they create. For better or worse, we now live in a post-AACR2 world. This volume reflects that fact while acknowledging that although some libraries may still be cataloging only in AACR2, most will be maintaining it for older copy-cataloged records, some libraries may not be using either format, and some readers may not be involved in cataloging at all.

NOTES

1. Of films nominated for Best Picture, 39.6 percent have been based on a preexisting novel, and a further 18.1 percent on a play. Nate Silver and Walter Hickey, "Best-Picture Math," *Vanity Fair,* March 2014, www.vanityfair.com/hollywood/2014/03/oscar-winner-predictions-nate-silver.
2. Melvil Dewey, "Library Pictures," *Public Libraries* 11 (1906): 10–11.
3. National Film Preservation Board, Frequently Asked Questions About the National Film Registry, 2013, www.loc.gov/film/filmnfr.html.
4. Joseph Carroll, Americans' Biggest Gripe About Going to the Movies: Cost, 2006, www.gallup.com/poll/25990/americans-biggest-gripe-about-going-movies-cost.aspx.
5. Charles A. Cutter, *Rules for a Printed Dictionary Catalogue* (Washington, DC: Government Printing Office, 1876), 10.

6. Nancy B. Olson, *Cataloging of Audiovisual Materials: A Manual Based on AACR2* (DeKalb, IL: Minnesota Scholarly Press, 1981).

7. DVD Cataloging Guide Update Task Force, Cataloging Policy Committee, Online Audiovisual Catalogers, Guide to Cataloging DVD and Blu-ray Discs Using AACR2R and MARC 21, 2008 Update, www.olacinc.org/drupal/capc_files/DVD_guide_final.pdf.

8. Metadata Department, Stanford University Libraries, Videos—Cataloging (RDA), 2014, https://lib.stanford.edu/metadata-department/clone-video-cataloging-guidelines.

9. Rick Lyman, "Marlon Brando, Oscar-Winning Actor, Is Dead at 80," *The New York Times,* July 2, 2004, www.nytimes.com/2004/07/02/movies/02CND-BRANDO.html.

10. Lori Widzinski, "The Evolution of Media Librarianship: A Tangled History of Change and Constancy," *Studies in Media and Information Literacy Education* 1, no. 3 (August 2001): 1.

11. James Monaco, *How to Read a Film: Movies, Media, Multimedia,* 3rd ed. (New York: Oxford University Press, 2000), 228.

12. *Library of Congress Subject Headings Manual* (Washington, DC: Library of Congress Cataloging Policy and Support Office, 2008–), Instruction Sheet H 1913.

CHAPTER 1

A BRIEF HISTORY OF FILM AND ITS FORMATS

A History of Film

The Early Years

The inventors of cinema are said to have called it "an invention without any future."[1] Yet in 1895, three days after Christmas, the Lumière brothers were the first to do something that would change the world.

It began in the Salon Indien of the Grand Café in Paris. Their father introduced ten of their films, each less than a minute long, to an audience of thirty-three spectators who had each paid one franc to gain entry. The first Lumière film, *La Sortie de l'Usine Lumière à Lyon* (*Workers Leaving the Lumière Factory in Lyon*), depicted the staged emergence of workers from a factory.

The brothers were not the first to film moving images, nor the first to show them publicly. They were not, as is popularly imagined, the inventors of film, but the inventors of the *cinema;* theirs was the first commercial public projection. The brothers had hosted private showings for audiences of industrialists, photographers, and engineers; they had even shown films at the Sorbonne. Though they quickly realized the potential of their new enterprise to generate more than thirty-three francs, they continued to view the motion picture as an extension of still photography, and were mainly interested in its industrial, scientific, and anthropological applications, as their matter-of-fact titles indicate. They embarked on a world tour the following year. Despite his success and the adulation heaped upon him, Louis, the director of the pair, retired from filmmaking in 1900.[2]

Among those in the audience that first night was a different type of would-be filmmaker. Georges Méliès was a cobbler, a theater-owner, and a magician. He offered the brothers 10,000 francs for one of their machines. When they turned him down, he built his own motion-picture camera. In contrast to Lumière productions, the Méliès films were full of monsters, haunted castles, scantily clad women, and magic tricks. His most famous film is a ten-minute fiction of man's first voyage to the moon, *Le Voyage dans la Lune* (*A Trip to the Moon*) (1902). Méliès directed 531 films over a seventeen-year career.[3]

The growth in filmmaking was rapid during the first few years of experimentation. In 1893, Thomas Edison had demonstrated both a motion picture camera, the kinetograph, and a device that allowed individual viewers to watch short films through an eyepiece, the kinetoscope.[4] Many innovations followed. Spurred by Edison's continuous modifications, trans-Atlantic rivalries, and an insatiable appetite for the new form of entertainment, the next decade saw engineering, commercial, and artistic talents combine to change the business of filmmaking from a hobby for nerdish technologists into an industry driven by showman capitalists. A set of definitive standards, such as frame speed (sixteen to twenty-four frames per second) and film width (35 mm), quickly coalesced. The first ten years of experimentation also saw the evolution of techniques recognizable as the grammar of film—multiple shots leading to the development of continuity, the construction of film narrative, innovations in storytelling that used close-ups, point-of-view shots, and action sequences.[5]

The first films were shown in vaudeville theaters and traveling shows. In 1906, a couple of enterprising businessmen set up a *nickelodeon*, a small storefront theater in Pittsburgh, dedicated to showing of motion pictures. By 1908, there were eight thousand nickelodeons and, two years later, twenty-six million Americans were making weekly visits. Over the next decade films grew longer, and the first "movie-stars" became objects of adoration and unceasing attention. Enhancements such as intertitles and musical accompaniment became part of audience expectation. Nickelodeons funded the expansion of production companies, first based in New York, before the stranglehold of Edison's patents led to a widespread decampment to Southern California, where filmmakers hoped to avoid Edison's lawsuits. The newly wealthy producers, and the stars they created, preferred the endless Pacific summers to the Big Apple's seasonality, and the scenery was conducive to the filming of Westerns, then the favorite genre of American moviegoers. By the 1920s, Hollywood had become synonymous with American film production. Powerful and efficient conglomerates developed the "studio system," producing hundreds of films every year, most now lost, driven and fronted by contract actors and actresses.[6] It was the age of Douglas Fairbanks, Mary Pickford, Buster Keaton, and Charlie Chaplin.[7]

The Coming of Sound and Hollywood's Golden Age

The first widely distributed sound film, *The Jazz Singer*, was released in 1927. By the end of 1929, nearly all films released by Hollywood were "talkies." As David Pierce has written recently, no other "artforms emerged as quickly, came to an end as suddenly, or vanished more completely than the silent film."[8] There are few better accounts of the chaos, structural change, and experimental flux brought about by the transition to sound than those produced by filmmakers themselves. If you want to know what happened in these years, watch *Singin' in the Rain* (1952) and *The Artist* (2011). If you want to know why the "Golden Age" ushered in by sound ended, watch *Sunset Boulevard* (1950) and *The Bad and the Beautiful* (1952).

Only the wealthiest studios had the capacity to invest in the expensive technologies needed for synchronous sound and image. Within a few years, five (20th Century Fox, Metro-Goldwyn-Mayer, Paramount Pictures, RKO Pictures, and Warner Brothers) became dominant. The Golden Age lasted about twenty years. During this time, the power of the five major studios was almost total. They held exclusive rights and ownership over everything—the sound stages, the equipment, and the people, because directors and actors were shackled by long-term contracts. Most importantly, the "Majors" owned the distribution mechanism, with power to insist that movie theaters showed only their releases.[9]

What seems almost incredible now is that so many great films came out of this narrow, cutthroat, commercial oligarchy. The era lasted for a generation.[10] Yet as the appeal of stars in melodramas waned, talented filmmakers were influenced by the more experimental cinema of postwar Europe, and found ways to work outside the studio system. Legislation fractured the monopolistic structures in the 1950s. Americans spent more of their free time in front of their new television sets and less in small-town picture-houses, though drive-in theaters increased in popularity as more people bought cars, and social mores became more relaxed.[11] These challenges spurred Hollywood to innovate once again—by the mid-1950s more than half of its productions were in color.[12]

From *Breathless* to Bilbo Baggins

On the other side of the Atlantic, a group of critics writing for the *Cahiers du Cinéma* magazine revolutionized filmmaking when they put away their typewriters and picked up hand-held cameras. The *Nouvelle Vague* (New Wave) married youthful iconoclasm with a deep appreciation for classic Hollywood. Its most lasting influence is the cult of the *auteur* director. American film school students influenced by the Nouvelle Vague in the 1960s (among them Francis Ford Coppola and Martin Scorsese) led the "New Hollywood" movement in the 1970s.

The movement first asserted itself with the release of *Bonnie and Clyde* in 1967. In one of his first reviews, Roger Ebert foresaw that it would become "a milestone in the history of American movies."[13] New Hollywood was committed to realism, influenced by the counterculture, narratively experimental, and pulsing with youthful vibrancy.

If the 1970s were the best decade for film since the Golden Age, the 1980s, in this author's opinion, must rank among the worst. Among the highest-grossing films in 1973 included the (now classic) *The Sting*, *The Exorcist*, *Serpico*, *Badlands*, and *Don't Look Now*. Ten years later the box-office hits were *Flashdance*, *Jaws 3D*, *Superman 3*, *Octopussy*, and *Staying Alive*. Though use of the term predates the 1980s, by the early years of that decade the blockbuster had become a genre in its own right and with it came the sequel.[14] Not all of these were bad films, but of the one hundred greatest American Films named by the American Film Institute to celebrate the centenary of film in 1998, only six were released in the 1980s (and only one, 1986's *Platoon*, in the second half of the decade).[15]

In the 1990s, intelligently expressed sentimentality seemed to offer producers guaranteed returns (*Forrest Gump* [1994], *Sleepless in Seattle* [1993],

Titanic [1997]). In the author's opinion, an interesting trend saw action stars problematize the Reaganite certainties they had once personified (Eastwood in *Unforgiven* [1990], Schwarzenegger in *Terminator 2: Judgment Day* [1991], Stallone in *Cop Land* [1997]). Computer-generated imagery became common, and payments to star actors rose to the tens of millions.

Shrinking DVD sales in the mid-oughts led to a scaling back of risk-taking. International box-office returns almost tripled between 2000 and 2010, with most revenues coming from big-budget action-based films and their sequels. Meanwhile, movie theaters have expanded their offerings to include live and high-definition recorded or streamed productions of operas, plays, and other performances. Some even rent out their screens to those wishing to play video games.[16] The ability to stream video across the globe (into both movie theaters and private homes) has upended the economics of film distribution.

Many releases today are sequels and prequels, remakes and "reboots," frequently based on preexisting, successful commercial products (computer games, toys, other films, and sometimes even board games (*Battleship* [2012]) and amusement park rides (the *Pirates of the Caribbean* franchise [2003–]). Critics have expressed concern about the health of an industry making films "financed on the basis of computer-generated spreadsheets, distributed according to first-weekend box-office figures, and projected by robots."[17] Steven Spielberg and George Lucas, no strangers to blockbusters and pyrotechnics themselves, predicted "a big meltdown" and an "implosion . . . of these mega-budgeted movies," due to changes in the entertainment landscape, when they spoke at the University of Southern California's School of Cinematic Arts in January 2013.[18]

But tightened purse-strings in Hollywood, and independent producers willing to invest in mid-budget dramas, made 2013 the best year for film in a decade.[19] The success of independent filmmaker (and cinematic existentialist) Christopher Nolan shows that, in today's film culture, critical and commercial interests can be aligned, as can the blockbuster and the drama. Critics have been worried about the death of cinema for about a hundred years; as film critic and historian David Thomson (who also believes that cinema is dying) has written, "year after year, the funeral has been observed."[20] So it ever has been.

A History of Film Formats

Celluloid was first developed as a replacement for ivory; its most common industrial application today is in the fabrication of ping-pong balls. The earliest experiments in motion pictures used strips of celluloid, covered with a coat of light-sensitive emulsion. Film length (in seconds) was determined by the physical length of film (in meters). The films made by the Lumière brothers were about fifty seconds long simply because that's how long it took to project seventeen meters of film at sixteen frames per second. The width of their film, known as the *film gauge,* was 35 mm, a size first standardized by Edison, which, remarkably, remained the established size for over one hundred years. Throughout the silent film period, the aspect ratio of width to height was fixed at 4:3. The need to store sound on film from the late 1920s led to the development of a 1.37:1 ratio. Every studio film made in 35 mm between 1932 and 1952 was shot in this format, known as the *Academy ratio.*

The physical properties of the medium, known as the *film stock,* have changed on a number of occasions.[21] Until the early 1950s, the base of film stock was plasticized nitrocellulose. That nitrocellulose was formerly called "guncotton" hints at its properties. Nitrate film is highly flammable—it will continue to burn even when submerged in water. The hot lamps used by projectionists led to cinema fires, as when a reel of nitrate film stock, ignited by a candle, was the cause of Ireland's second-worst fire tragedy: forty-eight lives were lost in the small town of Dromcoliher in 1926. Carrying nitrate film was even banned on the London Underground. The properties of nitrate film continue to be a concern to conservators today (see chapter 8 for conservation guidelines), and have even been used as a cinematic plot device, as in *Inglourious Basterds* (2009). *Safety film,* with an acetate base, began to be used in the 1930s, but professional use of nitrate wasn't entirely discontinued until the early 1950s. However, acetate is also prone to deterioration, and began to be replaced by polyester film stock in the 1970s.

Silent black-and-white films were sometimes hand-colored frame-by-frame, usually in a rudimentary way, to give the impression of greater realism. Colored film was a novelty until the late 1930s. Technicolor wasn't the first film color process, but it was the most widely used from its invention in 1916, until overtaken by Eastmancolor in the 1950s. Filming in Technicolor required a considerable amount of light, which made life uncomfortable for actors and production crew. The stages on which *The Wizard of Oz* (1939) were shot were "brutally hot," according to the film's cinematographer

Harold Rosson. Rosson spent $226,307 on lighting alone, almost a tenth of the film's total budget.[22]

Technicolor cameras didn't actually use color film. Light entered the camera and was split into three streams. These were then passed through filters and exposed onto three different rolls of film. By treating, then layering, these black-and-white film strips, color could be projected. The Technicolor process was expensive and produced highly saturated products, which may have suited *The Wizard of Oz,* but was inappropriate for realistic depictions of the world.

The introduction by Eastman Kodak of a single 35-mm film with three emulsion layers for the primary colors led to the end of Technicolor. From 1936 to 1966 the Academy of Motion Picture Arts and Sciences awarded two awards (i.e., the Oscars) annually for cinematography—one for black-and-white films, one for color. 1936 was also the last year in which all the nominees for Best Picture were in black and white. In 1960, *The Apartment* was the last film shot entirely in black and white to win until *The Artist* won Best Picture in 2012 (*Schindler's List* [1993], which won the Oscar for Best Picture in 1994, has four brief uses of color in an otherwise black-and-white film).[23]

The popularity of television in the 1950s, combined with the breakup of the distribution monopolies, challenged the traditional studio system in a number of ways. One of the most important innovations was the increased use of wider screen formats, a revolution that began with the release of *Shane* in a 1.66:1 ratio in early 1953. Paramount Studios filmed *Shane* in the Academy ratio, but the top and bottom of the frame were cropped to produce the first widescreen release. This didn't compromise the quality of the cinematography too radically: as is common in Westerns, it contained many long and medium shots. By the end of that year the major studios were releasing most of their biggest productions in widescreen, usually by cropping regular film. Universal and Columbia Pictures went one better by cropping to an aspect ratio of 1.85:1. Eventually, all Hollywood moved to this wider ratio, opening up new technological and artistic possibilities. Postwar Europe settled on 1.66:1. The vast majority of films are now filmed in 1.85:1 or 2.39:1. Also popular in the 1950s were CinemaScope, which used lenses that distorted an image onto standard film and then projected the film using another distorted lens onto a very wide, curved screen, and Cinerama, a widescreen process that used three synchronized cameras and projectors to show films in surround vision.[24]

More recent innovations have included the large-format IMAX (Image Maximum), which must be shown in specialist theaters, experimentation with film stock (e.g., *The Master's* [2012] use of 70 mm film), frame rates (*The Hobbit: An Unexpected Journey's* [2012] use of a forty-eight frames-per-second rate), the return of 3-D filmmaking from 1950s horror obscurity to blockbusting hyper-reality, and the increasing ubiquity of digital capture.

Digital Cinematography

There are distinct advantages to using digital photography in film. Alfred Hitchcock's *Rope* (1948) was an early example of a production filmed and edited to give the impression that the action took place in real time, captured in a single continuous shot. Hitchcock's cameras could hold only about twenty minutes of film, so *Rope* relies on cinematic trickery to achieve its effect. *Timecode* (2000) and *Russian Ark* (2002) were the first mainstream real-time films to use the conceit seamlessly. *Russian Ark* was captured on high-definition video which, instead of being compressed onto tape, as was the usual practice at that time, was transferred to a hard disc carried behind the cameraman—video itself has its technical limitations.

Digital cinematography has lowered the entry cost for filmmakers, and digital cameras are more portable than their film counterparts. In one sense, digital cinematography has removed much of the art from film photography. No longer must cinematographers wait for the perfect light or choose from a confusing array of film stocks—the camera's sensors and image-manipulation software automates and simplifies the process of filling the image with the desired optical characteristics. Digital cinematography allows filmmakers to immediately view what they have shot. But digital film can look harsh, and the granularity of film stock, so beloved of photographers and cineastes, is lost. Digital capture and photosensitive film result in different products; there is space for both cinematic formats. Many directors who eschewed digital capture have recently been won over by its possibilities, but we'll be living in a hybrid world for some time to come.

The Personalization of Film Watching: Home Video

Until the development of home video in the 1970s, films had little commercial life beyond their theatrical release, and opportunities to watch all but the most canonical older films were limited. Film fans who wished to see older films had to rely on television, theatrical re-releases, film societies, and a small number of revival houses. The introduction of VHS and Betamax changed this, turning old films back into marketable objects, and extending the lifespans of new releases to the limits of their commercial potential. DVDs have been a boon for film fans, who can now obtain copies of films previously known to them only by reputation. As selling films for home viewing became increasingly lucrative throughout the 1980s and 1990s, the attendant artistic and economic changes to filmmaking have been subtle and multifaceted. Films have become more violent and profane,[25] but also longer and more experimental. Many directors consider DVD and Blu-ray Disc features when filming, making sure to also create the bonus content consumers have come to expect. As the demand for physical media has begun to lessen with the rise of video streaming, it could be argued that Netflix, by far the most successful video streaming service, has led Hollywood develop more pyrotechnical films, which benefit from theatrical viewing (producers make far more money from ticket sales than from streamed views).[26] Home viewing continues to have a profound effect on the ways films are marketed, and thus how they are made.

Early Videocassette Tapes

Sony's U-Matic, a three-quarter-inch tape, was among the first formats to contain analog videotape inside a cassette. The costs of producing it were too high for many consumers, so Sony rebranded the product for industrial, educational, and broadcast use. The format retains a foothold in the broadcaster market today. In the early 1970s, many other formats were introduced by companies vying to develop the prevailing standard for television recording. Only two were successful, and one became dominant: VHS (Video Home System), a half-inch videocassette format, originated by engineers at Japan's JVC in 1971. Although thought inferior to its great rival, Sony's Betamax, it became the dominant system because of a characteristic many had thought a flaw—its comparatively large size. Though the quality of the picture stored on VHS was worse than on Betamax, standard Betamax tape could only store about two hours of film, which was shorter than many feature films.

VHS

VCRs (videocassette recorders) designed to play and record VHS were first sold in the late 1970s, becoming a ubiquitous feature of Western living rooms until the introduction of the DVD in the late 1990s. The death of the VCR has been swift. Within ten years of the first commercial DVD sale, most major film studios had stopped releasing films on VHS.

VHS is an analog system, which represents video as a continuous stream of waves. Compared to contemporary technologies, resolution is poor—equivalent to approximately 333 x 480 pixels. A VHS cassette can hold just over 400 meters of tape. VHS cassettes are 187 mm wide, 103 mm high, and 25 mm thick.

During the 1980s, a number of film directors, most notably the French auteur Jean-Luc Godard, experimented with filming on video instead of photochemical film. However, outside of art galleries and European art-house cinemas, video didn't take off until digital capture technology altered the boundaries of film production in the early twenty-first century.

CED

The popularity of VHS also doomed the Capacitance Electronic Disc (CED), popularly—if only briefly—known as the videodisc. Developed by the RCA Corporation, CED was a grooved, twelve-inch analog video disc based on phonograph technology. Development began in 1964, but the first CED player wasn't released until 1981. Each side of the disc, which was held within a plastic caddy, could hold about 60 minutes of video, with quality similar to VHS. Easily damaged, abandoned by its developers, the last CEDs were released in 1986.[27]

LaserDisc

The LaserDisc was a precursor to the much smaller optical discs of today. It offered sharper resolution and higher audio quality than VHS, but its cost prevented it from becoming anything but a niche format. LaserDiscs remained obscure, if desirable, products in the United States and Europe, though their popularity was greater in East Asia, particularly in the rental markets of Japan and Hong Kong.

Most LaserDiscs are 30 cm in diameter, similar to the size of a long-play vinyl disc, and like the LP, both sides are usually used. Music videos and short programs were sometimes put on 12-cm and 20-cm versions. Unlike LPs, LaserDiscs are made from two different pieces of acrylic, glued together. Three encoding formats, with differing rotation speeds, were developed, and all stored the video signal as analog data. The most common encoding formats, CAV (constant angular velocity) and CLV (constant linear velocity) discs, held thirty and sixty minutes of content, respectively, on each side. Viewers were inconvenienced by needing to flip over or change the disc. The final commercially available LaserDisc title was released in 2000. Pioneer, who made more than half of the almost seventeen million LaserDisc players sold worldwide, distributed its last player in 2009.

VCD

The VCD (Video CD), created in 1993, was the first format to make motion pictures available on a 12-cm optical disc. Image quality is similar to VHS. VCD was briefly popular in the United States, but the release of the DVD format in 1997 made it redundant in the West, although VCDs continued to grow in popularity in Asia as a cheaper alternative to DVDs. Unlike DVDs, VCDs have no regional coding, and so can be played anywhere in the world. Because of this, and the lack of any copy-protection, the illegal copying and sale of VCDs has been a problem in emerging markets. The audio and video tracks on a VCD are compressed, and a single VCD can hold 74 minutes of video, close to the 79 minutes of uncompressed audio on a CD.

DVD

In an echo of the technological and commercial battle over videocassettes twenty years earlier, two rival consortia began developing competing high-density optical disc formats in the early 1990s. A group of computer experts with representation from most of the nascent industry giants forced the convergence of a single standard by declaring that they would boycott both formats if independent development continued.[28] The resulting compromise was the DVD, which "stands for nothing, Digital Video Disc, or Digital Versatile Disc, depending on whom you ask."[29] Although the initial reception to the format was lukewarm (it took almost two years after first release for all the major Hollywood studios to commit to it), a critical mass soon developed, and in the early years of the twenty-first century growth became explosive.

DVDs are produced to dozens of specifications, differentiated by suffixing mathematical operators and letters (e.g., DVD-RAM, DVD-VR, DVD+RW). Only a few of these are relevant to the cataloging and collection of film (see chapter 4). Because DVDs provided higher image and sound quality as well as a raft of additional features, such as multiple audio tracks and support for widescreen images as standard, they revolutionized the way people could watch film, enabling home viewing to approach the cinematic experience more closely than ever before. Compared to VHS, DVD offers superior sound and picture quality; greater versatility, portability, and durability; and the capacity for interactivity.

HD DVD and Blu-ray Disc

Consumer satisfaction with DVD technology remains high as of this writing. The product is robust, so much so that successor technologies have used very similar media. As the DVD evolved from the CD, the HD DVD (high-definition DVD) and Blu-ray Disc both evolved from the DVD. HD DVD, essentially an extension of the DVD, was released before Blu-ray, the development of which faced technological hurdles. But a confluence of mergers, acquisitions, and commercial relationships sealed the dominance of the Blu-ray Disc within a couple of years. In June 2006, Luc Besson's *The Fifth Element* was the first film to be released in the format. The first HD DVDs, which had a lower capacity and data transfer rate than Blu-ray Disc, were released on April 18, 2006, and the last in 2008.[30]

Blu-ray Discs have the same diameter as DVDs, and like their predecessors they store information digitally as a series of binary pieces of data, physically encoded on a thin wafer of metal encased in plastic. However, they can hold more than five times the data, enough to store a high-definition film, or about thirteen hours of standard-definition video. In North America, the Blu-ray Disc "evolved to become the standard for home entertainment" in

2011, largely because of the parallel growth in sales of high-definition televisions, 3-D technology, and the wish by entertainment conglomerates to push a product with a higher profit margin.[31] The format is currently more dominant in the United States than elsewhere in the world, but DVD sales are falling everywhere as Blu-ray Disc sales increase. The technology continues to evolve. Blu-ray Discs embedded with dozens of data layers, which would massively increase storage capacity, are being developed. Sony and Panasonic have announced their intention to release a 300 GB optical disc (i.e., with over sixty times more storage than a standard DVD) in 2015, with an eye on the market for video archiving and cloud storage.[32]

It is quite possible that Blu-ray Discs will be the last physical storage medium for video to be adopted by the public. The exponential increase in storage capacity of hard drives and the emergence, encouraged by the behemoths of the technology world, of instant video streaming and cloud computing, could signal the end of the film as a portable, physical object in the living rooms and bookcases of private individuals. Chapter 8 will assess the implications of these emerging technologies.

A History of Audiovisual Librarianship

In 1924, the American Library Association set up the Visual Methods Committee and Committee on Relations Between Libraries and Moving Pictures. These committees recognized that film collections had become significant enough for the development of national policies. At this time, both school and academic libraries were already experimenting with film for teaching and research, while public libraries were using films to help popularize the books and authors Hollywood drew upon for inspiration. In 1929, the Kalamazoo Public Library in Michigan became the first public library to lend film.[33]

During the first half of the twentieth century, pressure to engage with film generally came from outside the library profession. The Visual Methods Committee was set up at the suggestion of a representative of the film industry. The first book to deal extensively with film librarianship, Gerald D. McDonald's *Educational Motion Pictures and Libraries,*[34] was published by ALA in 1942 with the support of the Rockefeller Foundation. This work came out of discussions that took place when the Foundation gave $5,500 to fund the Joint Committee on Educational Films, bringing together the

ALA, the American Film Center, the Association of School Librarians, and the American Council on Education. The Carnegie Corporation's campaigns to boost civilian morale during the Second World War brought funding for the ALA's Film Forum Project and involved forty libraries.[35] According to Palmer, it "represented the first large-scale use of films in public libraries,"[36] and its success led to the rapid expansion of library attempts at public education, assisted by the continued support of the Corporation.

The Library of Congress had been receiving deposits of film since the late nineteenth century. In 1912, copyright law was extended to cover motion pictures; wary of the dangers of nitrate film, LC didn't take up its rights to receive films under legal deposit until 1942.[37] From this date, they have collected selectively, though widely—in recent years 7,000 to 8,000 films have been added annually. Following its foundation in 1967, the American Film Institute began to deposit some of its archive collections in the Library of Congress. Unlike PCC libraries, which now use RDA for cataloging films, the Library of Congress continues to use the second edition of the *Archival Moving Image Materials* (AMIM) cataloging manual for its moving image materials. Although differences are generally minor, there is significant variation, and so catalogers are advised against using any LC records as templates. As the name suggests, this manual had its origins in the cataloging of archival, not library, material.

Early motion picture libraries of note include that of the Academy of Motion Picture Arts and Sciences, which set up a library only a year after it was founded in 1927. Its substantial collection (which consists primarily of works *about* film, rather than films themselves) is now funded by television revenues from the Oscars ceremony.[38] The Academy also contributed to the creation the University of Southern California's School of Cinematic Arts in 1929. This was a collaborative venture with the Academy, and early faculty members included prominent industry professionals, many of whom encouraged fellow actors and directors to donate their archives.[39]

Metadata standards have struggled to cope with audiovisual material. The Library of Congress took thirteen years to complete work on their *Rules for Descriptive Cataloging in the Library of Congress: Motion Pictures and Film Strips*, finally publishing a twenty-page guide in 1965. When the Anglo-American Cataloguing Rules were published in 1967, catalogers were dissatisfied with Part III's treatment of non-book materials, which drew heavily on the Library of Congress rules and the parallel projects devising standards for records and pictures, and was not subject to the same outside scrutiny as Parts I and II. A revised version of the chapter on audiovisual media and special instructional materials was published in 1975, and matters improved further with the publication of AACR2 in 1978, and its subsequent updates. Responses to RDA have been mixed, though audiovisual librarians were involved as test participants in the US national libraries' official RDA test.[40]

The organization On-Line Audiovisual Catalogers, Inc. (OLAC) was set up following a remarkable OCLC user group meeting at the 1980 ALA Annual Conference in New York.[41] A meeting about audiovisual cataloging snowballed, and after a thirty-minute adjournment, interested parties reconvened to set up OLAC. The group has done much to advance the cause of audiovisual cataloging in many fields, and has published helpful sets of cataloging guidelines. Nancy Olson chaired the first OLAC meeting and was its first president. The year after the conference saw the publication of Olson's seminal *Cataloging of Audiovisual Materials: A Manual Based on AACR2*, now in its fifth edition.[42]

NOTES

1. Something along these lines may have been said to Georges Méliès on that historic night in Paris, but by Antoine Lumière, father of the filmmaking brothers. It is usually misattributed to Louis Lumière. Lumière senior is supposed to have said: "My invention is not for sale; it would be the ruin of you. It might be exploited sometimes as a scientific curiosity: other than that it has no commercial future." The original French is quoted in C. W. Ceram, *Archaeology of the Cinema*, trans. Richard Wilson (New York: Harcourt, Brace and World, 1965), 11.

2. Guy Borgé, Marjorie Borgé, and Binernard Chardère, *Les Lumière* (Paris: Bibliothèque des Arts, 1985).

3. Elizabeth Ezra, *Georges Méliès: The Birth of the Auteur* (Manchester: Manchester University Press, 2000). *Hugo*, a 2011 film directed by Martin Scorsese, features Méliès as a major character, and his fall into relative obscurity as a plot device. The film is based on Brian Selznick's novel, *The Invention of Hugo Cabret* (New York: Scholastic Press, 2007).

4. For information on Edison's work as a filmmaker, see the extensive Library of Congress website devoted to the Edison companies, which includes digitized versions of hundreds of his films. Library of Congress, Motion Picture, Broadcasting, and Recorded Sound Division, Inventing Entertainment: The Early Motion Pictures and

Sound Recordings of the Edison Companies, www.loc.gov/collection/edison-company-motion-pictures-and-sound-recordings/.

5. Paul Anbinder, ed., *Before Hollywood: Turn-of-the-Century American Film* (New York: Hudson Hills Press, 1987).

6. A Library of Congress study has estimated that 70 percent of all American feature-length silent films have disappeared. See David Pierce, *The Survival of American Silent Feature Films, 1912–1929* (Washington, DC: Council on Library and Information Resources and The Library of Congress, 2013), www.clir.org/pubs/reports/pub158/pub158.pdf.

7. Eileen Browser, *The Transformation of Cinema: 1907–1915* (New York: Charles Scribner, 1990).

8. Pierce, *Survival*.

9. Scott Eyman, *The Speed of Sound: Hollywood and the Talkie Revolution, 1926–1930* (New York: Simon & Schuster, 1997).

10. David Bordwell, Janet Staiger, and Kristin Thompson, *The Classical Hollywood Cinema: Film Style and Mode of Production to 1960* (New York: Columbia University Press, 1985).

11. Mary Morley Cohen, "Forgotten Audiences in the Passion Pits: Drive-In Theatres and Changing Spectator Practices in Post-War America," *Film History* 6, no. 4 (Winter 1994): 470–86.

12. David Bordwell and Kristin Thompson, *Film Art: An Introduction*, 7th ed. (New York: McGraw Hill, 2004), 483–84.

13. Roger Ebert, "Bonnie and Clyde," *Chicago Sun-Times*, September 25, 1967, www.rogerebert.com/reviews/bonnie-and-clyde-1967.

14. For the earlier uses of the term "blockbuster," and its change in meaning following the success of *Jaws* (1975), see Steve Neale, "Hollywood Blockbusters: Historical Dimensions," in Julien Stinger, ed., *Movie Blockbusters* (London: Taylor & Francis, 2003), 48–50.

15. AFI's 100 Greatest American Movies of All Time. American Film Institute, www.afi.com/100Years/movies.aspx.

16. For example, Cineplex, the Canadian cinema theater chain, rents out its screens for "Xbox Big Screen Parties." See www.cineplex.com/Theatres/Birthdays/XBoxParties/.

17. Mark Kermode, *The Good, the Bad, and the Mulitplex* (London: Arrow Books, 2012), 13.

18. David S. Cohen, "George Lucas and Steven Spielberg: Studios Will Implode; VOD is the Future," *Variety*, June 12, 2013, www.variety.com/2013/digital/news/lucas-spielberg-on-future-of-entertainment-1200496241/.

19. See Derek Thompson, "Why Were There So Many Great Movies in 2013? An Economic Explanation," *The Atlantic*, January 17, 2014, www.theatlantic.com/

business/archive/2014/01/why-were-there-so-many-great-movies-in-2013-an-economic-explanation/283170/.

20. David Thomson, "American Movies are Not Dead: They are Dying," *The New Republic,* October 4, 2012, www.newrepublic.com/article/books-and-arts/magazine/107218/not-dead-just-dying/.

21. For further technical and historical details, see James Monaco, *How to Read a Film: The World of Movies, Media, and Multimedia—Language, History, Theory,* 3rd edition (New York: Oxford University Press, 2000). For the aesthetic consequences of different film stocks, see Bordwell and Thompson, *Film Art,* 229–33.

22. Aljean Harmetz, *The Making of the Wizard of Oz: Movie Magic in the Prime of MGM* (Chicago: Chicago Review Press, 2013), 231.

23. Ignoring its one scene of dialogue, *The Artist* was also only the second silent film winner. The first was *Wings* (1927), awarded the Outstanding Picture prize at the first Academy Awards ceremony in 1929.

24. Andrew Dowdy, *The Films of the Fifties: The American State of Mind* (New York: Morrow, 1973).

25. The Movie Body Counts website (www.moviebodycounts.com) provides a wealth of statistical data on violence in film. Only five films released in the 1960s had more than 100 on-screen violent deaths; the bloodiest was *The Wild Bunch* (1969), with 145. 28 films released in the 2000s had more than 100 such deaths. There are 836 violent on-screen deaths in *The Lord of the Rings: The Return of the King* (2003). For a brief historical overview of swearing in films, see Paul Burns, "Well, I Swear: A Brief F---ing History of Profanity in the Movies," *Sydney Morning Herald*, September 7, 2014, www.smh.com.au/entertainment/movies/well-i-swear-a-brief-fing-history-of-profanity-in-the-movies-20140901-10axdu.html. Hollywood's attitudes toward violence, sex, and profanity, and their potential social implications, are touched on in Kimberley M. Thompson and Fumie Yokota, "Violence, Sex, and Profanity in Films: Correlation of Movie Ratings With Content," *Medscape General Medicine*, 2004, www.medscape.com/viewarticle/480900.

26. For more on Hollywood's struggle to deal with the challenges posed by Netflix, see Matthew Garrahan, "Hollywood Feels Netflix's Cutting Edge," *Financial Times*, September 30, 2014, www.ft.com/cms/s/0/6b5e4c36-47ef-11e4-b5ad-00144feab7de.html.

27. Jim Taylor, Mark R. Johnson, and Charles G. Crawford, *DVD Demystified*, 3rd ed. (New York: McGraw Hill, 2006), 1–11.

28. Ibid., 21–26.

29. Jim Taylor, "DVD-Video: Multimedia for the Masses," *IEEE MultiMedia*, July 1999: 86–92, http://ivizlab.sfu.ca/arya/Papers/IEEE/Multimedia/1999/July/DVD-Video.pdf.

30. For a detailed history of the second audiovisual "format war," see Jim Taylor, Charles G. Crawford, Christen M. Armburst, and Michael Zink, *Blu-ray Disc Demystified* (New York: McGraw Hill, 2009), 213–27.

31. John Gaudiosi, "CES 2012: Blu-ray Discs Break $2 Billion Barrier for First Time in 2011," *Forbes,* October 1, 2012, www.forbes.com/sites/johngaudiosi/2012/01/10/ces-2012-blu-ray-discs-break-2-billion-barrier-for-first-time-in-2011/.

32. Daisuke Wakabayashi, "Sony, Panasonic Working on Next-Gen Optical Disc," *Digits: Tech News and Analysis from WSJ,* July 29, 2013, blogs.wsj.com/digits/2013/07/29/sony-panasonic-working-on-next-gen-optical-disc/.

33. John W. Ellison, ed., *Media Librarianship* (New York: Neal-Schuman, 1985), 79.

34. Gerald D. McDonald, *Educational Motion Pictures and Libraries* (Chicago: American Library Association, 1942).

35. Ellison, *Media Librarianship,* 80–81.

36. Joseph W. Palmer, "Contributions of the Carnegie Corporation to the Development of Public Library Film Service," *Journal of Library History,* 12 (Fall 1977): 327–28.

37. Leonard Maltin, *The Whole Film Sourcebook* (New York: Universe Books, 1983), 210.

38. About the Margaret Herrick Library, Academy of Motion Picture Arts and Sciences, 2014, www.oscars.org/library/about.

39. Cinematic Arts Library, University of Southern California, History, www.usc.edu/libraries/locations/cinema_tv/history/.

40. These tests resulted in three extensive discussion summaries. See Music Library Association (MLA) / Online Audiovisual Catalogers (OLAC) RDA Test Group, Discussion Summary Part 1: Major Issues with Access Points; Discussion Summary Part 2: Unresolved Issues for Further Investigation, Discussion and Follow-Up; and Discussion Summary Part 3: Resolved Issues, May 20, 2011, www.olacinc.org/drupal/capc_files/MLA-OLAC_RDAtest1.pdf, www.olacinc.org/drupal/capc_files/MLA-OLAC_RDAtest2.pdf, and www.olacinc.org/drupal/capc_files/MLA-OLAC_RDAtest3.pdf.

41. See On-Line Audiovisual Catalogers, *Newsletter,* 1, no. 1 (January 1981), http://olacinc.org/drupal/newsletters/1981January.pdf.

42. Nancy B. Olson, Robert L. Bothmann, and Jessica J. Schomberg, *Cataloging of Audiovisual Materials and Other Special Materials: A Manual Based on AACR2 and MARC 21* (Westport, CT: Libraries Unlimited, 2008).

CHAPTER 2

PRODUCTION AND DISTRIBUTION, CAST AND CREW

THIS CHAPTER DEALS WITH THE INDIVIDUALS AND CORPO-
rate entities involved in the creation and composition of film. This includes those who provide the organizational competencies and finance to allow production to begin (the producers, studios, and/or production companies); the people they employ, whose technical skills and imaginative faculties enable an idea to be realized as a series of carefully constructed photographs (the film crew); and the actors or other participants who speak the lines and perform the actions dictated by the screenwriter and director (the cast). Details of those who publish and distribute a film on a commercial basis, using physical or virtual formats such as DVD, Blu-ray Disc, or streaming media are also covered.

    The general public may know little about the contributions of some of these professionals. A small number of directors, and only a handful of producers, are known by the moviegoing public. Their reputations are deployed by the Hollywood marketing machine (the familiar "From the director of . . ."), but not always their names. Many actors, however, seek publicity like moths to a flame. Some retain a prominent media presence even though their films are of indifferent quality, or infrequently released. The other people involved in making a film are relegated to the small print on the film poster (if they're lucky), or more commonly the film credits, which grow longer by the year. *Nosferatu* (1922) listed sixteen names in its opening credits. When first released, *Star Wars* (1977) had closing credits listing 143 people. *Who Framed Roger Rabbit* (1988) had 743. The blockbusters of the twenty-first century are made by small armies, their production budgets larger than the annual expenditure of most Pacific nations. The end credits of *Alien vs. Predator* (2004) are twelve minutes long.

The first half of this chapter provides a guide to what these people and organizations do. The second half covers how to detail them in MARC 21 bibliographic records using RDA. The most significant contributors are recorded in field 245, in the statement of responsibility. They will also usually appear in access point entries for persons and corporate bodies (700, 710). Those lower down the cinematic chain of command are recorded in note fields for cast (511) and crew (508). Personal name main entries (100) can also be found in records for films, but only in unusual circumstances. This chapter also provides detail on the related MARC fields that describe identifying numbers (020, 024, 028), editions (250), publication (264), series (490, 830), awards (586), and the various fields that provide the spatial and temporal details of a production (043, 046, 257, 518).

What Film People Do

Citizen Kane (1941), a film of constant cinematic innovation, began with a title card and no credits, a practice almost unheard of at the time. Until the early 1970s, nearly every film began with opening credits and a title card displayed on a handful of frames before the start of the action. Films generally finished symphonically, with an authoritative "The End." Forty years ago the practice changed, and since then only a few of the most important cast and crew have been listed in opening credits, with more detailed credits at the end. It can be instructive to watch the complete list of closing credits. They'll often include something interesting or unexpected, and sometimes show visual or verbal jokes, or outtakes. Some Monty Python films list ridiculous and nonexistent crew members. Jackie Chan's films show footage of the stunts that went painfully wrong.

Credits moved from static cards accompanied by a song to a rolling list accompanied by orchestration because they simply became too long. Audiences will not put up with a thousand names appearing before or during the opening scenes, no matter how cleverly they are displayed. There are two reasons for the expansion. First, Hollywood's closed-shop guilds and unions required producers to acknowledge members' contributions to a film on screen. What may appear to outside observers as nonsensical arguments over credits have led to disputes between unions and filmmakers. George Lucas quit the Directors Guild of America after being fined for omitting opening credits in *Star Wars* (1977) and *The Empire Strikes Back* (1980). According to the Guild, the lack of opening credits meant that the work of the director hadn't been fully recognized. The irony of fining a director not known for his humility for failing to certify his own importance was lost.[1]

Second, cinematic productions have grown more complex. Much of this can be traced, as the preceding examples show, to the special effects that underpin most of today's blockbusters. Lucas's special-effects company, Industrial Light and Magic, employs over 500 digital artists. The name of the company, the powerful unions, and filmmaking's Byzantine arrangements demonstrate that making movies now takes place on an industrial scale. When cataloging a film, there is no need to record all the names listed in the opening or closing credits—it's sufficient to indicate the small number of people with the greatest creative, artistic, intellectual, and technical influence on the finished product.

But which crew members are the most significant?

First, and foremost, the director: yes . . . usually. But set aside the common assumption that elevates the director to a godlike role. The 2004 surprise hit *Primer* was made almost entirely by Shane Carruth. Recent technological advances have made it easier for talented individuals to produce high-quality films on small budgets, and Carruth's only help came from the friends who starred alongside him, and his family, who provided the catering.

Yet one-man bands are exceptions—films are collaborative projects. It is quite true that Orson Welles produced, directed, wrote, and acted in *Citizen Kane*, often regarded as the greatest film ever made, and the force of Welles's personality, and his creative genius, haunt every scene. But the actors of his Mercury Theatre company, who appeared in the film, were among the finest performers of the day. Editor Robert Wise went on to win two Academy Awards for directing—an honor never bestowed on Welles. With Gregg Toland behind the camera, Welles was working with Hollywood's greatest contemporary cinematographer. The script was coauthored (some say authored)[2] by the brilliant Herman Mankiewicz, whose work in the 1930s had "brought good-humored toughness to the movies, and energy and astringency."³ *Citizen Kane* would have been destroyed were it not for cantankerous and unpliable George Schaefer, President of RKO Studios, who released the controversial film against the wishes of almost the entire film industry and the most powerful media mogul America has ever known. *Citizen Kane*'s musical score was written by Bernard Hermann, whose later work for Alfred Hitchcock resulted in some of the most well-known music in the history of film.⁴

The gathering of so many great figures was no accident. Welles knew little about the mechanics of filmmaking when he started planning this film, then provisionally titled *The American*. If you can believe him (this being the director of *F for Fake* [1973], a pseudo-documentary about forgery, which revels in multiple layers of falsification), Welles's knowledge of direction came from watching John Ford's *Stagecoach* (1939) forty times over: "After dinner every night for about a month, I'd run *Stagecoach*. . . . It was like going to school."⁵ Part of his genius lay in his deployment of charm and intelligence, used to convince other talented people to work with him. These are the individuals we ought to consider including when creating catalog records for films.

The Producer

Producers are responsible for delivering the film to the studio, production company, or individuals who have financed it. They have the greatest influence over how a film should be made, and for ensuring that it is completed within budget. The producers are normally involved at the earliest stages of a project, in obtaining rights and developing the original idea. They collect the Academy Award for Best Picture. Producers often have responsibility for hiring the director and casting director, and frequently raise funds or a personally invest in the project.

Some of Hollywood's most significant producers began their careers as directors. It is not unheard of for actors to turn producer to develop a vanity project. More often than not, these actors, and many successful directors, become *executive producers*—people with a major financial interest, or representatives of someone with a major interest, in a film. But the title is ambiguous. Often the executive producer is the individual who purchased the idea for the film from the author of a preexisting literary text, and who then hired a producer to do further work on a project. A producer delegates the day-to-day production work to a *line producer*. Once production has begun, the executive producers rarely play any role in the technical or creative aspects of the film.

Important producers in the history of film include Robert Evans, Sam Goldwyn, Howard Hawks, David O. Selznick, and Jack Warner. Today's influential producers include Jerry Bruckheimer, Peter Jackson, Scott Rudin, Steven Spielberg, and Harvey Weinstein.

In the early days of Hollywood there emerged a handful of powerful film studios, vertically integrated conglomerates that retained monopolistic control over every aspect of a film, from its initiation to its final screening. By the 1920s, the "Big Five" (20th Century Fox, Metro-Goldwyn-Mayer, Paramount Pictures, RKO Pictures, and Warner Brothers) were all firmly established, making the vast majority of films on their own studio lots, distributed by their own distribution divisions, and shown in their own movie theaters. Performers and technical crew were contracted to these "Majors." A 1948 Supreme Court ruling outlawed these monopolistic practices, leading to the emergence of independent production companies. Today's major film studios provide financial backing and a distribution mechanism, on occasion renting studio space to other production companies. But behind the illusion of diversity, the old oligopoly still exists. The "Big Six" (Comcast/General Electric, News Corporation, Sony, Time Warner, Viacom, and The Walt Disney Company) can all trace their lineage to Hollywood's Golden Age in the 1930s and 1940s, and have a combined market share of over 85 percent. Lionsgate (founded in 1997), has recently challenged the dominance of this club.

The Director

The director handles the creative aspects of turning a script into a film, from pre-production through postproduction, overseeing the work of the rest of the production crew. Directors have control over the technical and artistic elements required to create and capture dramatic scenes on film or its digital surrogate. They tell the actors how they would like each scene performed, and tell the production crew how they would like each scene to look. Although employed by the producer, the director generally has the final say on the artistic and technical aspects of how the film is being made during production.

Any list of great directors will be notable for the figures it excludes. A selection of most influential and important directors in the history of film would include, but not be limited to, John Cassavetes, John Ford, Jean-Luc Godard, Jean Renoir, and Orson Welles. Among the significant directors working today are J. J. Abrams, Pedro Almodóvar, Joel and Ethan Coen, Christopher Nolan, and Martin Scorsese.

The Actors

After the director, the actors have the most visible influence on a film. The media are saturated with their on- and off-screen antics, and little needs to be said about what they do in their professional lives. The choice of which and how many of them to list in a catalog record is at the discretion of the cataloger, though they should certainly be recorded. The ability to find a film by searching for an actor is likely to be appreciated by your users. A list of significant and important actors seems unnecessary.

The Screenwriter

In *Sunset Boulevard* (1950), William Holden plays an unsuccessful screenwriter who complains that "audiences don't know someone sits down and writes a picture. They think the actors make it up as they go along." Writing a film is more complex than its audiences appreciate. Those projects not based on preexisting material such as novels, plays, videogames or the previous installment in a film series are generally initiated by screenwriters making a "pitch" to a film studio or production company. In *The Player* (1992), prospective screenwriters are asked to sell their idea in twenty-five words or less (one example: "So it's like a psychic political thriller comedy. With a heart. And not unlike *Ghost* meets *Manchurian Candidate*."). Screenwriters stay involved through the production process. For this they can thank their union regulations (in the United States there are two unions, the Writers Guild of America, East, and the Writers Guild of America, West; despite their similar names they are separate bodies).

However, fewer films are now based on original scripts, and many talented writers are concentrating on working for television (as, increasingly, are actors). Most films about films feature screenwriters as their heroes, unsurprisingly.

Important screenwriters in the history of film include Robert Benton, William Goldman, Ben Hecht, Joseph L. Mankiewicz, and Billy Wilder. Screenwriters writing some of the most interesting, or revenue-generating, films today include Michael Arndt, Charlie Kaufman, David Koepp, Terry Rossio, and Andrew Stanton. Many leading directors (such as Christopher Nolan, James Cameron, Wes Anderson, and Alfonso Cuarón) write their own films.

The Cinematographer

The cinematographer (sometimes called the director of photography, or with slightly different responsibilities, the lighting cameraman) is the unsung hero of filmmaking, responsible for much more than merely photographing the movement of the actors according to the director's instructions. A more heterogeneous role is described by the American Society of Cinematographers' manual: "Cinematography is not a subcategory of photography. Rather, photography is but one craft that the cinematographer uses in addition to other physical, organizational, managerial, interpretive and image-manipulating techniques to effect one coherent process."[6] The cinematographer has responsibility over both the camera and lighting crews. Cinematography combines art, science, and a little bit of mind-reading—the cinematographer must transfer the director's vision into a projectable series of moving images.

Among the most influential and talented cinematographers in the history of filmmaking have been Jack Cardiff, Conrad L. Hall, Sven Nykvist, Gregg Toland, and Gordon Willis. Innovative and award-winning cinematographers working today include Roger Deakins, Robert Elswit, Emmanuel Lubezki, Wally Pfister, and Robert Richardson.

The Editor

Editing is the most important part of a film's postproduction. Some have argued that the work of the editor most clearly distinguishes film from other arts. Most films are composed of thousands of different shots, and about fifty separate scenes. A shot is a continuous recording of multiple frames; a scene is a series of related shots. The editor pieces these together. Editing normally begins while filming is still taking place, leading to an "editor's cut" (also called an "assembly edit" or "rough cut"). Once the principal photography has been completed, the editor works with the director on a "director's cut." The collaboration between the editor and director is probably the most significant working relationship in film.

Many acclaimed and famous directors have had long-standing partnerships with particular editors. Many others, such as Akira Kurosawa, Stanley Kubrick, and today, the Coen brothers, have edited their own films. Editorial disagreements between producers and directors, although uncommon, are not unknown, and the final cut the editor produces can be different from the director's version. Orson Welles's cut for his second feature film, *The Magnificent Ambersons* (1942), was destroyed by the production studio, RKO, who thought that their own final version, with a happy ending, was more commercially viable. After cinematic release some films have been re-released with the director's preferred edits, also referred to as a *director's cut*. Recently, these have taken the form of commercial gimmicks: additional footage is added without much consideration for artistic merit, thus undermining the point of having a skilled editor in the first place. Six different versions of *Blade Runner* (1982) have been released.[7]

Among the greatest editors in film history are Dede Allen, Anne Coates, Walter Murch, Sam O'Steen, and William H. Reynolds. Notable editors working today include Stuart Baird, Michael Kahn, Pietro Scalia, Thelma Schoonmaker, and Dylan Tichenor.

The Composer

The composer of the original music can have a significant influence on the art of the film. From Sergei Prokofiev's score for Sergei Eisenstein's *Alexander Nevsky* (1938) to John Williams's compositions for films such as *Jaws* (1975) and the *Indiana Jones* series (1981–2008), the best musical scores become so intertwined with the images that it becomes difficult to think of one without also recalling the other. Preexisting classical and contemporary music is also used in film, perhaps most famously in *2001: A Space Odyssey* (1968), but the music needs to be chosen carefully. The use of "O Fortuna," from Carl Orff's cantata of *Carmina Burana,* may have seemed an original idea to director

John Boorman when he used it in his *Excalibur* (1981). Its overuse in films since has turned it into a cliché. The score should not be confused with the use of incidental sound, which can be no less complex and important, and the different audio formats discussed in chapter 4.

Other Significant Crew Members

Many other individuals have a significant creative input to the composition of a film. The director and producer are involved in the casting of the main actors, but the casting director also plays an important part by finding actors for the smaller parts and liaising between actors, directors, and production company in pre-production. The production designer works with the director and cinematographer to define the visual feel of a film. The art director has responsibility for sets and locations; the costume designer for what the actors wear; and the special effects supervisor for a range of practical, visual, or animation effects, from artificial rain and blood to car chases and space battles. Including any of these individuals in a catalog record would be unusual, but you may work in an institution in which these skills are taught or studied. If a film is known because of the influence of these crew members, it may be useful to include them. You will never need to include the best boy, foley artist, or dolly grip, but it's useful to know what these people do to answer crossword puzzles and trivia quizzes. The best boy is an assistant to the head of the electrical or camera department; a foley artist creates incidental sound; and the dolly grip operates the dolly, the vehicle on which the camera is mounted.

Cataloging

The following pages provide instruction on how to integrate the above-named individuals and corporate entities into catalogue records for film. These categories are understood broadly, so include, but are not limited to, the MARC 21 bibliographic fields describing the incidental details of a film's production and publication. Section headings take the form of MARC bibliographic fields, listed in ascending numerical order.

020 ISBN (R)

Publishers of instructional or educational DVDs and Blu-ray Discs issued in the United States may purchase International Serial Book Numbers (ISBNs) for these products from the U.S. ISBN Agency.[8] Entertainment releases are ineligible for ISBNs. Record an ISBN in subfield $a if it appears anywhere on the item (RDA 2.15.1.4), including ISBNs printed on the disc case, or on any accompanying material such as booklets.

As with monograph cataloging, subfield $c may be used to indicate the cost of the resource, and subfield $z in those rare cases when you have a canceled or invalid ISBN. Subfield $q may be used to add qualifying information when the resource has two or more ISBNs—perhaps one associated with the disc and one with an accompanying booklet.

Both indicators are undefined, and there is no end punctuation:

020 ## $a 9783831265237

024 Other Standard Identifier (R)

Only a few DVDs and Blu-ray Discs will have ISBNs—most barcodes on their cases will either be UPCs (Universal Product Code), or EANs (International Article Number, originally European Article Number). UPCs can be identified as a barcode with a twelve-digit number beneath. EAN barcodes generate a thirteen-digit number. Use first indicator "1" for UPC, or "3" for EAN. No information is usually given in the second indicator, though you may use it if you wish to note a difference between the scanned code and the number as printed: second indicator "1" indicates a difference, "0" indicates none. Do not include hyphens or spaces, and make sure to include all the numbers—particular care needs to be taken with UPC numbers, in which the first and last digits are usually printed in smaller type, sometimes outside the barcode. Identifiers for manifestations are an RDA core element, so UPCs and EANs must be recorded if printed on the resource (RDA 2.15.1.4). As with all 0XX fields, there is no end punctuation:

024 1# $a 711969114690

024 3# $a 5035673006542

Amazon web pages for optical discs contain a ten-digit alphanumeric ASIN number, generally beginning with the letter B. ASIN stands for

Amazon Standard Identification Number—ASINs and ISBNs are equivalent for books, but for other products the number is unique to Amazon. However, ASINs are not necessarily unique to products, only to individual Amazon marketplaces, of which there are a proliferating number. ASINs have been criticized by Wikipedia founder Jimmy Wales, among others, as a proprietary product identifier, and a threat to universal description.[9] Do not include them in catalog records.

028 Publisher Number (R)

A unique number assigned by the publisher can be found on most DVDs and Blu-ray Discs, generally on the top or bottom edge of the spine of the sleeve insert. They are sometimes also printed on the disc label (more commonly in the United Kingdom than in North America), and more frequently, on the back of the sleeve insert, on its lower half. There are no universal standards for videorecording numbers, and they appear in many arbitrary alphanumeric forms. Unlike the 024 field, there is no prescribed format for their transcription. As per MARC rules, "All spacing and punctuation internal to the number are carried in field 028" (www.loc.gov/marc/bibliographic/bd028.html).

RDA considers the publisher number to be a standard identifier (RDA 2.15.1.4), and therefore a core element. It is recorded in a 028 field with a first indicator "4." The second indicator covers the generation of the number as a note and/or added entry. Most libraries, and both MARC 21 bibliographic examples, record the second indicator as "2": "note, no added entry." The field has no end punctuation.

Record the number in subfield $a, and the name of the publisher or distributor in subfield $b. Use the form found on the spine, or among the information included on the back of the sleeve insert. Ignore all other identification numbers found on the disc. Commercially distributed DVDs and Blu-ray Discs sold in the United Kingdom will, unless they are exempt from classification, contain a number prefixed with the letters VF, beside, near, or under the British Board of Film Classification's ratings symbol. This is the unique registration number for each video work the Board classifies. Though they are often listed together, this number should not be confused with the publisher's videorecording number, and should not be recorded. For more on film certification, see chapter 3.

If there are several individual cases packaged as a set, use the number on the slipcase packaging in preference to the numbers included on the individual cases:

028 42 $a EKA40098 $b Eureka Video

043 Geographic Area Code (NR)

A 043 field may be used for non-fiction films about a particular place, by analogy with its use for monograph material. As with books, most libraries use the seven-digit MARC geographic area code in subfield $a, though local codes ($b) and ISO codes ($c) are also permitted. The field can contain more than one code: if multiple codes are used, list them in order of their relevance. Both indicators are undefined, and the field has no end punctuation:

043 ## $a zmo---

046 Special Coded Dates (R)

Some libraries code the year of a film's release in a 046 subfield $k, and the text of MARC does offer one example that supports the use of the 046 field for the release date of a film subsequently issued on DVD. Where the date of release differs from the date of production, a note (identified as belonging in the 046 $k and the 500 field) is a core element for moving images (RDA 6.4.1.3). Some libraries have read this instruction as justification for recording the year of the original cinematic release in subfield $k. The widespread use of this practice may ultimately force, and thus resolve, the issue, and using the field for this purpose is the only way of permitting searches limited by the year of release, as the information is useless for machine-processing in a 500 field.

However, this use is a liberal application of the field's scope in MARC 21. The PCC instruction is ambiguous, and the MARC text refers to different subfields ($o and $p). The conflation of the year of release with the year of creation (how the subfield is defined) is problematic (see the section on production/release history in chapter 4). In future, the granularity that such a defined field could offer would be of great use to library users and staff. But until MARC accommodates it and the majority of catalogers accept it, using the 046 field in this way has the potential to cause confusion.

Whether you wish to include a 046 field to code the year of original release is left to the cataloger's judgment. It has obvious benefits for users, but will be a local interpretation of the standard, and thus reliant on local systems and practices.

100 Main Entry—Personal Name (NR)

RDA is in agreement with this book's perspective that films are, by their nature, collaborative works. Though main entry access points for collaborative works are normally constructed for the individual or corporate body with principal responsibility for the work (RDA 6.27.1.3), an exception exists for films, for which the "preferred title for the work" is the authorized access point.

RDA does not list any films among its examples, but it does appear to allow catalogers to create a personal name main entry in certain circumstances (RDA 6.27.1.2). The inclusion of a 100 field would be valid if a single person performed all the major creative functions involved in making a film, though drawing up such an authoritative list of tasks and functions would be impossible, given film's inherent diversity. Orson Welles is a long way from qualifying for *Citizen Kane*. But for *Primer*, Shane Carruth was the sole practitioner of almost every one of the productive, creative, and artistic functions detailed above, so he may be included here. If in doubt, enter under title. Use the Library of Congress Name Authority File (NAF), an appropriate alternative authority file, or formulate the name according to your local guidelines. Use one of the terms in RDA Appendix I to qualify the entry with an appropriate relationship designator—this will usually be "filmmaker," defined by RDA as a creator "individually responsible for the conception and execution of all aspects of the film" (RDA Appendix I.2.1). Use of this field will be infrequent if your library collects mainly commercial discs. Film-school productions are the obvious exception. The field ends with a full stop, other mark of punctuation, or closing parenthesis:

    100 1# $a Carruth, Shane, $e filmmaker.

245 Title Statement (NR)

See chapter 3 for details on how to transcribe an appropriate statement of responsibility for individuals and corporate entities in the title statement field.

250 Edition Statement (R)

It can be difficult to assess whether a work on DVD or Blu-ray Disc is an edition or not. Film distributors use the word and concept more loosely than book publishers. But as abridgements and reworked versions of printed works can be understood as editions, so the alteration of films from projected to optical disc versions can sometimes be considered an edition too. If the DVD/Blu-ray Disc case contains the text "Widescreen edition," "Pan and scan edition" or similar, include this in an edition statement. However, the presence of the word "widescreen" on the sleeve insert does not, in itself, justify an edition statement. Before asserting that a resource counts as an edition, RDA advises the cataloger to identify certain words or statements indicative of alteration or difference (RDA 2.5.2.1). Use a general note (field 500) to describe these technical features as prescribed by RDA. A director's cut (see above) counts as an edition.

As per RDA instructions, "transcribe an edition statement as it appears on the source of information" (RDA 2.5.1.4). In order of preference, this should be a) the same source as the title, b) information shown within the disc presentation, c) information from the sleeve insert or printed on the disc, or d) any other external source (RDA 2.2.4). As with most RDA fields, if taken from an external source, place in square brackets (LC-PCC PS 2.2.4).

Neither indicator is defined. As RDA supports ISBD punctuation, the field must end with a full stop. RDA expands what can be included in an edition statement (RDA 2.5.2.1), and as a result, the 250 field was made repeatable in 2013:

    250 ## $a Director's Cut.

    250 ## $a 20th Anniversary Edition.

    250 ## $a 2nd ed.

    250 ## $a Special widescreen edition.

257 Country of Producing Entity (R)

An optional field, used specifically for films, in which the cataloger may record the country (never a lower jurisdiction or geographical area) where the central office of the film's main production company is based. Abbreviations may be used, but for consistency, the name of the country as listed in the NAF (as it was known at the time of the film's production), should be preferred. For international co-productions, or production companies with a considerable organizational presence in more than one country, list multiple countries separated by a space-semicolon-space. If uncertain about the appropriateness of a particular country, follow with a question mark and enclose in square brackets. A 500 note may be added to explain anything unusual, unclear, or ambiguous. You may include subfield $2 containing the MARC code that identifies the source of the country's form as indicated in subfield $a. Where the disc or discs contain more than one work, and their production companies are based in different countries, use multiple 257 fields.

Note that this field was redefined in October 2009, prior to which it was named "Country of Producing Entity for Archival Films," and was non-repeatable.

Both indicators are undefined. There is no internal punctuation. The field ends with a full stop or other mark of punctuation, unless the final word is an abbreviation or other data element that ends with its own mark of punctuation. A closing full stop should follow any closing bracket or parenthesis.

>   257 ## $a United States.
>
>   257 ## $a [Iceland?].
>
>   257 ## $a Congo (Democratic Republic).
>
>   257 ## $a Great Britain ; France ; Germany.
>
>   257 ## $a China $2 naf
>
>   257 ## $a [Country of production not identified].

260 Publication, Distribution, etc. (Imprint) (R)

Use the 264 field in RDA records to record information about publication and distribution.

264 Production, Publication, Distribution, Manufacture, and Copyright Notice (R)

The 264 field was created in response to the requirement in RDA to separate out elements formerly conflated in the 260 field. For example, AACR2 did not require a clear, coded distinction between publication, production, and distribution, though MARC subfields were available to record manufacturing information. RDA makes a distinction between these different functions. The field was not implemented until the second half of 2011, so some of the earliest RDA records still contain 260 fields. Update these when you encounter them.

Many independent filmmakers contend that making films is much easier than trying to get them distributed.[10] It was simple in the Golden Age of Hollywood, when a single company had absolute control over a film's life, from the first hazy idea in the mind of a scriptwriter under contract to the studio to the hour when a projectionist removed the last roll of film after its final showing in a theater owned by the same studio. Today, the distribution of film takes place in a more complex ecosystem. Although most of the larger studios maintain control over the distribution of films they have financed, many specialist firms now operate in a crowded and multifaceted marketplace.

Some companies handle more than one aspect of distribution—negotiating with, and delivering films to, theaters, creating promotional material and advertisement campaigns, selling discs and broadcast rights to cable and network television worldwide. Most money is still made from ticket sales, from which the producers and distributors retain the largest percentage (cinema owners receive very little—they turn a profit by charging high prices for cheap refreshments like popcorn and drinks).[11] The biggest cinema distributors, whether owned by studios or not, are most interested in the first month of cinematic release, when 95 percent of their gross income is made.[12] Ancillary rights, such as those for DVDs and Blu-ray Disc publication, are often sold on a time-limited basis to smaller firms, who may themselves sublicense to other, even smaller distributors, with tightly focused expertise in particular media or geographical markets. Theatrical distribution windows used to be phased, with releases to cinema screens, home entertainment media, and finally television, a drawn-out process. More recently, falling revenue from DVD sales has led to the theatrical window being reduced to about four months, at which time films are made available on physical and digital formats for sale and rental.

The distinction between the publisher and the distributor of a film on optical disc can be a fuzzy one, and the extra flexibility of the new 264 field is likely to add to, rather than repair, the confusion. Ascertaining the name of the publisher is difficult, and RDA's circular definitions of publisher and distributor don't help. In the context of DVDs and Blu-ray Discs, what librarians understand the definition of "publisher" to be is generally the same as how film people would define "distributor." They should be assumed to be equivalent, unless a clear distinction is made on the resource. An appreciation of the difference between producers, publishers, and distributors is not always recognized by those with responsibility for packaging design, so take care that you transcribe the name of the correct firm (i.e., don't transcribe the film's original production company). The publisher/distributor can be inferred from the prominence and position of its name and logo on a disc. Look also at the text running close to the edge of the disc, and the small text on the sleeve insert. Often, the publisher's name is printed on the spine of the sleeve insert.

$A PLACE OF PUBLICATION

Transcribe the place of publication in subfield $a. Take this from the same source as the publisher's name, and transcribe it exactly as it appears. If the place of publication cannot be found at this source, take it from another source within the resource. Failing that, refer to the list of sources given at RDA 2.2.4. The place of publication often doesn't appear on the resource at all, but it can usually be found on the publisher's website. Bracket the place of publication if taken from an external source. Spell the place out in its full, unabbreviated form, and qualify it with the name of the jurisdiction or country, unless obvious. Only one place of publication needs to be transcribed—in RDA there is no longer a requirement to add a place of publication in the country where the cataloger is based, or to privilege that place when multiple places are listed.

If the place of publication cannot be determined, enter the phrase "Place of publication not identified" in square brackets (RDA 2.8.2.6, LC-PCC PS 2.2.4), and transcribe the place of distribution or manufacture in an additional 264 field (RDA 2.9, RDA 2.10).

$B PUBLISHER

Transcribe the publisher in subfield $b. When there is more than one publisher, only include the first (RDA 2.8.2), unless it would be overtly misleading for it to stand alone. If you do include more than one, include all within the same 264 field. Transcribe the name of the publisher as it appears on the resource. Alternatively, record a more concise form of the publisher's name if the additional vocabulary is not required for identification (RDA 2.8.1.4).

If the publisher cannot be determined, enter the phrase "Publisher not identified" in square brackets (RDA 2.8.4.7, LC-PCC PS 2.2.4). When the distributor can be determined, transcribe this in an additional 264 field (RDA 2.9). If no publisher or distributor can be determined, but you know the name of the manufacturer, transcribe this in an additional 264 field (RDA 2.10). Distribution or manufacturer statements need only be used when you lack sufficient information to identify the publisher.

Publisher information, including place of publication, is only relevant to discs intended for distribution (usually on a commercial basis). Noncommercial productions, such as locally produced copies created for the purpose of conservation, probably require only a date, though RDA 2.7 is ambiguous on this.

$C PUBLICATION DATE

Record the publication date of the disc in subfield $c. Don't record an incomplete date—if you cannot determine it then estimate or infer it based on available information, and enclose it in square brackets (RDA 1.9.2, RDA 2.8.6.6, LC-PCC PS 2.2.4). The publication date can be inferred from the copyright date, which will be printed on most DVDs and Blu-ray Discs. To dissuade piracy, the film industry is keen on explicit claims of copyright. *Night of the Living Dead* (1968) owes something of its fame to the fact that it immediately entered the public domain on release, the distributors having inadvertently dropped the copyright notice when they changed the film's name on its title card.[13] Prior to the Copyright Act of 1976, copyright owners were required to place such a notice on the final prints of films.

Take care that you don't mistake the copyright date for the film's theatrical release date. Copyright renewal dates, or copyright dates for packaging materials, are often printed on the disc too. Packaging redesigns do not justify the creation of a new record. Some libraries have a policy of transcribing standalone copyright dates if present on the resource. Others only transcribe the copyright date if it differs from the publication date. Copyright dates are only a core element in RDA if neither the publication nor distribution date is present on the resource (RDA 2.11).

Keep in mind that DVDs were not sold in Japan until 1996, in the United States until 1997, in Europe until 1998, and in Australia until 1999. No DVD published in these areas can have publication dates prior to these dates. Similarly, no Blu-ray Disc can have a publication date prior to 2006.

INDICATORS AND PUNCTUATION

The first indicator is usually entered as a blank. A second indicator "1" is used for publisher information, "2" for a distributor, "3" for a manufacturer. When transcribing a copyright date in an additional field, the second indicator must be "4."

A second indicator "0" is used for unpublished material (though it is somewhat unclear what constitutes publication in RDA). MARC defines a field coded in this way as one that indicates the presence of a production statement. This does not refer to film production, or film producers, as described earlier in this chapter.

264 fields follow the same punctuation practices as 260 fields, except those fields in which the copyright date is transcribed, which do not have any end punctuation. All other fields should end with a full stop, comma, other mark of punctuation, or a closing parenthesis, bracket, or angle bracket. As per ISBD rules, each set of bracketed elements must be enclosed in its own set of square brackets (RDA D.1.2.1). The usual rules about capitalization, which generally advise to transcribe as found, apply:

```
264 #1   $a London : $b BBC Films, $c 2009.
264 #4   $ ©2010

264 #1   $a [Place of publication not identified] : $b Turner Home
         Entertainment, $c [2013]
264 #2   $a Burbank, Calif. : $b Warner Home Video, $c [2013]
264 #4   $c ©2013

264 #1   $a [Irvington, New York] : $b The Criterion Collection, $c [2013]
264 #4   $c ©2013

264 #0   [Between 1997 and 1999?]
```

490 Series Statement (R), 830 Series Added Entry— Uniform Title (R)

Transcribe series information as you would with books, but keep two additional things in mind when cataloging DVDs and Blu-ray Discs.

First, the word *series* should only be understood as it applies to bibliographic description. RDA defines a series thus: "A group of separate resources related to one another by the fact that each resource bears, in addition to its own title proper, a collective title applying to the group as a whole" (RDA Glossary). When speaking informally about a series on optical disc, we may be referring to vocabulary chosen by the publisher/distributor to link separate productions, usually films. Or we might be talking about a set of television episodes linked by a common cast, production crew, and situation, often featuring a continuously developing plot. Only the first concept is transcribed in the 490 and 830 fields. For details on how to record television series, miniseries, and serials, see chapter 5.

Second, it can be quite difficult to determine whether a set of words indicates a series, distributor branding, alternative or additional title, or merely marketing language. If you are unsure, the uncertain phraseology can be included within quotation marks in an additional 500 field note.

Transcribe the series as it appears on the disc or on-screen, in a 490 field (RDA 2.12.2.3, which advises following RDA 2.3.1.4's basic instructions on recording titles). If the series name cannot be found on the carrier then take it from, in order of preference, the case, any accompanying material, a published description (such as a catalog), or any other available resource. When including an 830 field, the first 490 indicator should be "1." If your record lacks an 830 field (i.e., when no authorized form of the series is found in the NAF), the first indicator should be zero. The second indicator is undefined. Include any initial articles in the 490 field entry. The field has no end punctuation.

Transcribe the 830 field as it appears in the NAF. The first indicator is undefined; the second "0." The 830 field ends with a full stop, other mark of punctuation, or closing parenthesis.

Where appropriate, include numbering. Transcribe as displayed on the item in the 490 field, and as indicated in the NAF for the 830 field:

    490 1# $a The Herzog collection
    830 #0 $a Herzog collection.

PRODUCTION AND DISTRIBUTION, CAST AND CREW | 49

```
490 0#   $a Jean-Luc Godard—the ultimate collection

490 1#   $a The Masters of Cinema Series ; $v. no. 17
830 #0   $a Masters of cinema series ; $v 17.

500 ##   $a 'Widescreen collection' on DVD sleeve insert.
```

508 Creation/Production Credits Note (R)

Most of the significant individuals or corporate entities described in the first half of this chapter should be recorded in this field. Record the names of any crew members that are considered to be important, with each individual (or group of individuals) prefixed with a statement of his or her function (RDA 7.24.1.3). The list of those included will differ by genre, with the addition of animators and art directors for animated films, special effects supervisors for science fiction and fantasy, choreographers for musicals, etc. The order is at the cataloger's discretion, but for a film, it is most useful to list the director first. The information can come from any source (RDA 7.24.1.2). Some have interpreted RDA to suggest that only crew members who do not appear in the 245 field's statement of responsibility should be included in a 508 note field. The text of RDA does not state this, and though it may confuse the library user to include the same information twice or more, an incomplete list of prominent crew members would be even more misleading. The 508 field is rarely, if ever, used to record production companies, though its definition and scope does not preclude this. Punctuation, aside from the full stop at the end, is at the cataloger's discretion: the examples below offer only a guide. Both indicators are undefined. The field ends with a full stop or other mark of punctuation. A closing full stop should follow any closing bracket or parenthesis.

Include performers, narrators, and presenters in a 511 field.

The following examples show possible contents of a 508 note for *One Flew Over the Cuckoo's Nest* (a 1975 feature film), *Finding Nemo* (a 2003 animated film), and *Mary Poppins* (a 1964 musical film):

```
508 ##   $a Director, Milos Forman; producers, Michael Douglas, Saul Zaentz;
         screenplay by Lawrence Hauben, Bo Goldman; cinematographer,
         Haskell Wexler; editors, Sheldon Kahn, Lynzee Klingman; original
         music, Jack Nizsche.
```

508 ## $a Director, Andrew Stanton; producer, Graham Walters; screenplay by Andrew Stanton, Bob Peterson, David Reynolds; cinematographers, Sharon Calahan, Jeremy Lasky; editor, David Ian Salter; original music, Thomas Newman; supervising technical director, Oren Jacob; supervising animator, Dylan Brown; art directors, Ricky Vega Nierva (characters), Robin Cooper (shading), Anthony Christov and Randy Berrett (environments).

508 ## $a Director, Robert Stevenson; producer, Bill Walsh; screenplay by Don DaGradi, Bill Walsh; cinematographer, Edward Colman; art directors, Carroll Clark, William H. Tuntke; editor, Cotton Warburton; original music, Richard M. Sherman, Robert B. Sherman; costume designer, Tony Walton; choreographers, Marc Breaux, Dee Dee Wood.

511 Participant or Performer Note (R)

List actors, narrators, and voice actors (for animated films) in this field. Which actors, and how many to include, is at your discretion—RDA merely advises listing those that are deemed "important for identification, access, or selection" (RDA 7.23.1.3). One rule of thumb might be to include everyone named in the narrative summary at the back of the sleeve insert. Alternatively, you might decide to include the actors listed in the opening credits, or on the sleeve insert's "billing block," the condensed-typeface list of cast and crew used on film posters and advertising paraphernalia. If the accompanying material notes that an actor's performance led to a significant award, you ought to include their name, no matter how incidental the performance (e.g., Beatrice Straight won the 1977 Academy Award for Best Actress in a Supporting Role for *Network* [1976], though she was only on screen for five minutes and forty seconds).

The form of the actors' names is left to the cataloger's judgment, but it is advisable to use the form most familiar to audiences; generally listed in IMDb, though once again any source of information can be used (RDA 7.23.1.2). IMDb is the best source for disambiguating film people with the same or similar names—it uses Roman numerals in parentheses after names to differentiate them, for example, Colin Higgins (I); Colin Higgins (II). Both the Screen Actors Guild and Equity (the United Kingdom actors' union) require members to use unique names, which is the reason some actors use a middle initial. Many actors trade under a different name than that printed on their birth certificates, because they don't want to be confused with someone else with the same name (Michael Keaton was born Michael Douglas), because a new name was more saleable or memorable than the original (Michael Caine grew up as Maurice Joseph Micklewhite, Marilyn Monroe as Norma Jeane Mortenson), or, during the Golden Age, because they wanted to disguise their Jewishness (for example, Tony Curtis, Kurt Douglas, Lauren Bacall, and Ernest Borgnine).

A first indicator "1" is used to generate the display content "Cast:" so there is no need to include this word in your listing. Some libraries prefer to use first indicator "0," followed by the phrase "Cast includes," which avoids the ambiguity over the list's completeness. Always use first indicator "0" for other contributions, and qualify them as in the examples below. The second indicator is undefined, and the field ends with a full stop or other mark of punctuation. A closing full stop should follow any closing bracket or parenthesis:

> 511 1# $a Harrison Ford, Rutger Hauer, Sean Young, Edward James Olmos, M. Emmet Walsh, Daryl Hannah.
>
> 511 0# $a Voices include: Tim Curry, Samantha Mathis, Christian Slater, Jonathan Ward, Robin Williams, Grace Zabriskie.
>
> 511 0# $a Narrator: Morgan Freeman.
>
> 511 0# $a Melvyn Bragg interviewing Dennis Potter.

518 Date/Time and Place of an Event Note (R)

The scope of this field is broad. It is most commonly used to provide further detail on the place (RDA 7.11.2.3) and date (RDA 7.11.3.3) of the recording of a live performance, most obviously a play or opera. It can also record temporal and location details for documentary films if this is important for access or description.

The place and/or date may be placed in repeatable $p and $d subfields, with the information in controlled or uncontrolled form. Both indicators are undefined. The field ends with a full stop or other mark of punctuation. A closing full stop should follow any closing bracket or parenthesis:

518 ## $a Performed live at the Olympia Theatre, Dublin, August 8, 1997.

518 ## $a Filmed on location in the Korengal Valley, Kunar Province, Afghanistan, between June 2007 and June 2008.

518 ## $d 11 July, 2013 $p BP Lecture Theatre, British Museum, London.

7XX Added Entries for Persons, Corporate Bodies, and Related Works (R)

A creator, that is, "a person, family, or corporate body responsible for the creation of a work" (RDA Glossary) is an RDA core element. You must include creators of films in your record using the guidelines in RDA 9.2 and 19.2, qualified by an appropriate relationship designator from RDA Appendix I.2.1. The most common of these, for practically every film, will be "screenwriter."

Other possible relationship designators for films include "librettist" (for filmed versions of operas), "lyricist," and "composer" (films of non-dramatic musical works); "choreographer" (ballet, or other dance work); "filmmaker"; "interviewee" and "interviewer" (for films composed of a single or small number of interviews—not documentaries that contain interviews mixed with other footage).

Everyone else is optional. Record persons, families, or corporate bodies associated with a work if you deem them important for access (RDA 19.3.1.3). Use an appropriate relationship designator from RDA Appendix I.2.2.

Of the crew listed earlier in the chapter, those that should be recorded include "film director" (which, for reasons known only to the authors of RDA, is not included in the list of creators, and therefore not a core element), "director of photography," "film producer," and "production company." Add others if you think it would be useful or practical to do so. It may be desirable to record a distributor or publisher if they have been the driver for a major alteration or re-production, such as scanning and digital manipulation of the original print for a Blu-ray Disc re-release.

Optionally, record any further relationship designators for contributors associated with expressions, using the appropriate relationship designations. Examples in RDA 20.2 include the additional access points provided by a library for *Brokeback Mountain* (2005). Seven actors are included under the set of examples for "performer." Under "other contributor," the art director, editors, musical composer, costume designer, and production designer are listed. All these have appropriate relationship designators in RDA Appendix I.3.1, but note that film editors are qualified by "editor of moving image work."

If necessary, provide access points for individuals, families, or corporate bodies associated with items or manifestations, using the appropriate relationship designator (RDA Appendix I.4, RDA Appendix I.5). For guidelines on recording individuals associated with related works, such as a novel or play on which the film is based, see chapter 3.

Because the Library of Congress authority files exist to permit "clear identification of authors and subject headings," you will find them lacking when it comes to authority control of film professionals.[14] If you cannot find a name in the NAF or an alternative authority file, formulate it according to cataloging rules and appropriate local guidelines.

Use indicators in access points for films as you would for books. In a 700 field, first indicator "0" is used for forename, "1" for surname, and "3" for family name. In a 710 field, use first indicator "0" for an inverted name, "1" for a jurisdiction name, and "2" for a name in direct order. The second indicator must either be blank or "2," used for access points to analytical titles for certain types of works within a resource (covered in chapter 3). For both 700 and 710 relationship designators, use subfield $e, usually preceded by a comma. Repeat this subfield in cases where "the same entity has multiple roles" (see guideline 10 of the PCC Guidelines for the Application of Relationship Designators in Bibliographic Records).[15] Relationship designators may be omitted if the individual or organization's relationship to the film cannot be determined. Relator codes may be used in subfield $4. The field ends with a full stop, other mark of punctuation, or closing parenthesis, unless subfield $4 is the last subfield, when no final punctuation should be present:

> 700 1# $a Reagan, Ronald, $e actor.
>
> 700 0# $a Andre, $c the Giant, $d 1946-1993, $e actor.
>
> 700 1# $a Nixon, Richard M. $q (Richard Milhous), $d 1913-1994, $e interviewee.
>
> 700 1# $a Welles, Orson, $d 1915-1985, $e screenwriter, $e film director.
>
> 700 1# $a Dubus, Marie-Sophie, $e editor of moving image work.

710 2# $a Republic Pictures Corporation, $e production company.

710 2# $a Library of Congress. $b Motion Picture, Broadcasting, and Recorded Sound Division.

830 Series Added Entry—Uniform Title (R)

See this chapter's entry on MARC 21 field 490.

NOTES

1. Marcus Hearn, *The Cinema of George Lucas* (New York: Harry N. Abrams, 2005), 132.
2. Ben Hecht, the most influential Hollywood screenwriter at the time, wrote of the film, in the newspaper *PM*, that "this movie was not written by Orson Welles. It is the work of Herman J. Mankiewicz." Quoted in Pauline Kael, "Raising Kane," *For Keeps* (New York: Dutton, 1994), 235–325, 274. Kael's essay was controversial at the time of its publication (1971), and her impressionistic and opinionated style has been criticized by film historians. Her choice of sources is selective. The critical consensus, then and since, is that Welles had considerably more involvement in the writing of *Citizen Kane* than Kael and Hecht give him credit for.
3. Kael, "Raising Kane," 247.
4. For more on the film's troubled history, and Welles's collaborators, see Kael, "Raising Kane." For a more balanced take on the early Welles, and the production of *Citizen Kane*, see Simon Callow, *Orson Welles; vol. 1: The Road to Xanadu* (London: Vintage, 1996).
5. Orson Welles and Peter Bogdanovich, *This is Orson Welles* (New York: Da Capo Press, 1998), 28–29.
6. John Hora, *The American Cinematographer Manual*, 9th ed. (Hollywood, CA: ASC Press, 2004), 1.
7. Paul M. Sammon, *Future Noir: The Making of Blade Runner* (London: Gollanz, 2007), 500.
8. U.S. ISBN Agency, ISBN Guides: Basic Information, www.myidentifiers.com/sites/default/files/images/MYID+Basic+Information.pdf. Note that the U.S. ISBN Agency is not a federal agency, but rather a for-profit division of Bowker, a publishing industry support company.
9. Jimmy Wales, "Ten Things That Will Be Free." Keynote lecture, Wikimania 2005, Frankfurt am Main, August 5, 2005, https://archive.org/details/wikimania2005_JimmyWales_1/.

10. See the various concerns raised in Geoff King, Claire Molloy, and Yannis Tzioumakis, *American Independent Cinema: Indie, Indiewood and Beyond* (London: Routledge, 2013).

11. Brad Tuttle, "Movie Theaters Make 85% Profit at Concession Stands," *Time*, December 9, 2009, http://business.time.com/2009/12/07/movie-theaters-make-85-profit-at-concession-stands/.

12. Alexandra Cheney, "Jeffrey Katzenberg Predicts 3-Week Theatrical Window in Future," *Variety*, April 28, 2014, http://variety.com/2014/film/news/jeffrey-katzenberg-predicts-3-week-theatrical-window-in-future-1201166052/.

13. Jonathan Bailey, "How a Copyright Mistake Created the Modern Zombie," *Plagiarism Today*, October 10, 2011, www.plagiarismtoday.com/2011/10/10/how-a-copyright-mistake-created-the-modern-zombie/.

14. This problem is discussed by Michelle Emanuel in "A Fistful of Headings: Name Authority Control for Video Recordings," *Cataloging and Classification Quarterly*, 49, no. 6 (2011): 484–99.

15. PCC Guidelines for the Application of Relationship Designators in Bibliographic Records, www.loc.gov/aba/pcc/rda/PCC%20RDA%20guidelines/Relat-Desig-Guidelines.docx.

CHAPTER 3

CONTENT

THIS CHAPTER DEALS WITH THE ARTISTIC AND INTELLECTUAL content of DVDs and Blu-ray Discs. It discusses the MARC fields which cover titles (130, 240, 245, 246, 730, 740), language (008/35–37, 041, 546), physical description (300, 306, 336–338, 340), notes indicating content (505, 520), form of work (380), and subject and genre headings (6XX).

Cataloging

008/35–37 Fixed-Length Data Elements/Language (NR), 041 Language Code (R), 546 Language Note (R)

When it comes to the recording of language, MARC 21 is overdesigned, and the three places it offers for the coding and description of linguistic data all serve different purposes. Films on optical disc can contain many different kinds of language content, and while only a small amount of this information will be of interest to library users, a full and detailed account of the language content will become more important as catalogs develop, and discovery layers offer a greater variety of faceting tools.

LANGUAGE IN THE 008 FIELD

The default language of the soundtrack or intertitles (for silent films, see below) should be entered in the 008 field, positions 35–37. If it is necessary to choose between language tracks before watching a film, code the language of the film's original release, if an option. If this language is not available, code the language displayed most prominently on the packaging and menu options. Code "zxx" when there is no spoken or sung language, and no intertitles; code "sgn" when sign-language is more prominent than any spoken language.

LANGUAGE IN THE 041 FIELD

It is only necessary to include the 041 field for discs containing more than one language. It enables the cataloger to expand on the language information provided in the 008 field, and add coded data indicating the presence of, most commonly, other soundtracks or subtitles. All languages on the disc must be recorded (RDA 6.11.1.4).

041 $A SPOKEN LANGUAGE

Use 041 subfield $a to record the language coded in the 008 (for spoken-language films), any other language(s) with a substantial spoken presence, and the language(s) of any additional audio tracks, including all dubbed versions. List the language indicated in the 008 field first.

041 $B LANGUAGE OF SUMMARY

Subfield $b may be used to record the language of an accompanying summary if different from the language recorded in subfield $a, such as information which may be present on the back of the sleeve insert. However, the utility of this subfield is questionable for films on optical disc, and it is not obvious how its use would be helpful to catalog users. Likewise, subfield $g may record the language of the packaging if it differs from the first language listed in $a, but library users are unlikely to find this additional information beneficial.

041 $H ORIGINAL LANGUAGE

Subfield $h may be used to record the original language of the film; that is, the language the actors were filmed speaking, or the language of the original intertitles. Include this information if is not apparent from the rest of the description, or if the disc lacks the original language version. However, changes to MARC in 2011 enable this field to be used even when the film is not a translation, allowing libraries to index by the language of original production. Prior to this change, use of subfield $h was broader, so take care when copy cataloging.

041 $J LANGUAGES IN WRITTEN FORM

Use 041 subfield $j to record the languages that appear in written form: subtitles, intertitles, and captioning.

Subtitles, which display as text at the bottom of the screen, provide a transcription of the words spoken and/or translations of the characters' speech into different languages. Subtitles may be encoded as part of the image or provided as a digital overlay. The former cannot be turned off, but the latter are usually optional, and may be selected from the disc menu, or among the remote-control and system options. Subtitles for the hearing-impaired provide additional descriptions of non-spoken audio.

Intertitles appear in a separate frame between the action sequences of silent films, usually providing a summary of the action, or implied conversation. They cannot be selected or turned off. Early twentieth-century Europe was a more linguistically diverse place than is generally realized, and it was quite common for continental productions to create content in more than one language.

Closed captioning was an early version of subtitling that provided a description of the non-spoken audio elements and other contextual information in addition to transcribing the spoken text, designed to help the deaf and hard of hearing. Captions are visible as white letters against a black background. Captioning was developed first for television broadcasts, then later for VHS. It was embedded in the video signal, and did not transfer particularly well to digital formats, which can struggle with decoding. Region 2 DVDs (see chapter 4 for an explanation of DVD regional coding) do not carry closed captioning and Blu-ray Discs cannot do so. Instead, additional subtitle tracks are often provided for the hearing-impaired. Closed captions are so called because in early broadcasts they were purposely hidden from viewers who lacked the technology to receive them. *Open captions*, permanently visible, are rarer still.

041 INDICATORS AND PUNCTUATION

Usually the first indicator of a 041 field will be "1," indicating that the item is, or includes, a translation. Subtitles, dubbing, and alternative language tracks are all examples of translation. Use first indicator "0" for a film in which more than one language is spoken, and for which no translations have been provided. The second indicator will usually be "#," which notes that the field contains MARC language codes. A second indicator "7," with an appropriate subfield $2, should be used if other language codes are used. The field has no end punctuation.

546 LANGUAGE NOTE

Use a 546 note field to clarify or expand upon information given in the 008/35–37 and 041 fields. The 041 subfields lack the complexity required to differentiate between different types of language content. There is no minimum number of words for inclusion of a language, so cataloger's judgment should be used. Arnold Schwarzenegger's catchphrase "Hasta la vista, baby" does not justify the coding of Spanish in a record describing *Terminator 2: Judgment Day* (1991), but if the use of a language is more than a token, it may be helpful to include it in a 546 field note. Both indicators are undefined. The field ends with a full stop or other mark of punctuation. A closing full stop should follow any closing bracket or parenthesis.

EXAMPLES

Spoken language English. Additional Spanish sound track. Optional subtitles in English, French, Portuguese, and Spanish. English packaging and menus:

    008/35-37 eng
    041 1# $a eng $a spa $j eng $j fre $j por $j spa $h eng
    546 ## $a In English with optional dubbed Spanish soundtrack; optional English, French, Portuguese, or Spanish subtitles.

Spoken language French, Arabic, and Corsican, with brief Italian sequences. French subtitles for sequences in Arabic and Corsican. French packaging and menus:

    008/35-37 fre
    041 1# $a fre $a ara $a cos $j fre $h fre $h ara $h cos
    546 ## $a Soundtrack a mixture of French, Arabic and Corsican, with brief sequences in Italian; French subtitles for sequences in Arabic and Corsican.

Spoken language English. Optional French, German, and Spanish sound tracks. Close-captioned in English. Subtitles in English, French, Spanish,

German, Arabic, Russian, Chinese, Chinese (simplified), Bahasa Malaysian, and Urdu. English packaging and menus:

> 008/35-37 eng
> 041 1# $a eng $a fre $a ger $a spa $j eng $j fre $j spa $j ger $j ara $j rus $j chi $j ind $j urd $h eng
> 546 ## $a In English with optional dubbed French, German or Spanish soundtracks; optional subtitles in English, French, Spanish, German, Arabic, Russian, Chinese, Chinese (simplified), Indonesian or Urdu. Close-captioned in English.

English sound track. Original production in Spanish and German. English packaging and menus:

> 008/35-37 eng
> 041 1# $a eng $j eng $h spa $h ger
> 546 ## $a In English. Original production was in Spanish and German.

DVDs and Blu-ray Discs can store up to eight audio tracks, though these are often used for commentary tracks and additional audio formats (e.g., stereo and surround sound) in addition to different languages. Thirty-two subtitle tracks can be stored.

See OLAC's best practice document for video language coding for further information and examples.[1]

130 Main Entry—Uniform Title (NR)

The use of an authorized access point for a film itself is uncommon. However, because it is an RDA core element, the cataloger should carefully consider whether one is required. It may be used to record the preferred title of a work, that is "the title in the original language by which the work has become known either through use in resources embodying the work or in reference sources" (RDA 6.2.2.4). This title may differ from what appears on the title frame which, when present, is the source of the information entered in a 245 field.

A 130 field is used most commonly for films that have the same title as one or more other items in the catalog, which happens with films based on novels or plays. It also occurs when different filmed versions of a story exist, or when different films share the same title—a common occurrence, since

Hollywood producers have a habit of borrowing older film titles for contemporary blockbusters. If there is a potential for conflict, check first the catalog, then the NAF or IMDb. Where a title has been repeated, the advantages of disambiguation using a 130 field should be considered. When necessary to distinguish the film from works in other formats, add "Motion picture" in parentheses after the title (RDA 6.27.1.9). Although this phrase may confuse the library user, and although elsewhere in RDA it is used to refer to a contiguous set of images on photochemical film, it is the only applicable form in the list provided at RDA 6.3.4.3. Add the year of release if more than one film exists with the title (RDA 6.4). If two or more films with the same name were released in the same year, add the surname of the director in the format shown below (RDA 6.6, LC-PCC PS 6.27.1.9):

130 0# $a Remains of the day (Motion picture)

130 0# $a Hamlet (Motion picture : 1996)

130 0# $a Noise (Motion picture : 2007 : Saville)

A 130 field may be used when a film has been released under different titles in the same language. This may happen when an American film uses vernacular, cultural, or geographical references that would be unfamiliar to viewers in other English-speaking countries, or vice-versa. An authorized access point may therefore be useful when the screen title differs from the release title, or when the same film has different titles in different jurisdictions:

130 0# $a Ice cold in Alex (Motion picture)
245 10 $a Desert attack . . . [2]

130 0# $a Hoosiers (Motion picture)
245 10 $a Best shot . . .

Some kinds of translations may also use 130 fields. Most commonly, they should be used for a single film dubbed into one other language, which can only be watched in this language. Subfield $1 should include the language into which the film has been dubbed. Similarly, silent films with intertitles in a language other than that of the original release may be provided with an authorized access point. However, a uniform title in a foreign language can be problematic, as many systems will display a 130 in preference to a 245 field. Check this with a systems librarian or vendor if unsure.

```
130 0#   $a Shichinin no Samurai. $1 English.
245 10   $a Seven samurai . . .

130 0#   $a Cabinet des Dr. Caligari. $1 English.
245 14   $a The cabinet of Dr Caligari . . .
```

For all uses of a 130 field, the first indicator notes the number of non-filing characters, for titles that begin with an article. Most libraries follow OCLC practice, which implements the LC suggestion that initial articles may be deleted, and titles entered without them. The second indicator is undefined. Field 130 ends with a full stop, other mark of punctuation, or closing parenthesis.

A 130 field cannot be used if any other 1XX field is present, and should only contain an authorized form of the title. If multiple films are present on the resource, enter uniform titles in 730 fields. The LC-PCC PS for RDA 6.27.1.9, which covers additions to access points representing works, offers many more cases where authorized access points are constructed for a film itself.

240 Uniform Title (NR)

A 240 field will only be necessary when a 100 field is present. As noted in the previous chapter, a 100 field would be somewhat unusual in a catalog record for a film. Where the inclusion of a uniform title is required, use a 130 or 730 field.

245 Title Statement (NR)

The title of a film is usually obvious, but the title statement probably causes more difficulty for the audiovisual cataloger than any other MARC bibliographic field. In part, this is due to RDA's difficulties with film, reflected in language that is often inapplicable to the medium, in ambiguous examples, and in a failure to appreciate the complexity of film production. But the landscape of film is diverse, and a film's opening credits (in which the title often appears) reflects this diversity of form, professionalization, and financing mechanisms. The way a title displays is often integral to the artistic form and purpose of a film, and often helps to establish its genre, style, and content. Title screens and sequences have many functions beyond the informational.

SOURCE OF TITLE IN $A

While the title of a film is usually fairly obvious, it can be difficult to tell the cataloger where to locate it, and how to transcribe it. Most of the time this is easy—the source of information for a film's title is the title frame or frames (applied to film in RDA) or title screen (applied to digital resources) (RDA 2.2.2.3). The title is customarily displayed close to the start, or at the very end, of the film's opening credits or title sequence. Opening credits are shown over the action of the film. Title sequences, most familiar from the *James Bond* films, are distinct and discrete mini-films in their own right, which list cast and crew in a stylized sequence used to set a mood, and often played against the backdrop of a commissioned song. The credits detail, in a calibrated and negotiated way, the names of the individuals who were most significant to the film's creation, and appear on-screen during the first few minutes. But sometimes there is a wait—thirteen minutes in the case of *Raising Arizona* (1987), so fast-forward with discretion.

Not all films have a title frame or title screen. In recent years, it has become fashionable to dispense with opening credits entirely. This is an idiosyncratic signature favored by directors such as Clint Eastwood and Christopher Nolan, and also occurs frequently in films built on the conceit of "found footage" (such as *Paranormal Activity* [2007] and *Cloverfield* [2008]). The title of these films usually, though not always, appears before the end credits. For films that lack a title frame or screen, take the title, in order of preference, from a version printed on the disc label, from the container, or from the disc menu (RDA 2.2.2.3.1). If the cataloger thinks that the title printed on the disc label is more appropriate than the on-screen version, RDA authorizes using it in preference (RDA 2.2.2.3). This alternative may be helpful for foreign-language films, particularly when the film is known by the translated title, or when the title frame is in an unfamiliar language. It also makes it possible to ignore the stylistic features of a film title presented in an unusual way. Include a concise 500 note if the title is taken from a source other than the title frame or screen. The title frame or screen should not be confused with the title in the disc menu.

RDA allows the cataloger to replicate the stylistic peculiarities sometimes displayed in the capitalization of film titles, but the capitalization practices of RDA Appendix A (effectively the same rules as in AACR2) are more likely to serve the needs of the user.

$B PARALLEL TITLES AND SUBTITLES

If the title appears in more than one language, transcribe the version in the language of the film's content in subfield $a, then include the other version(s) in subfield $b, and/or as variant titles in a 246 field, as appropriate. Where the resource contains more than one parallel title, transcribe each within the same subfield $b, or chose the title most relevant to the user. An English-language title frame is sometimes inserted into foreign-language productions released in English-speaking countries. More commonly, an English title will appear as a subtitle. This form of parallel title should be transcribed in subfield $b, preceded by an equals sign (RDA 2.3.3.1). A parallel title may be taken from any source (RDA 2.3.3.2). That is, subfield $a could transcribe the title in one language as taken from the title frame, and subfield $b a parallel title in another language taken from the disc case. A note may be made in such cases if the source of the parallel title is considered important. Subtitles (in the cataloging sense of the word, not the cinematic one) can also be transcribed using the more familiar subfield $b preceded by a colon.

$C STATEMENT OF RESPONSIBILITY

A statement of responsibility is a core RDA element, though only one is required (RDA 2.4.2). Transcribe it as it appears on the source of information (RDA 2.4.1.4), normally the opening credits. In RDA, a statement of responsibility relates "to the identification and/or function of any persons, families, or corporate bodies responsible for the creation of, or contributing to the realization of, the intellectual or artistic content of the resource" (RDA 2.4.1.1). Many of the individuals and corporate bodies detailed in chapter 2 meet these criteria, yet the text also implies that performers, producers, and those "who have contributed to the artistic and/or technical production" should be recorded elsewhere, usually in note fields. It is, therefore, unclear who remains to be transcribed in the 245 field's statement of responsibility.

RDA's examples add to the uncertainty. RDA 2.4.1.6 offers a television broadcast in which the producer, writers, directors, animator, and editor are all included. Only one of the examples appears to describe a film: the text reads: "directed and produced by the Beatles." Unfortunately, it is impossible to map this to a real-world resource—The Beatles did not direct and produce any of their five feature films—but it does appear to justify the transcription of directors and producers. As outlined in the previous chapter, these are usually the two most important "responsible entities" for films, and their collocation is the typical combination of words prefixing an opening credits title frame, in the form "Library Pictures presents a film by Melvil Dewey." Because a screenwriter must be included in an additional access point field (see chapter 2), any screenwriters whose names appear in the credits must also be included.

Therefore, transcribe the author(s) of the screenplay, producer(s), and director(s) in the form, language, and order they appear on the screen. Producers and production companies differ in the degree of their involvement, so will not always be listed together. Take care with the word "production"—it can, after all, refer to the film in its entirety. In the mid-twentieth century, the phrase "a Jane Doe production" in the opening credits often meant that Jane Doe was the film's director: nowadays the phrase would read "a Jane Doe film." For foreign language material, statements of responsibility can be transcribed from the subtitles; they do not need to be in their original language.

Record other names listed in the credits in 508 and 511 note fields. It is uncertain whether these lists should exclude those names listed in the statement of responsibility. This confusion, and the general lack of clarity about statements of responsibility for film, can be traced to RDA's uncritical adoption of the ambiguous rules found in AACR2 7.1F and 7.6B6. At the time of writing, a CC:DA task force is looking at these issues, in particular the inconsistencies between RDA sections 2.4, 7.23, and 7.24.

RDA 2.4.1.4 offers an option for the abridgement of statements of responsibility. The accompanying LC-PCC PS advises against this, but used judiciously, this can help prevent the title statement from becoming overly long, and grants the cataloger a helpful degree of flexibility. A mark of omission (. . .) should not be used to indicate any exclusion. Omissions may be summarized in square brackets when a single statement of responsibility names more than three persons or corporate bodies performing the same function (e.g., ". . . produced by Mark Gordon [and seven others] . . .") (RDA 2.4.1.5), though once again the accompanying LC-PCC PS advises against it. For mainstream productions it is only necessary to consider this for producers. The Directors Guild of America allows only a single director to be listed in credits for feature films. The Writers Guilds permit three credits at most, though teams of two may be credited as one if separated by an ampersand!

PREFATORY WORDS

Film titles are often prefaced and introduced with the name of the principal production company or director, and on occasion the writer or producer. Words that serve as an introduction to the title should not be transcribed (RDA 2.3.1.6). The text of RDA includes examples of production companies and corporate copyright owners. Therefore, all words such as "Disney presents," "Universal Pictures presents" and "DC Comics presents" should be ignored when transcribing titles, though these versions may be added as a variant in a 246 field if it may assist identification or access.

However, when it comes to names, families, and corporate bodies, RDA seems to recommend including them in transcriptions when certain criteria hold. That is, if "the title includes a name that would normally be treated either as part of a statement of responsibility or as the name of a publisher, distributor, etc., and the name is an integral part of the title (e.g., connected by a case ending) then record the name as part of the title" (RDA 2.3.1.5). No films are offered as examples.

It makes little sense to rule that a film with the words "Disney's Sleeping Beauty" in the title frame should be transcribed as "Sleeping Beauty," but that "Steven Spielberg's Amistad" should be transcribed as "Steven Spielberg's Amistad." The title of *Sleeping Beauty* is "Sleeping Beauty," the title of *Amistad,* "Amistad." It would actually be more useful to append the word "Disney" to the first title, to differentiate its production from two other films with the same name. This rule privileges the word order and grammatical rules of the English language.

There is a clear conflict with the RDA instruction above and the instruction at 2.3.1.6: "Do not transcribe words that serve as an introduction and are not intended to be part of the title." Because the names of directors or writers are not intended to form part of a title (there are exceptions), the author advises against their transcription in a 245 field. However, if they appear on the title frame, or in any of RDA's other prescribed sources, treat them as variant titles and record in a 246 field.

If a title cannot be determined from any source, devise a brief title that indicates the form and subject, "e.g., names of persons, corporate bodies, objects, activities, events, geographical area and dates" (RDA 2.3.2.11) of the work. The title should be in English (LC-PCC PS 2.3.2.11) and enclosed within square brackets (LC-PCC PS 2.2.4).

MULTIPLE WORKS ON DISC(S)

When a disc contains multiple works, but one is dominant, transcribe the title of this work in the 245 field (RDA 2.1.2.2), with information on the additional titles recorded elsewhere as appropriate. Most obviously, the other works should be listed in a 505 formal contents note, and additional access points provided in 700, 710, 730, or 740 fields, as for a single work.

When a disc contains multiple works, and none is dominant, record a collective title if present on the resource (RDA 2.1.2.2, 2.3.2.6). Add a 505 note, and the appropriate 7XX additional access point fields, to provide information about individual titles. If the resource lacks a collective title, list the titles of all parts (RDA 2.1.2.2) in a 245 field, accompanied by statements of responsibility if they differ from title to title, though this can cause display issues, as subfields $a, $b, and $c are not repeatable.

INDICATORS AND PUNCTUATION

Punctuation, and use of indicators, follow familiar MARC practice, and the field ends with a full stop, even if another mark of punctuation is present. An additional full stop is unnecessary if the final word is an abbreviation containing its own full stop:

> 245 00 $a Enter the dragon / $c Warner Bros. presents ; written by Michael Allin ; produced by Fred Weintraub and Paul Heller ; in association with Raymond Chow ; directed by Robert Clouse.

> 245 00 $a Drive / $c produced by Marc Platt, Adam Siegel, John Palermo, Gigi Pritzker, Michel Litvak ; based on the book by James Sallis ; screenplay by Hossein Amini ; directed by Nicholas Winding Refn.

> 245 04 $a The girl with the dragon tattoo / $c Columbia Pictures and Metro-Goldwyn-Mayer Pictures present ; a Yellow Bird production; a David Fincher film ; producers Scott Rudin, Søren Stærmose, Ole Søndberg, Ceán Chaffin ; based on the book by Stieg Larsson ; screenplay by Steven Zaillian.

> 245 00 $a Dr Strangelove : $b or, how I learned to stop worrying and love the bomb / $c Columbia Pictures Corporation presents ; a Stanley Kubrick production ; screenplay by Stanley Kubrick, Terry Southern, and Peter George, based on the book 'Red Alert' by Peter George.

245 00 $a Letyat zhuravli = $b The cranes are flying / $c postanovka Mikhaila Kalatozova ; proizvodstvo ordena Lenina kinostudii "Mosfil'm."

245 00 $a [Five short documentaries about European nuclear power stations in the 1960s and 1970s].

246 Varying Form of Title (R)

Record variants of the title transcribed in the 245 field if deemed important for identification or access (RDA 2.3.6.3). Only use the 246 field for discs that contain variations on single or collective titles. Discs containing separate works should be given additional title listings in 730 or 740 fields.

Add a variant title where stylistic peculiarities, such as numbers, abbreviations, acronyms, and symbols, could make search and discovery difficult. However, do not overlook the greater flexibility of RDA when it comes to the content of the 245 field:

245 00 $a Se7en . . .
246 3# $a Seven

245 00 $a Turner & Hooch . . .
246 3# $a Turner and Hooch

245 00 $a Force 10 from Navarone . . .
246 33 $a Force ten from Navarone

Add a variant title for any parallel title previously provided in a 245 subfield $b:

245 00 $a À bout de souffle = $b Breathless . . .
246 31 $a Breathless

Add a variant title for a widely used shorter form of the title:

245 00 $a Indiana Jones and the temple of doom . . .
246 30 $a Temple of doom

Add a variant title for a widely used, if incorrect, form of the title, using subfield $i where appropriate.

245 00 $a First blood . . .
246 1# $i Also known as: $a Rambo

Inaccuracies in the title statement are transcribed in RDA. When the corrected title is considered important for access, a variant title may be added:

    245 00 $a Pirates of the Carribean . . .
    246 #1 $i Corrected title: $a Pirates of the Caribbean . . .

As noted above, there appears to be a conflict in RDA between the rule that advises against the transcription of prefatory words, and the formulation of a title prefaced by the name of a person, family, or corporate body in the possessive case. Where such formulations do occur, add them as a variant title in a 246 field, using subfield $i where appropriate. Provide any other displayed or printed version of the title that includes introductory or prefatory words if it would improve access, or is necessary for identification:

    245 00 $a They live . . .
    246 33 $a John Carpenter's They live

    245 00 $a Sleeping beauty . . .
    246 33 $a Disney's Sleeping beauty

    245 00 $a Pet Sematary . . .
    246 14 $i Title on container: $a Steven King's Pet Sematary

As with the cataloging of monographs, do not try to infer user behavior. Catalogers cannot presume to know what information users lack.

The first indicator follows the practice with monograph material regarding the generation of a note and/or added entry. The second indicator qualifies the type of title. For appropriate second indicators, chose among "# - No type specified," "0 - Portion of title," "1 - Parallel title," and "3 - Other title." The other indicators could be interpreted in ways analogous to their use for monograph materials, but the text of the MARC 21 bibliographic standard provides no justification for doing so. Omit initial articles (LC-PCC PS 2.3.6.3). The field has no end punctuation.

300 Physical Description (R)

$A NUMBER OF OBJECTS, AND DURATION OF FILM

RDA retains the term "videodisc" from AACR2. This word has been used to describe many different physical objects on which a contiguous set of still images have been stored, so the lack of more familiar vocabulary is unfortunate. But "videodisc" is the only appropriate word for DVDs and Blu-ray Discs in the approved list of carrier types (RDA 3.3.1.3).

However, alternative vocabulary is permitted if a) the carrier "is in a newly developed format" not on the list, b) none of the listed terms is appropriate, or c) an alternative term is preferred by the cataloging agency preparing the description (RDA 3.4.1.5). The third condition has been used by some libraries to justify the use of "DVD" and "Blu-ray Disc" in their descriptions. If this approach is preferred, make sure it is a matter of policy and not personal inclination. Otherwise, commercially distributed discs (i.e., DVDs encoded with MPEG-2 files on the DVD-Video standard, and Blu-ray Discs encoded with MPEG-2 or MPEG-4 files on the BD-Video standard) should be described using the singular or plural of the word "videodisc" in subfield $a, prefixed by the number of units (RDA 3.4.1.3). DVD-ROM and BD-ROM discs containing video files that must be opened using computer programs should be described using the singular or plural of the words "computer disc."

Despite its phobia of abbreviations, RDA still recommends contracted vocabulary for units of duration (RDA Appendix B.7), so give the length in minutes in parentheses, abbreviated as "min." Information on duration may be taken from any source contained within the resource. The running time should indicate the length of the film, not the combined length of film and supplementary material. If the cataloger knows that the running time differs from that stated on the source of information, this may be indicated by recording the stated playing time, followed by the words "that is," then the actual running time. However, be aware that the differing global broadcast standards reflected in geographical encoding variations mean that the running times of films on optical disc may differ from the running times of their theatrical projection (see chapter 4). It is, therefore, important to ascertain the running time from the resource, and not an external source such as IMDb. The running time can also be affected by shorter or longer end titles, distributor information, copyright notices, and geographically varied alterations due to censorship rules. If the disc(s) contain more than one film, give the running times of each, separated by semicolons (RDA 7.22.1.5).

$B SOUND AND VISION

In subfield $b, indicate whether the film contains sound (RDA 7.18.1.3). Note that silent movies are rarely silent for the purposes of cataloging. Use "sound" if the film is accompanied by an audio track, "silent" if there is none. Also in subfield $b, indicate whether the film is in color, in black and white, or both (RDA 7.17.3). RDA does not prescribe the spelling of colour/color, so either form may be used. Films that combine color and black and white are not uncommon. The combination is used most famously in *The Wizard of Oz* (1939), which changes from black and white to color when Dorothy arrives in Oz. Other notable examples include *Singin' in the Rain* (1952), *If . . .* (1968), *Solaris* (1972), *Schindler's List* (1993), and *Pleasantville* (1998). When encountered, try to provide concise detail on the mixture.

For early film, note whether the images are toned or tinted. Toning and tinting were both processes that gave a degree of color to black-and-white film—by the 1920s, most films had some degree of tinting. Tinting was a simple process that involved bathing black-and-white film in one or more colored dyes. Toning was a more complex and subtle chemical process that used film stocks embedded with different metals to achieve color effects. Indicate the presence of toning or tinting in parentheses.

$C DIAMETER OF DISC

Again, in contrast to RDA's metric preferences, the diameter of the disc should be recorded in inches in subfield $c, abbreviated as "in." (RDA 3.5.1.4.4, LC-PCC PS 3.5.1.4.4, LC-PCC PS 3.5.1.3). For DVDs and Blu-ray Discs, this will generally be "4 3/4 in.":

> 300 ## $a 1 videodisc (122 min.) : $b sound, color ; $c 4 3/4 in.
>
> 300 ## $a 1 videodisc (36 min.; 62 min.) : $b silent, black-and-white (tinted) ; $c 4 3/4 in.
>
> 300 ## $a 2 videodiscs (approximately 289 min.) : $b sound, black-and-white with a brief color sequence ; $c 4 3/4 in.
>
> 300 ## $a 1 videodisc (89 min., that is, 98 min.) : $b sound, color with black-and-white introductory and closing sequences ; $c 4 3/4 in.

$E SUPPLEMENTARY PHYSICAL MATERIAL

The disc on which a film has been embedded is, of necessity, "the predominant part of the resource" for audiovisual catalogers. Only this part of a resource should be recorded in subfield $a (RDA 3.3.1.3). But RDA's rules do not preclude the recording of other accompanying material, if substantial.

Many DVDs and Blu-ray Discs, especially those of historical or cultural interest, are issued with booklets. On occasion, catalogers will encounter "special editions" of films, accompanied by books or audio CDs. Provide a general note for anything unusual. If the accompanying material has been, or could be, published separately, add a 700, 710, or 730 field. Otherwise, anything with its own title should be included in a 740 uncontrolled related or analytical title added entry field (LC-PCC PS 2.3.6.3), omitting the initial article if present. Such objects may, of course, be cataloged separately. See chapter 7 for advice on "combo packs" or "dual format editions," which contain both Blu-ray Discs and DVDs in a single release.

Accompanying material may be recorded either in subfield $e, or an additional 300 field. In general, use $e for material that is supplementary to the film (e.g., booklets), otherwise add additional 300 fields (LC-PCC PS 3.1.4). The subfield can also contain information that would usually go in $b and $c, punctuated according to ISBD rules.

The details of special features included on the disc, or on an accompanying disc, are not recorded here, but in a 500 note.

INDICATORS AND PUNCTUATION

Both indicators are undefined. The field ends with a full stop if the record contains a 4XX field, but may end with another mark of punctuation or closing parenthesis if a 4XX field is not present:

    300 ## $a 1 videodisc (90 min.) : $b sound, black-and-white ; $c 4 3/4 in. + $e 1 booklet (32 pages : illustrated ; 19 cm)

    300 ## $a 1 videodisc (90 min.) : $b sound, color ; $c 4 3/4 in. + $e 1 book (129 pages : illustrated ; 21 cm) + 1 audio disc (stereo ; 4 3/4 in.)

    500 ## $a Accompanied by: Titanic : the story / by Henry Hirst. London : Go Entertainment, 2011 ; The band played on (CD).

    740 02 $a Titanic: the story.

    740 02 $a Band played on.

    300 ## $a 1 videodisc (145 min.) : $b sound, color ; $c 4 3/4 in.

    300 ## $a xii, 457 pages : $b illustrations, maps ; $c 24 cm.

    500 ## $a Accompanied by: The Baader-Meinhof complex / Stefan Aust ; translated from the German by Anthea Bell. London : Bodley Head, 2008.

    700 1# $a Aust, Stefan. $t Baader Meinhof Komplex. $1 English.

306 Playing Time (NR)

An uncommon field of six numeric characters, in the pattern "hhmmss" (hours minutes seconds), may be used to record a machine-readable version of a film's running time. For films shorter than one hour (and, analogously, shorter than a minute), record the hour (or minute) as two zeros. It is difficult to ascertain a film's length precisely (see chapter 4), and this field is really best confined to the cataloging of sound material.

336 Content Type (R)

Fields 336–338 are perhaps the most obvious immediate change in MARC 21 brought about by RDA. They dispense with the need to use the unsatisfactory 245 $h [videorecording] GMD, and break down ill-defined elements of the 007 and 008 fields into exclusive categories to better help differentiate the elements of film on disc. It's a shame that some of this clarity could not have been brought to the vocabulary used in these fields, which does not reflect common use. The elements are also somewhat random, lacking philosophical cohesion and terminological rigor.

RDA 6.9.1.3 provides a list of content types for the 336 field—record as many of these as are applicable in subfield $a. In most cases only "two-dimensional moving image" will be needed, but records may include "performed music," "spoken word," "still image," or "text" if they are a "form of communication through which a work is expressed." Most obviously, record "text" for any accompanying booklet substantial enough that users might search for it separately, or for a disc with substantial textual content. The RDA Glossary appears to imply that "three-dimensional moving image" should be used for 3-D films, although the images are flat and the illusion of depth is artificial.

Three-character MARC codes exist for each of the content types offered in RDA table 6.1 (www.loc.gov/standards/valuelist/rdacontent.html). If used, record these codes in subfield $b. The textual form, or the three-character code, may be used separately or together. Most libraries either use the textual form alone, or use both. The codes for "two-dimensional moving image" and "text" are "tdi" and "txt," respectively. The code for "performed music" is "prm," for "spoken word" "spw," and for "still image" "sti."

The authors of RDA do not appear to have considered that more than one element may need to be described in a bibliographic record, or if they did, they did not consider the practical difficulties of recording multiple elements. There are two ways of doing this in the 33X fields, neither of them satisfactory.[3] The different materials may be qualified using subfield $3. There is no controlled vocabulary for this text, so prefer common terms (book, DVD, Blu-ray Disc, etc.). Alternately, subfield $a may be repeated. The first option will result in a more user-friendly display, but the second is more open to system interpretation and manipulation. Both indicators are undefined, and the field does not contain any internal or end punctuation.

336 subfield $a should be in agreement with, and used in conjunction with, Leader position 06 (i.e., usually "g - Projected medium"). Take care to include the appropriate $2 codes, as shown in the examples below:

> 336 ## $a two-dimensional moving image $2 rdacontent
>
> 336 ## $3 book $a text $2 rdacontent
>
> 336 ## $3 Blu-ray Disc $a three-dimensional moving image $2 rdacontent

337 Media Type (R)

The 337 field is meant to reflect "the general type of intermediation device required to view, play, run, etc., the content of a resource" (MARC 21 bibliographic field 337), that is, the kind of machinery needed to access the type of content indicated in the 336 field. In general, this will be "video" for carrier technologies from videocassette through to Blu-ray Disc. However, in the unusual case of a video being encoded on a CD-ROM, DVD-ROM, or BR-ROM (i.e., using a type of video-file encoding such as Flash, QuickTime, etc., which may only be opened on a computer), this will be "computer." This term is somewhat incongruous, since "computer" is not a "medium" in the way the other terms provided in RDA 3.2 are.

The textual form of the media type is recorded in subfield $a, and the one-character MARC code in subfield $b (www.loc.gov/standards/valuelist/rdamedia.html). The code for "video" is "v."

See the above entry on field 336 for indicators, punctuation, the coding of subfield $2, and the options available for recording additional materials.

337 subfield $a should be in agreement with, and used in conjunction, with 007/00 (Category of material) (i.e., usually "v - Videorecording," or "c - Electronic resource"):

> 337 ## $a video $2 rdamedia

338 Carrier Type (R)

The 338 field describes the object on which the content is stored. Record as many terms as are applicable from the list provided in RDA 3.3.1.3. Take care with vocabulary that borrows from library standards, not necessarily literary warrant—the list includes "computer disc" and "audio disc," yet, without a space, "videodisc" (on the model of "videocassette"). Add a 338 field with "volume" in subfield $a if you have recorded the presence of an accompanying booklet in the 300 subfield $e.

The textual form of the carrier type is recorded in subfield $a, and the two-character MARC code in subfield $b (www.loc.gov/standards/valuelist/rdacarrier.html). The code for "videodisc" is "vd," for "computer disc" "cd," for "audio disc" "sd," for "videocassette" "vf," and for "volume" "nc."

See the preceding discussion of field 336 for indicators, punctuation, the coding of subfield $2, and the options available for recording additional materials.

338 $a should be in agreement with, and used in conjunction with, 007/01 (Specific material designation) (i.e., usually "d - Videodisc"):

> 338 ## $a videodisc $a volume $2 rdacarrier

340 Physical Medium (R)

The little-used 340 field contains details of the material substance and dimensions of an object. The diameter of discs may be indicated here (RDA 3.5.1.4.4), and some libraries do so as a matter of policy. Because it repeats information provided in the 300 field, its use is best limited to discs of unusual size, though it may also be helpful for describing formats such as videodiscs and photochemical film (see chapter 6). RDA's examples record the diameter of discs (including one videodisc of peculiar size) in centimeters, but most libraries follow LC practice, both here and in the 300 field, and record the diameter of discs in inches (LC-PCC PS 3.5.1.4.4).

Both indicators are undefined, and the field ends with a full stop, unless it contains a $2, in which case no punctuation is required. There is no internal punctuation:

> 340 ## $b 4 3/4 in. $2 rda

380 Form of Work (R)

This optional field allows catalogers to define the work by genre or form. It is most usefully deployed to indicate whether the resource contains a film or television recording in cases where it is not evident from other data in the record. It is a core element in RDA "when needed to differentiate a work from another work with the same title or from the name of a person, family, or corporate body" (RDA 6.3). Catalogers are free to use vocabulary of their choosing, though a term from any subject heading list or thesaurus may be used if qualified by a subject source code abbreviation in subfield $2. The author recommends the use of the terms "motion picture," "television program," or "television series" where necessary. Both indicators are undefined, and the field has no end punctuation:

    380 ## $a Motion picture

505 Formatted Contents Note (R)

A 505 field usually records the titles of separate works, or parts of single works, and may be used to provide a description of the content when the resource being described is on multiple discs, each containing separate titles. For resources containing a single dominant work with additional bonus features, use a general note field (500), as described in chapter 4. A good rule of thumb is to include a more detailed formal contents note if any of the additional features could be shown as distinct works in their own right.

The most commonly encountered example of this would be a resource with two discs—one containing the film, the other containing a documentary or documentaries about it, or shorter works by the same filmmaker. The field may also be used for longer works that need to be encoded on more than one disc, especially if indicated by numbered or named parts. The information may be recorded in a single field, or the contents of each disc can be listed in successive fields.

Where the resource contains multiple discs, and each disc contains both a film and additional features (such as documentaries, trailers, etc.), record only the main feature in the 505 field, with bonus material listed in a 500 field note.

Record the title from the source that provides the "best identification" (LC-PCC PS 25.1.1.3): normally the title frame, container, or disc menu, in that order. Record the first statement of responsibility if they differ for each title, along with any other individual or corporate body for which an access point entry has been created. There is no limit to the number of works that may be recorded.

Use a space-dash-space to separate components. The first indicator controls the generation of an introductory phrase: "0" for "Contents:" "1" for "Incomplete contents:" "2" for "Partial contents:". Use "8" if a phrase is not required. A blank second indicator records that the content designation is basic, while enhanced content designations are coded "0." Basic contents notes include all data in a single subfield $a, separated by ISBD punctuation where necessary. Enhanced notes use additional subfields: $g for miscellaneous information (such as duration or year of production), $r for statements of responsibility, $t for titles.

The field ends with a full stop, other mark of punctuation, or a closing angle bracket (used to record information about individual volumes in records containing temporary data). A full stop should follow any closing bracket or parenthesis:

> 505 0# $a disc 1: Parts 1-3 (184 min.) - disc 2: Parts 4-6 (201 min.) - disc 3: Parts 7 and 8 (130 min.).
>
> 505 2# $a disc 1: L'Atalante (1934) - disc 2: À propos de Nice (1930). Taris (1931). Zéro de conduite (1933).
>
> 505 00 $t Battleship Potemkin / $r directed by Sergei Eisenstein ; written by Nina Agadzhanova $g (1925). $t Drifters / $r New Era presents ; directed and edited by John Grierson $g (1929).
>
> 505 8# $a Main feature - Excerpts from 'Jean Renoir, le patron : la règle et l'exception' (1966), a French television program by film-maker Jacques Rivette - Part one of 'Jean Renoir,' a two-part 1993 BBC documentary by film critic David Thomson - Interview from a 1965 episode of the French television series 'Les écrans de la ville' in which Jean Gaborit and Jacques Durand discuss their reconstruction and rerelease of the film.
>
> 505 0# $a disc 1: Koyaanisqatsi / Francis Ford Coppola presents ; an IRE presentation ; produced and directed by Godfrey Reggio (86 min.,

1983, 1.85:1) – disc 2: Powaqqatsi / a Golan-Globus production ; a Francis Ford Coppola and George Lucas presentation ; directed by Godfrey Reggio ; produced by Mel Lawrence, Godfrey Reggio, Lawrence Taub ; written by Godfrey Reggio and Ken Richards (99 min., 1988, 1.85:1) – disc 3: Naqoyqatsi / Miramax Films and Steven Soderbergh present ; written and directed by Godfrey Reggio ; produced by Joe Beirne, Godfrey Reggio, Lawrence Taub (89 min., 2002, 1.78:1).

505 80 $g disc 1. $t Alien / $r a Brandywine – Ronald Shusett production ; directed by Ridley Scott ; screenplay by Dan O'Bannon ; story by Dan O'Bannon and Ronald Shusett ; produced by Gordon Carroll, David Giler, Walter Hill ; directed by Ridley Scott -

505 80 $g disc 2. $t Aliens / $r a Brandywine production ; story by James Cameron, David Giler, Walter Hill ; screenplay by James Cameron ; produced by Gale Anne Hurd ; directed by James Cameron -

505 80 $g disc 3. $t Alien / $r Twentieth Century Fox presents ; a Brandywine production ; story by Vincent Ward ; screenplay by David Giler, Walter Hill, Larry Ferguson ; produced by Gordon Carroll, David Giler, Walter Hill ; directed by David Fincher.

506 Restrictions on Access Note (R)

If film certification (see the discussion below on MARC field 521) is used to restrict access, or if access is restricted for any other reason, include a 506 note. This note should complement, not replace, a 521 note, used to record information provided by the appropriate national rating system. The first indicator may contain either a blank, "0" (no restrictions), or "1" (restrictions apply). The second indicator is undefined. The field ends with a full stop or other mark of punctuation. A full stop should follow any closing bracket or parenthesis:

506 1# $a Access restricted to those aged 18 and above.

506 1# $a Access restricted to those registered on the Master's program in Screen Media.

520 Summary, Etc. (R)

RDA recommends a summary "if it is considered to be important for identification or selection," and suggests that audiovisual resources fulfill this requirement in its parenthetical guidelines (RDA 7.10.1.3). However, none of its nine examples is an audiovisual work. The appropriate use of summaries can certainly assist the library user in making a selection, and gives the resource more visibility in the catalog. But by increasing the number of words indexed in the database, summaries can diminish the usefulness of keyword searching.

Information for a summary can be taken from any source (RDA 7.10.1.2), but may most easily be found on the back of the container, or respected online sources such as IMDb. Container summaries exist to sell a product, not to provide a "brief objective summary of the content" that RDA and library users require. Compare IMDb's summary of *Transformers* (2007): "An ancient struggle between two extraterrestrial clans, the heroic Autobots and the evil Decepticons, comes to Earth, with a clue to the ultimate power held by a young teenager,"[4] with the container's "From director Michael Bay and executive producer Steven Spielberg comes a thrilling battle between the AUTOBOTS™ and the DECEPTICONS™." The latter is particularly unhelpful because Bay (and perhaps Spielberg) will already be included in the record. Neither summary mentions robots (the film's subject), though these summaries may be edited to include significant keywords, if they are not present elsewhere in the record. If the summary is taken from a physical or digital source, provide it in quotation marks, with an attribution.

Avoid summaries containing spoilers that give away plot twists or might lessen any intended suspense or audience surprise (e.g., for films like *The Sixth Sense* [1999] or *The Crying Game* [1992]). Additional guidelines on writing summary notes can be found in OLAC's *Summary Notes for Catalog Records* (www.olacinc.org/drupal/?q=node/21).

A selection of first indicators generate various display constants. An undefined first indicator generates the content "Summary:". The second indicator is undefined. Subfield $b may be used for an expansion of the summary note, but as a general rule, summaries ought to be short enough not to require this. The field ends with a full stop or other mark of punctuation. A full stop should follow any closing bracket or parenthesis:

520 ## $a "In Nazi-occupied France during World War II, a plan to assassinate Nazi leaders by a group of Jewish U.S. soldiers coincides with a theater owner's vengeful plans for the same." Unedited summary from the Internet Movie Database.

520 ## $a "Silent movies are giving way to Talking Pictures – and a hoofer-turned-matinee idol is caught in that bumpy transition with his buddy, prospective ladylove and shrewish co-star." Edited summary from container.

521 Target Audience Note (R)

Most countries certify newly released films using a rating system, which provide advice to audiences by classifying according to the amount of on-screen sex, violence, profanity, and other adult themes.

The systems most familiar and relevant to readers of this volume are likely to be the ratings issued by the Motion Picture Association of America (MPAA); the British Board of Film Classification (BBFC); and Canada's two ratings agencies, the Canadian Motion Pictures Distributors Association (CMPDA) and the Régie du cinema. As a starting point for general information on film classification systems used in other jurisdictions, see Wikipedia's extensive entry on the subject (http://en.wikipedia.org/wiki/Motion_picture_rating_system), which provides descriptions of, and website links to, most of the rating systems used around the globe.

UNITED STATES

The Motion Picture Association of America (MPAA) (www.mpaa.org) is a trade association representing the six biggest Hollywood studios. The association has a broad mandate, but it is best known for its campaign against file-sharing and its film rating system. Small studios, and production and distribution companies, can submit their films to the association for a rating.[5] Films may be released without rating, though many theaters refuse to show unrated films.

The MPAA ratings are:

- G (General audiences)
- PG (Parental guidance suggested/some material might not be suitable for children [previously, the initials GP and M were used instead of PG])

- PG-13 (Parents strongly cautioned/some material may be inappropriate for children under the age of 13)
- R (Restricted/under 17 not admitted without parent or adult guardian)
- NC-17 (No one 17 and under admitted [NC-17 replaces the earlier X rating])

MPAA ratings have no legal force, and are simply meant to provide advice to the consumer. However, movie theaters in the United States adhere to them and often avoid films with explicitly adult themes.[6]

DVD and Blu-ray Disc releases are not considered to be different films from their associated theatrical versions, so MPAA ratings appearing on titles on optical disc are the same ratings given at the time of theatrical release. However, if the film has been substantially altered—perhaps as a re-edited director's cut—the optical disc releases will be given an unrated status. Re-released films can be resubmitted to reflect contemporary categories and social prejudices.[7]

GREAT BRITAIN

The BBFC (www.bbfc.co.uk) started out as the British Board of Film Censors, and was set up by the film industry in 1912. It is run on a not-for-profit basis, and is funded by the fees it charges for the classification of cinema releases, videorecordings, and video games. Its recommendations for cinematic releases have no legal basis—under law, the power to decide which films are shown to which audiences resides with local government, though BBFC's advice is generally followed by British cinemas.

The BBFC was renamed the British Board of Film Classification in 1984, when it was given the statutory responsibility to classify the vast majority of videorecordings made available for hire or purchase.[8] This authority was expanded and clarified with the Video Recordings Act 2010.[9] Cinema-release and home video versions of films usually receive the same classification, though on occasion videorecorded versions receive a more restrictive rating, due to bonus features, and their potential to be accessed by unsupervised children.

Since 2002, the BBFC categories applied to videorecordings have been:

- U (Universal, suitable for all ages)
- PG (Parental guidance)
- 12 (No one under the age of 12 may purchase or rent [the category 12A relates only to cinematic releases—classification guidelines are

the same as the 12 rating, but children under the age of 12 must be accompanied by an adult])
- 15 (No one under the age of 15 may purchase or rent)
- 18 (No one under the age of 18 may purchase or rent)
- R18 (Can only be sold in licensed sex shops or shown in licensed adult cinemas, in both cases to those aged 18 or over)

Material exempt from classification (e.g., educational films) need not display any symbol, but a white E in a green triangle is sometimes provided. Uc (Universal Children, particularly suitable for children under 4) was used until 2009.

IRELAND

Distribution companies offering films for sale and rental in Ireland often use the same packaging as films distributed in the United Kingdom. These containers will often print the relevant label from the Irish Film Classification Office (IFCO) (www.ifco.ie). It may be useful (and in the case of those cataloging in Ireland, essential) to indicate this category in the record.

CANADA

The classification of cinematic releases in Canada is the legal responsibility of the provinces, and there are six provincial film classification offices (the territories, and some provinces, use ratings assigned by neighboring provinces). The Canadian Home Video Rating System (CHVRS), administered by the Canadian Motion Picture Distributors Association (www.mpa-canada.org/en/), averages out the ratings for cinematic releases provided by participating provinces to provide a consistent display for all films made available for rental or sale. "Information pieces" are also supplied under a variety of standardized categories.

There are slight variations among the provinces that use the CHVRS, but the categories are usually:

- G (General audience, suitable for all ages)
- PG (Parental guidance)
- 14A (14 Accompaniment, those under 14 should view with an adult, no rental or purchase below this age where prohibited by law)
- 18A (18 Accompaniment, those under 18 should view with an adult, no rental or purchase below this age where prohibited by law)

- R (Restricted to those aged 18 or over, no rental or purchase below this age where prohibited by law)
- A (Adult, films whose explicit purpose is the portrayal of sexual activity and/or violence)

A government agency in Quebec, the Régie du cinema (www.rcq.gouv.qc.ca/), rates all cinematic releases and videorecordings. Its four classifications are:

- G (Visa général, may be viewed, rented, or purchased by those of any age)
- 13+ (13 Ans et plus, may not be rented or purchased by those under the age of 13—when applied to cinematic releases children under 13 to be admitted only when accompanied by an adult)
- 16+ (16 Ans et plus, may not be viewed, rented, or purchased by those under the age of 16)
- 18+ (18 Ans et plus, may not be viewed, rented, or purchased by those under the age of 18)

RECORDING TARGET AUDIENCE INFORMATION

The MARC 21 bibliographic standard provides ambiguous advice about where to record these classifications. 520 first indicator "4" displays the constant "Content advice:". Subfield $2 is used for the "Source code for the particular classification system used [for example, the MPAA (USA) and BBFC (UK) film classification systems] to construct the content advice statement recorded in subfield $a" (MARC 21 biographic field 520).

However, though imperfect and slightly misleading, 521 seems a better fit. Most studio productions are made with the probable classification in mind. As such, film classifications do indicate a target audience (though they are better understood as content advice). If included in a 520 field, they risk being misrepresented under the catchall of a summary. The MARC 21 bibliographic standard supports this interpretation by listing an MPAA rating as one of its 521 examples. RDA seems to be in agreement, defining an "intended audience" as "the class of user for which the content of a resource is intended, or for whom the content is considered suitable" (RDA 7.7.1.1). RDA links the intended audience to a 521 target audience note in Appendix D.2.

First indicators "0," "1," "2," "3," and "4" generate a variety of display constants that are mostly inapplicable to film. First indicator "8" generates no display constant, and should be used for most records, but if the cataloger wishes to generate the display constant "Audience:" this may be done using a blank. The second indicator is undefined. List the name or standard acronym for the organization(s) that provided the rating, followed by the rating itself. It may be useful to indicate if the rating has been superseded. Include content advice if helpful to library users. Where the classification has been misprinted (most frequently in Canada, because of CHVRS's complexity), include the correct classification. The field ends with a full stop or other mark of punctuation. A full stop should follow any closing bracket or parenthesis:

521 8# $a MPAA rating: PG-13.

521 8# $a BBFC rating: 15; Irish Film Classification Office rating: 18.

521 8# $a Exempt from classification.

521 ## $a CHVRS rating: R (should be 18A).

546 Language Note (R)

See this chapter's entry on MARC 21 field 041.

586 Awards Note (R)

This field may be used to record any prize awarded to the production. The text of the MARC 21 bibliographic standard offers this example: "586 ## $a Academy Award for Best Picture, 1987." RDA also provides instructions (RDA 7.28), and gives the example: "Academy Award: Best Actress, Diane Keaton; Best Director, Woody Allen; Best Picture; Best Writing, 1978."[10] If users will benefit from this information, record it here. If, like actor George C. Scott, the cataloger believes that the Academy Awards are "a public display with contrived suspense for economic reasons"[11] he or she may prefer to ignore the existence of this field, though there are, of course, other significant awards in the film industry too.

6XX Subject Access Fields (R)

Fields 600 (Subject Added Entry—Personal Name), 610 (Subject Added Entry—Corporate Name), 650 (Subject Added Entry—Topical Term), etc., may be used to record the subject content of audiovisual material in ways analogous to monograph material. Subject headings should be assigned for all important topics mentioned in the 520 summary statement field (LCSH Manual H 2230). The LCSH subject heading "Action and adventure films" would be appropriate for a 650 field for works *about* action/adventure films, not for works that *are* action/adventure films (though a handful of action films are about action films, such as *Last Action Hero* [1993]). When cataloging fictional works, add the genre subdivision "$v Drama" to subject access fields (LCSH Manual H 2230). LCSH has many headings of the form "[Topic] in motion pictures," used for works about these topics in film, not the films themselves.

The LC authorities FAQ (http://authorities.loc.gov/help/auth-faq.htm) advises that "works about 'movies,' 'motion pictures,' 'cinema,' and 'films' are all entered under the established subject heading 'Motion pictures.'" The scope note for the heading suggests that

> Works about the technical aspects of making motion pictures and their projection onto a screen [should be] entered under Cinematography. Works about the technical aspects of making video recordings, i.e., creating and storing moving images in an electronic form and displaying them on an electronic display are entered under Video recording.

Field 655 (Index Term—Genre/Form) meets a different need. In the second edition of *Nonbook Materials: The Organization of Integrated Collections*, Weihs, Lewis, and Macdonald noted that the increased popularity of film courses and availability of videocassettes had "resulted in patrons asking for motion pictures other than by subject matter. Librarians and media specialists would like headings for mood, technique, and genre, and classification for animated and experimental films."[12] The development of a distinct thesaurus of genre and form terms (LCGFT) has allowed catalogers to meet this challenge, and shows what can be achieved when the bibliographic control of audiovisual materials is informed by a careful mix of expert knowledge, user priorities, and literary warrant. The inclusion of genre is essential for assisting the user to find and select film. As LC's *Moving Image Genre-Form Guide* states, it "serves as a shorthand for archivists, scholars, and filmmakers, having become the single best recognized and intrinsically appropriate way to categorize film and television works into readily understood classifications."[13]

Genre headings in 655 fields describe what type of film the resource contains, not what the film is about. LCGFTs may be used for both fiction and non-fiction genres. "Genre" refers to a broadly understood category of film defined by a particular style, usually involving certain narrative elements, settings, stock characters, or themes. Familiar examples include Westerns, comedies, and science-fiction films. Films can encompass many genres.

In practical terms, "form" is a more problematic word, referring to films of a certain format, such as TV movies or documentaries. The text of the MARC 21 bibliographic standard offers a confusing, multifaceted definition that interprets form as a kind of material or subject, as opposed to genre's style or technique.

The Library of Congress began to develop distinct genre and form terms for films in 2007. These were published in the 2009 edition of *Library of Congress Subject Headings Supplemental Vocabularies: Free-Floating Subdivisions, Genre/Form Headings, Children's Subject Headings*. In 2011, they were separated out into their own distinct thesaurus, and LC discontinued the supplemental vocabularies book. The list is now included in the six-volume Library of Congress Subject Headings, and can also be searched as a distinctive set on Classification Web.

They are based on literary warrant, usually offer advice on alternative, broader, and related terms, and are often accompanied by useful guidance, for example, Apocalyptic Films:

> This heading is used as a genre/form heading for films set in a world or civilization after a catastrophic event (e.g., nuclear war, an alien invasion), sometimes also including the period immediately preceding the event. Films set in an uncertain future, in a society ruled by an ineffectual, corrupt, or oppressive regime or by aliens, robots, etc., are entered under Dystopian films.

When using these terms in a catalog record, code "lcgft" in subfield $2. Terms from other lists or thesauri may be used if accompanied by the appropriate code, in subfield $2, from the list of Genre/Form Code and Term Source Codes published by the Library of Congress' Network Development and MARC Standards Office. OLAC's Guidelines for the Usage of Moving Image LC Genre/Form Headings (http://olacinc.org/drupal/capc_files/moving-image-genre-guidelines-draft.pdf) offers additional advice and guidelines.

The Library of Congress, Academy of Motion Picture Arts and Sciences, American Film Institute, and British Film Institute all define a "feature film" as one that is more than forty minutes long. This definition is by no means universal, and the Screen Actors Guild maintains that a feature film must be at least eighty minutes long. When cataloging a film of forty minutes or longer, include the LCGFT genre term "Feature films" in a 655 subfield $a.

Next, determine whether the resource is fictional or non-fictional, and add a 655 field containing the term "Fiction films" or "Nonfiction films" as appropriate.

Add additional 655 fields containing appropriate terms from LCGFT, listing major genres before minor ones. LCGFT terms may not be subdivided.

LCSH headings can be used in lieu of LCGFT terms, but only if the scope note states that the subject heading is to be used for works of a certain type, not works about a particular topic. Where no scope note is present, catalogers may use their judgment. The source of these headings is coded by the inclusion of a second indicator "0," and does not require a subfield $2.

Though a welcome innovation, the use of genre and form terms is considered by some to be far from satisfactory. Some critics have argued that the idea of genre is so subjective, vague, and normative that it is nearly meaningless.[14] While this taxonomic problem is real and important for film theorists, genre terms are meaningful for audiences. More practically, Martha Yee has identified ten types of headings in the precursor terms to LCGFT that are neither genre/form, nor topical subject headings.[15] These are headings for films made for a particular audience, type of broadcast or distribution, films made by a filmmaker belonging to a particular group of people, films made from a particular point of view, unfinished films, the cost or production values of a film, styles and movements, films in a series, fictitious character, and radio or television time slot. Yee's paper was published in 2001, so does not take account of LC's creation of the separate thesaurus of genre and form terms, but most of the issues she identified still exist. However, lacking the easy pointers found in monographs (publisher descriptions, chapter titles, introductions, CIP data, etc.), the application of subject and genre access points to films can be difficult for librarians not versed in the language of cinema. The fuzziness of the two thesauri (LCSH and LCGFT) is therefore quite helpful. By definition, the application of subject or genre access terms is an inexact science.

Avoid subject headings containing spoilers. For LCSH fields, use the appropriate indicators familiar from cataloging monograph materials, and end all fields with a full stop, other mark of punctuation, or closing parenthesis. In 655 fields, the first indicator is blank, and the second "7." When ending with subfield $2, the field should contain no end punctuation; instead, the subfield preceding $2 should end with a mark of punctuation or closing parenthesis:

    600 10 $a Senna, Ayrton, $d 1960-1994.
    650 #0 $a Automobile racing drivers $z Brazil $v Biography.
    655 #7 $a Feature films. $2 lcgft
    655 #7 $a Nonfiction films. $2 lcgft
    655 #7 $a Documentary films. $2 lcgft
    655 #7 $a Sport films. $2 lcgft

    600 10 $a Mendez, Antonio J. $v Drama.
    610 10 $a United States. $b Central Intelligence Agency $v Drama.
    650 #0 $a Iran Hostage Crisis, 1979-1981 $v Drama.
    655 #7 $a Feature films. $2 lcgft
    655 #7 $a Fiction films. $2 lcgft
    655 #7 $a Thrillers (Motion pictures). $2 lcgft

700 Added Entry—Personal Name (R), 730 Added Entry—Uniform Title (R), 740 Added Entry—Uncontrolled Related/Analytical Title (R)

This section describes how to create additional access points for titles. For the more familiar use of a 7XX field to record the names of individuals and corporations involved in the production of a film itself, see chapter 2.

Create additional access points for related works. Access points should also be created for analytical works, that is, distinctive parts of the resource when the resource as a whole has already been given a comprehensive description.

RELATED WORKS

For a novel or play from which the film has been adapted, create an author-title access point using a 700 field. For adaptations of preexisting cinematic or televisual works such as remakes, prequels and sequels, etc., create a 730 field. Record related works in their catalog entry, or preferred title, format, which precludes the use of 740 fields.

Relationships to other works are cinematically important, both commercially and artistically. Of the ten 2013 releases with the highest box-office receipts in the United States, four were sequels, two prequels, and one a "reboot" of an earlier film. Six were based upon preexisting novels, stories, or comic books. Only one, *Gravity*, had an original screenplay.

A *sequel* maintains continuity of character, storyline, or setting from another film. The action can begin directly with the ending of a prior film, as with *[Rec]* (2007) and *[Rec]²* (2009), or at any time in the future (fifty-seven years pass between *Alien* [1979] and *Aliens* [1986]). *Prequels* are set temporally prior to a previously filmed work. They are less frequently produced, and usually made only because most of the original characters have died in previous films, or the storyline has come to a natural end point. Sequels and prequels do not have to cohere with what came before. The films of the *Terminator* (1984–) franchise contain notorious contradictions and internal inconsistencies.

There are many kinds of remake, from films with similarity in plot and character (*Rio Bravo* [1959] and *El Dorado* [1966]), to precisely constructed shot-by-shot re-productions (the 1960 and 1998 versions of *Psycho*). Successful European and Asian films are often remade as American productions. Directors who have filmed a story with a small budget early in their careers have sometimes returned to the same story when they become established Hollywood players (Michael Mann's *LA Takedown* [1989] and *Heat* [1995]; Alfred Hitchcock's *The Man Who Knew Too Much* [1934 and 1956]). Film producers and directors can find dramatic resonance in earlier films that echo contemporary concerns, justifying their re-creation. The endemic violence associated with Italian-American gangsters' control over illegal alcohol in 1930s Chicago (*Scarface* [1932]) inspired Al Pacino to pursue production of a film about the murderousness of Cuban-American cocaine distributors in 1980s Miami (*Scarface* [1983]).

A more recently developed Hollywood ploy is the *reboot*, where the concept behind a previous film or series is liberally shaken up, so that nothing but the core details and characters remain. Reboots differ comprehensively from the earlier version—continuity can be ignored, nonessential elements ditched. The reboot is a clever, if cynical, product. Frequently based on a cult or genre series, ironic and self-referential elements ensure that large existing fan-bases are placated, while an originality of style aims to attract new audiences. Reboots have a tendency to either be commercially and critically successful (the new *Star Trek* [2009–] and *Batman* [2005–2012] franchises), or complete flops (*Conan the Barbarian* [2011], *Total Recall* [2012]). Expect many more in years to come.

Preface the related work using subfield $i with the appropriate relationship designator as listed in RDA Appendix J (RDA 24.5.1.3), followed by a colon. Most commonly, this will be "Motion picture adaptation of (work)," but there is scope among these designators for abridgements, expanded versions of, remakes, prequels, and sequels to other works. Relationship designators may also be used for adaptations, etc., of expressions—see RDA Appendix J.3.

Internal punctuation of 700 fields for related works follows practices familiar from the cataloging of monographs, though the relationship designators that would usually follow the individual's name should be omitted (PCC Guidelines for the Application of Relationship Designators in Bibliographic Records, Guideline 12). The first indicator will normally be "1," the second undefined. The field ends with a full stop, other mark of punctuation, or closing parenthesis.

Compile and punctuate a 730 field as with a 130 field (RDA 24.4.2, 6.27.1.3). The first indicator should be "0," the second undefined. The field ends with a full stop, other mark of punctuation, or closing parenthesis.

Ideally, additional access points would to be created for authors, where cinematic works are based upon characters they have created, such as the countless films that have been made about Count Dracula, Frankenstein's monster, and Sherlock Holmes. Unfortunately, no appropriate designator exists in RDA Appendix I. Some libraries include these authors with the relationship designator "creator" in subfield $e, but this implies that the author is a creator of the work being cataloged. More granular kinds of relationships may be given designator terms with the publication of RDA Appendix L, still a work in progress. In the meantime, a generic note contained in a 500 field will have to suffice:

> 700 1# $i Motion picture adaptation of (work): $a Grass, Günter, $a 1927-. $t Blechtrommel.
>
> 730 0# $i Remake of (work): $a Total recall (Motion picture : 1990)
>
> 730 0# $i Remade as (work): $a True grit (Motion picture : 2010)
>
> 730 0# $i Sequel to (work) : $a The hustler (Motion picture : 1961)

ANALYTICAL WORKS

Additional access points for analytical works will include the titles of individual films where the resource contains multiple works, physically or digitally separate language versions of a single film, accompanying works, or additional bonus materials that have been issued separately at some point. When recorded in a 730 field, the title should be preceded by subfield $i, containing the relationship designator "Container of (work)" or "Container of (expression)" (changed from "Contains (work)" and "Contains (expression)" in RDA's April 2014 update). A 740 field may record cases when the title on the resource differs from the information recorded in the 730 field, or when the cataloger determines that additional uncontrolled titles may be usefully included.

Where a disc containing multiple works lacks a collective title, and all titles have been recorded in the 245 field, create additional access points for each title after the first, if the following titles have been listed after the first title's statement of responsibility.

Where a disc has been cataloged under a collective title, create additional access points for each of the films. Variant titles, such as the English title of foreign-language works, may be added as additional uncontrolled titles.

Dubbed versions of films, films shot in more than one language version, and films with intertitles in more than one language may be recorded as additional expressions. If these versions are recorded in 730 or 740 fields, record the original version in addition, as per the examples below. Include subfield $l containing the language, for versions in all languages except the original.

Analytical works can contain subfields $n and $p, detailing parts of sections, though their use should rarely be required for films.

For analytical works in a 730 field, the first indicator should always be "0," the second always "2." The field ends with a full stop, other mark of punctuation, or closing parenthesis.

For analytical works in 740 fields, the first indicator notes the number of non-filing characters. As with the 130 field, many libraries follow the OCLC practice of entering titles without initial articles, coding the first indicator "0." The second indicator for analytical entries is always "2." The field ends with a full stop, other mark of punctuation, or closing parenthesis:

> 700 12 $i Container of (work) : $a Aust, Stefan. $t Baader Meinhof Komplex. $l English.
>
> 730 02 $i Container of (work) : $a Red river (Motion picture)
>
> 730 02 $i Container of (expression) : $a Magnificent Ambersons (Motion picture)

730 02 $i Container of (expression) : $a Magnificent Ambersons (Motion picture). $l Spanish.

700 12 $i Container of (work) : $a Chekhov, Anton Pavlovich, 1860–1904. $t D︠i︡ad︠i︡a Van︠i︡a.

740 02 $a Uncle Vanya.

NOTES

1. OLAC Cataloging Policy Committee: Video Language Coding Best Practices Task Force, Video Language Coding: Best Practices, 2012, www.olacinc.org/drupal/capc_files/VideoLangCoding2012-09.pdf.

2. Ellipsis points within sample MARC 21 bibliographic fields are used in this volume to indicate that the field is presented in an abbreviated form.

3. For an overview of the display problems this creates, and the advantages and disadvantages of different approaches to description, see Music Library Association and Online Audiovisual Catalogers, RDA Test Group Discussion Summary Part 2: Unresolved Issues for Further Investigation, Discussion and Follow-Up, 2011, www.olacinc.org/drupal/capc_files/MLA-OLAC_RDAtest2.pdf.

4. Internet Movie Database, *Transformers* (2007), 2013, www.imdb.com/title/tt0418279/.

5. The Association has been accused of rating the releases of its constituent studios more leniently than independent productions. See Doug Atchison, "Separate and Unequal? How the MPAA Rates Independent Films," in John Landis and Jason Shinder, eds., *The Best American Movie Writing 2001* (New York: Thunder's Mouth Press, 2001), 59–69.

6. Gary Susman, "Whatever Happened to NC-17 Movies?," *Rolling Stone*, November 26, 2013, www.rollingstone.com/movies/news/whatever-happened-to-nc-17-movies-20131126.

7. Classification and Rating Administration, Motion Picture Association of America, Inc., Agreement to Submit Motion Picture for Rating, 2012, www.filmratings.com/downloads/cara_submittal_paperwork.doc.

8. British Board of Film Classification, About the BBFC, www.bbfc.co.uk/about-bbfc.

9. *Video Recordings Act 2010. Chapter 1,* www.legislation.gov.uk/ukpga/2010/1/pdfs/ukpga_20100001_en.pdf.

10. This is ironic, because Allen is the most famous non-attendee at the Oscars ceremony; he has only turned up once, in 2002, to thank Hollywood for supporting his home town of New York after the 9/11 attacks.

11. Anthony Holden, *Behind the Oscar: The Secret History of the Academy Awards* (New York: Simon and Schuster, 1993), 62.

12. Jean Weihs, Shirley Lewis, and Janet Macdonald, *Nonbook Materials: The Organization of Integrated Collections,* 2nd ed. (Ottawa: Canadian Library Association, 1979), 7.
13. Brian Taves and Judi Hoffman, *Moving Image Genre-form Guide,* 1998, www.loc.gov/rr/mopic/migintro.html.
14. See Robert Stam, *Film Theory* (Oxford: Blackwell, 2000).
15. Martha M. Yee, "Two Genre and Form Lists for Moving Image and Broadcast Materials: A Comparison," *Cataloging and Classification Quarterly* 31, nos. 3–4 (2001): 247–95.

CHAPTER 4

TECHNICAL FEATURES

THIS CHAPTER BEGINS BY OFFERING A BRIEF HISTORY OF DVDs and Blu-ray Discs, and an outline of their differing standards and formats. It moves on to cover the MARC 21 bibliographic Leader and control fields (007, 008), and the new fields covering sound (344), video (346), and digital file (347) characteristics. It then looks at the different uses to which general (500) and system details notes (538) can be put.

DVD

Cassette tapes may have been more convenient than vinyl records, but they sounded awful. The developers of CD technology promised to marry the portability and accessibility of tapes with the audio quality of records. Arguments over whether CDs or records sound better continue to this day. The grooves of a vinyl record copy the waveforms of the sound they represent—they are literally an analog of that sound. CD recordings break these waves into one of 65,536 values, recorded 44,100 times per second, in binary format, on a layer of metal encased in a plastic disc. A CD player, amplifier, and speakers reconstruct the sound waves. Something is displaced in the process. Audiophiles often say that the warmth of vinyl has been lost in the adoption of more efficient digital formats (though CDs respond much better to changes in frequency, and have a much greater dynamic range—the ratio between the softest to the loudest possible sound).

DVD technology developed from the CD. An analog medium (photographic film), which is continuous, gradual, and progressive, is split up into digital units, and encoded on a disc that is indistinguishable, to the naked eye, from a CD. But DVDs *are* physically different. A CD encases a thin sheet of metal within a single piece of plastic. A DVD's transparent metal film separates two molded pieces of clear plastic, glued together, which makes DVDs firmer than CDs, thus reducing wobble. Both formats store data in pits and grooves along a single spiral track that starts at the center of the disc. CD and DVD players read this data using a laser.

This increase in storage capacity, which is great enough to encode films in higher resolution than had been possible with videotape, was enabled by two technological advances. The first was evolutionary—a DVD's data track is narrower than a CD's, and therefore longer (12 km); its microscopic bumps are smaller and closer together. The second advance was the development of high-ratio compression software (along with the programming and processing power required to decompress large amounts of data quickly and accurately). DVD video signals are typically compressed at a ratio of 40:1, using a compression standard called MPEG-2. So though they have the diameter (12 cm) and thickness (1.2 mm) of CDs, standard DVDs can store at least seven times more data.

A still frame from a DVD film is usually 480 or 576 pixels high, and 720 pixels wide. That is, each frame contains over 350,000 distinct pixels. At these resolutions, a typical DVD can hold about two hours of video; films with longer running times may be encoded by using lower resolutions, or by storing data on two separate physical layers. Some DVDs store data on both sides.

DVDs come in a variety of different physical and application formats. The former govern the amount of data that can be recorded, and whether it can be recorded to once or multiple times. The latter are concerned with the different standards for storing and reproducing data.

Non-recordable commercial discs come in four different physical formats, depending on whether one or both sides of the disc are used to store data, and whether each side has one or two layers. Most commercial discs are single-sided—either single-layer (also known as DVD-5) or dual-layer (also known as DVD-9). Single-sided, single-layer discs hold up to 4.70 GB of data, and single-sided, dual-layer discs up to 8.50 GB.[1]

There are five recordable physical formats. They can be identified by their disc label or color, but if in doubt, the free software tool K-probe (www.k-probe.com) can confirm the type of disc.

> **DVD-R/DVD+R (DVD RECORDABLE):** These are single-use recordable DVDs, employing slightly different technologies. They can be differentiated by their color. DVD-R uses a dark purplish dye as a recording medium; DVD+R is silver. DVD-R is more tolerant of low temperatures, higher humidity, and rapid environmental variations. It is the most compatible format, and the older of the two. Some libraries have reported problems using radio-frequency identification (RFID) tags with this format. DVD+R discs are written to and read from more efficiently. Data recorded on dye tends to degrade more quickly than that recorded on pressed, commercial discs.
>
> **DVD-RW AND DVD+RW (DVD RE-RECORDABLE):** There are competing standards for rewritable discs, though both types of discs work in most players. They can be rewritten about a thousand times.
>
> **DVD-RAM (DVD REWRITABLE):** An erasable format, these discs can be rewritten more than one-hundred thousand times. They have zoned segments, built-in defect management, and come in a disc cartridge. Most DVD drives cannot read DVD-RAM, and the format is used almost exclusively for archival and computer storage.

There are many different DVD application formats. The most common are:

> **DVD-VIDEO:** The type of DVD cataloged most often. It is the usual, and almost universally accepted, format for storing and distributing film, and what most people mean when they say "DVD." In this book, "DVD" almost always means a disc containing the DVD-Video format.
>
> **DVD-AUDIO:** A format for storing up to eight hours of standard audio, or for storing audio at higher fidelity than is possible on CD. The market for DVD-Audio is small, partly because the benefits of higher fidelity only become apparent with expensive equipment, and partly because of rivalry with the Super Audio CD (SACD) format.

DVD-ROM (DVD READ ONLY MEMORY): These only work in computers, and are mostly used for software applications and data storage. The abbreviation is ambiguous, however, because it also refers to discs that have been mass-produced for commercial distribution, stamped with a glass master, and thus impossible to erase or write to. That is, most of the DVD-Video discs purchased by libraries will also, in one sense, be DVD-ROMs. In catalog records, the abbreviation will only refer to the earlier definition.

Blu-ray Disc

The development of Blu-ray Disc from DVD was both evolutionary and revolutionary. A process called *sputtering* creates discs with the recordable layer closer to the surface, upon which a hard, scratch-resistant coating is applied to prevent damage. Storing data on this part of the disc allows the use of a laser with a shorter wavelength, and the blue laser beams used to read Blu-ray Discs are two and a half times narrower than the red lasers used to read DVDs, The color of the laser gives the disc its name—the "e" was left out of Blu-ray intentionally, since ordinary words cannot be registered as trademarks. Improvements in technology enabled pits and grooves to become even smaller, making the data track even narrower. Unlike the sandwiched layers of the DVD, Blu-ray Discs are composed of a single piece of polymer plastic. All Blu-ray Disc players are backward-compatible (so will also play DVDs and CDs), as DVD players are backward-compatible with CDs.

Standard Blu-ray Discs also deploy more efficient data encoding. High-definition audio and video can be stored on the medium, with a pixel resolution of 1920 x 1080 as standard. That is, a still frame from a Blu-ray Disc film will contain more than two million individual pixels. Blu-ray Discs come in sizes of eight and twelve centimeters, though smaller discs are only used with consumer electronics devices such as digital camcorders. Like DVDs, Blu-ray Discs can store information on both sides. Single-layer discs have a capacity of twenty-five gigabytes.

Standard 12-cm Blu-ray Discs come in different configurations, with distinct physical characteristics:

BD-R (BLU-RAY DISC, RECORDABLE): A single-use recordable format akin to DVD±R. Data is written onto a thin layer of an inorganic alloy. Single- and dual-layer discs are available.

BD-RE (BLU-RAY DISC, REWRITEABLE): A rewritable format akin to DVD±RW. Using a phase-change alloy as a recording medium allows the disc to be rewritten at least 1,000 times. Single- and dual-layer discs are available.

BD-RE XL AND BD-R XL (BLU-RAY DISC, EXTRA LARGE): These configurations were launched in Japan in 2010. Using a third—and in the case of BD-R XL, a fourth—recording layer, increases storage capacity even further. Triple-layer discs can store just over 33.33 GB per layer, and quadruple-layer discs 32 GB per layer. It is unclear whether there will be much consumer demand for these formats. Consumer demand is also likely to dictate whether BD Hybrid discs move from the laboratory into homes and offices. These discs could hold Blu-ray Disc, DVD, and CD layers simultaneously, though different layers would need to be read by different lasers.

BD-ROM (BLU-RAY DISC, READ-ONLY MEMORY): As with DVD-ROM, this abbreviation has two meanings. As a physical format, it refers to any disc that has had data impressed on it before distribution.

Blu-ray Discs, like their DVD predecessors, use a variety of different application formats, though they show less diversity. Most discs are in the BD-MV (or BDMV [Blu-ray Movie]) format, the standard for commercial releases of films. BD-AV (or BDAV [Blu-ray Disc Audio/Visual]) is a less technically complex format, aimed at amateur filmmakers.

Blu-ray Discs containing 3-D versions of films have been available since 2010. The specifications of Blu-ray 3-D players include backward compatibility with 2-D discs. The market is small, but likely to grow with time. At present, many 3-D Blu-ray Disc films are released "flat" (i.e., 2-D) on theatrical release, and converted in postproduction.

Another emerging technology is 4K ultra-high-definition resolution, the still frames of which contain 3840 x 2160 pixels, that is, four times the amount of visual information stored on regular Blu-ray Disc.

Late 2013 saw the release of the first slew of 4K films, driven in part by manufacturers with interests in selling the latest generation of expensive televisions. Although the change from analog to digital, and from standard to high-definition, brought marked increases in picture quality, increases in resolution beyond those offered by standard Blu-ray Disc and high-definition televisions only become apparent on enormous screens.

Leader (NR)

Code DVDs and Blu-ray Discs "g - Projected medium" in Leader position 06 (Type of record).

007 Physical Description Fixed Field (R)

All records for DVDs and Blu-ray Discs should contain a 007 field. It is the only place in a MARC record to record certain types of machine-readable data integral to optical disc formats. Different categories of material are described by different sets of codes. DVDs and Blu-ray Discs are coded as "videorecordings," not as "motion pictures," the phrase used in MARC (and RDA) to describe films on rolls and reels (see chapter 5). The coding for both types of disc is:

POSITION 00 (CATEGORY OF MATERIAL)
Always "v - Videorecording."

POSITION 01 (SPECIFIC MATERIAL DESIGNATION)
Always "d - Videodisc."

POSITION 02 (UNDEFINED)
Always "# - Undefined."

POSITION 03 (COLOR)
Use "b" for black and white, "c" for color, "m" for films with both black and white and color sequences (e.g., *The Wizard of Oz* [1939], and *Ivan the Terrible, Part II, The Boyars' Plot* [1946]).

POSITION 04 (VIDEORECORDING FORMAT)
Use "s" for Blu-ray Disc, "v" for DVD. Records for DVDs created prior to 2002 may be coded "g," formerly used for all laser optical videodiscs. The code is now used only for LaserDiscs. The code for DVD was created in 2001, and that for Blu-ray Disc in 2008, so the earliest releases in those formats may be misdescribed in older records.

POSITION 05 (SOUND ON MEDIUM OR SEPARATE)

Normally "a - Sound on medium," but very infrequently "# - No sound (silent)" when the disc is devoid of sound, not a "silent film," which usually contains at least one sound track of accompanying music.

POSITION 06 (MEDIUM OF SOUND)

Normally "i - Videodisc," but very infrequently "# - No sound (silent)."

POSITION 07 (DIMENSIONS)

Always "z - Other."

POSITION 08 (CONFIGURATION OF PLAYBACK CHANNELS)

Use "m" for mono sound, "s" for stereo, "q" for surround, "k" for mixed (quite common, because films on optical disc will often contain sound in more than one format), "n" for discs lacking a sound track, and "u" for unknown. This coding should be in agreement with the 344 subfield $g.

008 Fixed-Length Data Elements (NR)

Character positions 00–17 and 35–39 are generic for all types of material. Code positions 18–34 as per the MARC 21 bibliographic instructions for visual materials. All coding is the same for both DVD and Blu-ray Disc.

POSITIONS 00–05 (DATE ENTERED ON FILE)

Usually system generated.

POSITION 06 (TYPE OF DATE/PUBLICATION STATUS)

Insert "s" for a single known, inferred, or estimated date, which should match the date recorded in the 264 subfield $c.

When an additional 264 field records a copyright date, insert "t," even if the copyright date and the date of publication are the same. Alternately, insert "s," and a single date, if both dates are the same.

Use date type "r" for locally produced reproductions.

The value "m" may be used when a set of discs recording a single work has been published over a number of years.

Use date type "q" where a range of questionable dates have been recorded in a 264 field.

The inclusion of subtitles, additional language tracks, bonus materials, etc., are changes in content that justify regarding a film on optical disc as a different work (in the MARC sense, not the FRBR one) to the version shown in movie theaters. When discs lack these features, many libraries judge the content to be identical to the original release, and code the work "p," which records a change of medium, but not content. The MARC 21 bibliographic standard states: "For moving images, if a work with identical content but in a different medium has a later release date than the original work, code p is used (e.g., a videorecording released in 1978 that was originally produced as a motion picture in 1965)." But the technical and artistic alterations required to convert a film from a cinematic to home-video version (outlined later in this chapter) are much more artistically and creatively significant, and alter the content far more radically, than the inclusion of, for example, a subtitle track. The author does not think the current MARC definitions and audio-visual best practice make sense, and would argue against the use of date type "p" for films on optical disc.

POSITIONS 07–10, 11–14 (DATE 1, DATE 2)

The year of publication, as recorded in the 264 subfield $c, should be entered here, and always recorded, even for uncertain or inferred dates. If position 06 has been encoded with a value of "p," "m," "q," or "t," record a second date, otherwise four blanks. List values "m" and "q" in chronological order. For value "p," first record the release date of the disc, followed by the release date of the original production. For value "t," record the publication date first, the copyright date second.

POSITIONS 15–17 (PLACE OF PUBLICATION, PRODUCTION, OR EXECUTION)

This two- or three-digit alphabetic code must agree with the information recorded in the 264 field. This records the location of the disc's publisher, not the original production company. Locally produced copies should still record the place of the original publication.

POSITIONS 18–20 (RUNNING TIME FOR MOTION PICTURES AND VIDEORECORDINGS)

These positions should record the running time of the main feature, not including additional material. The data must contain three digits—films with running times less than 100 minutes should be prefixed with a zero (e.g., a 99-minute film would be recorded as 099). When the running time exceeds 999 minutes, enter "000." When the running time is unknown or cannot be determined enter "---." The running time must agree with subfield $a in the 300 field. Take from the resource rather than any external sources.

POSITION 21 (UNDEFINED)
Always "# - Undefined."

POSITION 22 (TARGET AUDIENCE)
This data is rarely necessary, and it can be difficult to define. Do not attempt to code, unless a matter of local policy. See the text of the MARC 21 bibliographic standard for further details.

POSITIONS 23-27 (UNDEFINED)
Always "# - Undefined."

POSITION 28 (GOVERNMENT PUBLICATION)
For government publications, see the text of the MARC 21 bibliographic standard for extensive details. For discs that are not government publications, insert a blank ("#").

POSITION 29 (FORM OF ITEM)
Codes "o - Online" and "q - Direct electronic" were introduced in 2010 to disaggregate resources that had formerly been coded under the umbrella of "s - Electronic." These new fields allow the cataloger to separate out online resources, and discs encoded with the DVD-ROM or BD-ROM application formats (i.e., those which require a computer to play). However, much confusion has been caused by the failure of MARBI/MAC to make "s" obsolete, and the MARC 21 bibliographic standard's inadequate explanations of the three codes.

Until these issues have been resolved, it is probably best to leave this position blank.

POSITIONS 30-32 (UNDEFINED)
Always "# - Undefined."

POSITION 33 (TYPE OF VISUAL MATERIAL)
Always "v" for videorecording.

POSITION 34 (TECHNIQUE)

Code "1" for live-action (i.e., with regular actors and actresses, not a cartoon), "a" for animation, "c" for a combination of live-action and animation.

POSITIONS 35–37 (LANGUAGE)

The three-character MARC code for the default language of the soundtrack or intertitles (for silent films) is entered here. See chapter 3 for more details on the coding of language.

POSITIONS 38 AND 39 (MODIFIED RECORD, CATALOGING SOURCE)

Follow local policy for monograph materials.

344 Sound Characteristics (R)

THE NEW "CHARACTERISTICS" FIELDS

Fields 344, 345, 346, and 347 are newly established in the MARC 21 bibliographic standard to support RDA. Many legacy systems will be unable to utilize these fields, and many small libraries lacking their own systems librarians will be unable to take advantage of them. The data recorded in the 34X fields is read by computers, not people, so until the ILS market catches up, the cataloger should continue to record information in a human-readable format, too. For the moment, the new fields will often duplicate data recorded elsewhere, most obviously in the 300, 500, and 538 fields. However, the potential of the new fields to better encode, and thus express more precisely, a faceted granularity should not be overlooked, and their use is encouraged. Some of the data may appear redundant, but they are indicative of the type of description that may be encountered in a post-MARC world, and will make the transition to such standards easier.

WHY SOUND MATTERS

Film critic James Monaco has written of sound in film that, "[i]deally, the sound of a film should be equal in importance with the image." He continues, "Sadly . . . sound technology in film lags far behind not only the development of cinematography but also the technology of sound recording that has developed independently from film."[2] At its best, sound can define a film. *Apocalypse Now* (1979) not only gave the Vietnam War a look, it gave it a soundtrack. Films such as *The Conversation* (1974) and *Berberian Sound Studio* (2012) explicitly draw audience attention to the filmic use of captured and reproduced sound.

Sound and image were unified in the defining cinematic technology of the early twentieth century. Sound was possible in the earliest years of cinema, but the equipment would have been bulky and noisy, and the sound discontinuous with the image. In 1919, a system for translating sound into electrical signals, and hence to light that could be imprinted onto film, was patented. This system continued almost unchanged until the digital revolution of recent years. In the 1970s and 1980s systems were developed for recording multiple simultaneous tracks on film stock. Technologies developed by Dolby Laboratories led to improved fidelity and reduced the inherent background noise that had plagued cinema performances until that time. Sophisticated surround-sound systems became a mark of pride and a promotional tool for movie theaters.

$A AND $B RECORDING METHOD AND MEDIUM

Field 344 allows for the recording of a variety of optical disc technical specifications. For both DVDs and Blu-ray Discs, subfields $a and $b will always be coded as "digital" and "optical," respectively.

$G MONO, STEREO, AND SURROUND SOUND

RDA asks us to record the configuration of playback channels and any special sound characteristics if the information is readily available (RDA 3.16.8.3, 3.16.9.3) and important for identification or selection (RDA 3.16.8.4, 3.16.9.4). "Configuration of playback channels" refers to the number of sound channels used in a recording. RDA offers mono, stereo, quadraphonic, and surround: record these terms in subfield $g. These data should be in agreement with the 007 fixed field, position 8. If these terms are not sufficient, catalogers may choose their own terms, once concisely stated. Contrary to many style guides, RDA regards mono and stereo as single words, not abbreviations. See appendix B for the symbols used to indicate playback configuration.

Mono is single-channel sound, the standard in film until the second half of the twentieth century. Films contained a single sound track—if multiple microphones were used on set they would be mixed into a single signal path. Mono sound is sometimes indicated by the phrase "1.0 sound."

Experimentation with *stereo* sound began in the 1930s, but it was not until the 1950s that stereo, or the ability to create the illusion of directionality, began to be used in the surround and 3-D formats popular at that time. The emergence of widescreen cinema formats permitted more than one sound track to be encoded on a film using magnetic tracks instead of optical ones, but also required multiple channels to fill the wider field of the screen. These magnetic tracks were of lower quality than the optical tracks previously used. Dolby stereo reintroduced optical tracks in the 1970s. Technical advances have come thick and fast since this time, though certain directors preferred to record in mono until recently, following director Stanley Kubrick's principle that good mono is always better than bad stereo. Stereo sound is often indicated by the phrase "2.0 sound," sometimes "2.1 sound," or an appropriate symbol.

Quadraphonic was a format developed in the 1970s, the first commercial attempt at surround sound. It never achieved more than a specialist interest, and failed due to format incompatibilities, awkward technology, and expensive equipment. It has sometimes been converted to modern sound formats and released through a variety of technologies, but it is hardly ever found on films released commercially on optical disc. In today's terminology, it would be called 4.0 surround sound.

Surround sound has a variety of technical and vernacular uses when applied to film. Look for the number 5.1 (and for Blu-ray Discs, 7.1), which refers to the attempt to replicate the position of the five different speaker types present in most movie theaters. The ".1" refers to sound provided by a subwoofer, which reproduces low frequencies.

$H EQUALIZATION AND NOISE-REDUCTION SYSTEMS

Two competing surround sound formats dominate the market: Dolby Digital and DTS. Both are "lossy," meaning that some audio information is lost when the sound is compressed into a format that will fit on the disc.

As Blu-ray Discs can hold more data than DVDs, DTS and Dolby developed new formats (Dolby Digital Plus and DTS-HD High Resolution) that enabled more audio information to be stored and processed by more simultaneous audio channels. Blu-ray Discs can also accommodate the two competing lossless compression formats (Dolby TrueHD and DTS-HD Master

Audio), as well as Linear PCM, a raw, uncompressed audio format, the highest fidelity sound currently offered for films on optical disc.

Playback characteristics should be recorded in subfield $h, though RDA offers a woefully incomplete list of terms with which to describe them. The only option is "Dolby"—DTS is not included in the list. But RDA does permit the cataloger to "use another concise term or terms to indicate the special playback characteristics" in cases where "none of the terms in the list is appropriate or sufficiently specific" (RDA 3.16.9.3).

When using vocabulary taken from the lists in the text of RDA, end the field with a subfield $2 containing "rda." Catalogers may use their own term(s) in an additional 344 field, and/or include further details in a 538 note field. If using a term outside RDA's list, replicate the form of words, numbers, and letters found on the carrier.

Both indicators are undefined, and there is no internal or end punctuation:

> 344 ## $a digital $b optical $g stereo $h Dolby $2 rda
>
> 344 ## $a digital $b optical $g surround $2 rda
> 344 ## $h Dolby Digital 5.1

346 Video Characteristics (R)

See the description of MARC 21 bibliographic field 344 for general guidelines on the new 34X fields.

BROADCAST STANDARDS

The projection of film and the receipt of television broadcasts are based on fundamentally different technologies. The implications of this incompatibility are far-reaching.

Films were first captured and projected at 24 frames per second because the illusion of motion is suitably convincing at this speed (a principle known at the persistence of vision). Early filmmakers gained little by capturing more images per second. Twenty-four is also an easily, and multiply, divisible number—just as film stock was expensive, so was the time of editors, and cutting a film took less time if half, a third, a quarter, a sixth, etc., of a second could be calculated quickly. Nowadays most films are projected at 48 frames per second to minimize flicker—each frame is projected twice.

American television signals were broadcast at sixty frames per second (in reality, thirty frames, each shown twice) because the electrical standard for alternating current was set to 60 Hz (switching polarity from positive to negative, and then back again, sixty times per second). Europe and Australia have AC frequency rates of 50 Hz.

It gets worse. Three different encoding systems are used for analog color television broadcasts. The geographical dispersal of these systems is complex, and the listing below offers only an approximate guide.

The National Television Systems Committee (NTSC), the first system to be developed, was used in North America, the Caribbean, most of South America, and some East Asian countries, including Japan. NTSC broadcasts have two interlaced fields per frame, for a total of 525 lines, refreshing at a rate of 30 frames per second. NTSC receivers have built-in line control to perform color correction. This unsatisfying solution to a technical problem led the to the system being dubbed "Never The Same Color."

Phase Alternate Line (PAL) was developed later, in an attempt to solve the color-quality issues of NTSC, and was used throughout most of Europe, Africa, and the Middle East; Australia and New Zealand; the Indian subcontinent; and China. It contains 625 lines per frame, with a refresh rate of 25 frames per second. The signal is interlaced, like NTSC, into two fields, composed of 312 lines each, but unlike NTSC it corrects phase errors in the transmission of the signal. Because fewer frames are displayed per second, a flicker can sometimes be seen in the image, much like the flicker that is noticeable when a projected film is watched closely. PAL offers a higher-resolution image and better color stability.

Séquentiel Couleur à Mémoire (Sequential Color with Memory, abbreviated SECAM) was used in France, francophone Africa, and most of the countries of the former Soviet Union. It uses memory to store lines of information to solve the color issues so problematic for NTSC. Information is transmitted in alternate lines, and a video line store is used to combine the signals, which halves the vertical color resolution relative to PAL and NTSC.

HOW BROADCAST STANDARDSARE REPRESENTED ON DVD

Digital systems, such as DVD and Blu-ray Disc, transmit information not as analog waves, but as a series of bits, which solves problems of color quality and allows for much higher resolution. DVD could have become a universal, worldwide system. But a combination of inertia and a wish by production studios to retain powers limiting distribution meant that two formats were developed for DVD, mimicking the screen resolution and refresh rates of the PAL/SECAM versus NTSC divide. The acronyms are misleading when applied to DVDs. The information is digital, so analog color distinctions no longer apply (also, most television broadcasts are now digital, and use different standards, with NTSC nations migrating to the ATSC standard, and most PAL and SECAM nations moving to DVBT). Because films released on optical disc in North America still have different picture resolutions and frame rates from those released elsewhere, the two terms are still used, providing an easy shorthand for the geographical distinction.

The broadcast/resolution/refresh rate standard is not always indicated on the DVD. While it is probably safe to assume that the encoding of a disc will match the standard in the jurisdiction it was created for, it can also be determined using most computer media players. If using Windows Media Player, open the "File" menu, then select "Properties," and look for "Video Size." If using VLC Media Player, open "Tools," then "Codec Information," and look for "Resolution." NTSC films are usually 720 x 480 pixels (sometimes 352 x 240), and PAL/SECAM 720 x 576 (sometimes 352 x 288). Regular DVDs cannot handle high-definition resolutions.[3] All PAL DVD players can also play NTSC discs, but few NTSC players play PAL discs; most television screens sold in Europe can display both formats. Computers can read from, and display the contents of, both kinds of disc.

Filmmakers do not shoot an extra six shots per second to splice into DVD releases of their films. 24 frames-per-second projections are converted into 30 NTSC-compatible frames per second ones through a process called *3:2 pulldown*. Frames are repeated according to a mathematical pattern, so that only twenty-four different frames are projected each second. The effect is noticeable when a film is watched closely; one of the reasons, besides its greater resolution, that film enthusiasts prefer PAL to NTSC. However, PAL has its own problems. Every second it displays 25 frames of a film shot at 24 frames per second, so PAL-encoded films play 4 percent faster than NTSC ones, and 4 percent faster than their creators intended them to be viewed. The increase in speed also raises the pitch of the accompanying sound.

HOW BROADCAST STANDARDS ARE REFLECTED ON BLU-RAY DISC

When it comes to the high-definition standards on Blu-ray Disc, the underlying technology and aspect ratios (16:9 or 1.78:1) are shared worldwide, though the standard has multiple variants. HDTV comes in two different display resolutions (1280 x 720 and 1920 x 1080), two different scanning systems that govern the interlacing of broadcast pictures, and most problematic of all, two different frame rates, retaining the NTSC and PAL/SECAM refresh frequencies. For television broadcasts, the 25 versus 30 frame-rate divide between the two sides of the Atlantic is likely to remain for the foreseeable future, because the majority of video playback devices, such as VCRs, analog camcorders, and many DVD players plugged into HDTVs remain configured for local settings.

These issues have not carried over to Blu-ray Disc. Films on Blu-ray Disc are usually stored at 1920 x 1080 pixels, with a refresh rate of 24 frames per second. So the NTSC/PAL distinction will not apply to high-definition material in a library's collection, though it may still apply to any additional content in standard definition, such as trailers and extras. A high-definition television or monitor is needed to see the benefits of the higher-resolution encoded on a Blu-ray Disc, and not all screens and monitors can translate the various standards detailed above.

When using vocabulary taken from the lists in the text of RDA (RDA 3.18.3.3 offers HDTV, NTSC, PAL, and SECAM), end the field with a "$2 rda" subfield. The indicators are undefined, and there is no internal or end punctuation. The cataloger may wish to add a note in the 500 field to advise users of possible problems with playback if the disc's broadcast standard differs from that used in the local jurisdiction:

```
346 ##    $b NTSC $2 rda

346 ##    $b PAL $2 rda
```

347 Digital File Characteristics (R)

See the description of MARC 21 bibliographic field 344 for general guidelines on the new 34X fields.

$A FILE TYPE

Record "video file" in subfield $a (RDA 3.19.2.3).

$B DVD OR BLU-RAY DISC

In subfield $b, record the encoding format, taken from the list provided at RDA 3.19.3.3, usually "DVD video" or "Blu-ray."[4] For a video file that must be played on a computer, determine the file format, then record the form displayed in the list.

$C FILE SIZE

Only record the file size in subfield $c for discs containing a single video file that must be played on a computer.

WHY DISCS DIFFER ACROSS THE GLOBE

Subfield $e may be used to record regional coding, which was consigned to a note field in AACR2.

Film producers used to make most of their money from ticket sales in the United States. Until recently, less attention was paid to international distribution. During Hollywood's Golden Age, films often had multiple local premieres before opening nationwide (*Gone with the Wind* [1939] premiered first in Atlanta, then four days later in New York, nine days after that in Los Angeles, and nationwide three weeks later). Copies were then shipped to the larger South and Central American nations (Brazil was always an important market) and Canada. A while later the film would open in the United Kingdom, then Australia, then Europe. Distribution elsewhere was haphazard, and sometimes prevented by geopolitical events. *Gone with the Wind* did not premiere in France until 1946 and the Soviet Union until 1990.

These practices continued into the era of home video, and VHS releases frequently took place in the United States before the film had received its theatrical premiere in other countries. This led to problems with piracy and copyright theft, which became worse with the rise in popularity of the VCD, especially in China, where the government permitted few theatrical releases of Hollywood productions.[5]

The industry's solution was twofold—cinema releases became global marketing events (as a rule of thumb, an additional 50 percent of a film's production budget is now spent promoting it) with consequently shortened release and distribution cycles, and regional encoding was established. Shortly after their development, DVDs were encoded to play only on hardware sold in discrete geographical regions.

DVD REGIONAL CODING

Regional coding is applied to DVD-Video and games, but rarely to DVDs in other formats. It is also optional. It is not a form of encryption, but simply information that a player checks. Each region is represented by a computer bit, and because there are eight bits in a byte, there are eight regions. DVDs may operate in more than one region. The regional code for DVDs is usually indicated by a number superimposed on an image of a globe inside a square box with rounded corners.

Prior to 2000, most DVD-ROM drives did not have in-built regional coding, and region management was determined by the software or operating system. From January 1, 2000, manufacturers of DVD drives were required to impose a regional code. The code may be changed up to five times by the owner of the disc. The eight regions are:

1. North America, and the unincorporated territories of the United States
2. Europe, Turkey, the Middle East, South Africa, Japan, and most British and French overseas territories
3. Southeast Asia and South Korea
4. Australia, New Zealand, Papua New Guinea and the Melanesian islands to its east, Central America, and South America
5. Africa (except South Africa and Egypt), countries of the former Soviet Union, Central Asia, the Indian subcontinent, and North Korea
6. China
7. Reserved for future use
8. Nontheatrical international venues, such as airplanes and cruise ships

The term "Region 0" is sometimes used for region-free discs.

BLU-RAY DISC REGIONAL CODING

Regional codes were simplified for Blu-ray Discs because theatrical release windows have become shorter. Very few of the first discs released by studios contained regional coding, and even now many discs lack it—in the age of Amazon, distributors realize that overseas audiences can order and watch the American release. There are three Blu-ray Disc regional codes: A, B, and C, sometimes referred to as 1, 2, and 3. Regions are defined for the whole disc on DVDs, but Blu-ray Discs can be programmed to determine the region on a title-by-title basis. The regional code for Blu-ray Disc is usually indicated by a letter superimposed on an image of a globe inside a six-sided polygon. The three regions are:

A. North, Central, and South America, Southeast Asia, Japan, and North and South Korea
B. Europe, Africa, the Middle East, Australia, and New Zealand
C. Countries of the former Soviet Union, Central Asia, and the Indian subcontinent

Most library users are unaware of regional coding; patrons are unlikely to know what it means. If the library's collection contains discs encoded for a region other than your own, the addition of a 5XX note, or a note in the holdings record, is advisable, as is a prominent label on the disc container, and/or a pop-up message in the ILS. If a library has facilities for showing films (perhaps in support of a film studies department), investing in a multi-region player would be advantageous. If users try to play a disc encoded for a different region on their own computers, they are given the option to change the default region, but this is not advisable, because after a number of changes the region becomes locked. VLC media player (www.videolan.org/vlc/index.html) is an established and free open-source program that will play discs from all regions.

Does RDA Acknowledge Regional Coding?

It is unclear whether RDA provides a list of regional codes—RDA 3.19.6.3 lists only "region 4" and "all regions." Record these in subfield $e if relevant; otherwise additional 347 fields will be necessary if using vocabulary beyond the controlled list.

The indicators for 347 are undefined, and the field has no final punctuation. When using vocabulary taken from the lists in the text of RDA, end the field with a "$2 rda" subfield. However, the lists provided by RDA are not definitive. For example, it may be desirable to indicate that a disc contains a file encoded in the Flash Video format, even though "Flash" is not on the designated list at RDA 3.19.3.3. Add as an additional field when using uncontrolled vocabulary. As with the broadcast standard recorded in the

346 field, an additional 500 note field could warn users of possible playback issues related to discs coded to other regions:

347 ## $a video file $b DVD video $e all regions $2 rda

347 ## $a video file $b Blu-ray $2 rda
347 ## $e region 1

347 ## $a video file $2 rda
347 ## $b AVI $c 427 MB

500 General Note (R)

Use a 500 note to record valuable information that cannot be accommodated in another field, or to expand upon information recorded elsewhere. The MARC 21 bibliographic standard does not provide enough note fields for cataloging film, so the potential scope of this field is broad. Some technical features can now be included in the new (machine-readable) 34X fields, while other technical information is more appropriate in the (human-readable) 538 field.

Use individual 500 notes to record information about additional and special features, aspect ratio, production and release history, regional coding, and related works. A 500 note may also be used to clarify information provided in other MARC fields.

ASPECT RATIO

Aspect ratio is the ratio of the horizontal width of the image to its height, an important component of a film's style (see chapter 1). The MARC 21 bibliographic standard gives no field in which to record this, so place in a generic 500 note, if readily ascertainable (RDA D.2.1, 7.19). Modern widescreen televisions have a tendency to distort images to fill the entirety of the screen, but wider does not mean better if it means stretching a film beyond its intended dimensions. Discs in the "Masters of Cinema" series, released by Eureka!, advise viewers on how to avoid such manipulation, calling them "a distortion and corruption of the original artwork, which travesty the integrity of both the human form and cinematographic space." Take detail from the resource, accompanying material, or container. If desired, additional information may be provided from other sources (RDA 7.19.1.2).

The aspect ratio of widescreen HDTV television is 1.78:1 (16:9), close to the 1.85:1 standard for widescreen cinema. When a film shot in one of the earlier, narrower, formats is shown on a HDTV television, black vertical bars are added to the sides of the screen, a process known as *pillarboxing*. An alternative is the *tilt and scan technique,* which horizontally crops the image at top and bottom. Still more familiar is *letterboxing*, for viewing widescreen film on older types of television and computer monitors. Black lines are imposed on the top and bottom of the screen, creating a letterbox shape. More controversial is *pan and scan,* sometimes called full frame, where the sides are cropped off the widescreen image by an editor who has panned back and forth across the original image using a scanner to capture and center the action. Because this technique is arbitrary and can result in significant loss of directorial vision (especially with 2.35:1 images, where 45 percent of the original can be removed), it is unpopular among filmmakers.

In the production and projection of film, *anamorphic widescreen* refers to the practice of using a distorted concave lens in filming, which creates a vertically elongated image when printed onto standard 35 mm motion picture film. A convex lens attached to the projector then recreates the image in widescreen format. When applied to DVDs, the phrase describes the technique used to store widescreen images using the frame size of full-screen video (i.e., 4:3) by making the shape of the pixels wider—DVD players can detect this and adjust the image proportionally. Blu-ray Discs also support this distortion technique, but because Blu-ray Discs were designed to support wider, high-definition resolutions, it is rarely used.

Because widescreen televisions will render widescreen films more sympathetically, some libraries record information about aspect ratio in the 538 system requirements field. But the aspect ratio bears little relation to other information in this field. The 500 field is a more appropriate fit.

Many DVDs and Blu-ray Discs contain the main feature in a widescreen format, with additional features in 4:3, though this will rarely be indicated on the container. Because additional features are usually incidental, do not indicate their aspect ratio unless this information is present on the resource itself.

Unfortunately, the RDA rules governing the description of aspect ratio are particularly unhelpful, misleading and captious. The text of RDA asks us to use one of three terms to describe the aspect ratio. The definition of these terms is mathematically neat but is otherwise unknown in cinema. RDA uses "full screen" for ratios of less than 1.5:1, "wide screen" (note the space) for ratios of 1.5:1 and above, and "mixed" "for resources that include multiple aspect ratios within the same work" (RDA 7.19.1.3). RDA does not prohibit the use of the correct (if ill-defined) technical terms, which are more helpful to the library user in any case. The author advises their parenthetical use in records.

RDA also requires numerical ratios, if known, to be recorded with a denominator of 1 (RDA 7.19.1.3). Presumably this requires converting 4:3 to 1.33:1 and 16:9 to 1.78:1—once again, arbitrarily. But RDA does not preclude recording the ratios in their more familiar style, and the author recommends both be used.

When the resource is described as being a modification of the cinematic release, record the original aspect ratio in addition to the aspect ratio of the expression. To avoid confusion, record these in separate fields.

RDA also requires that the cataloger "record the specific method used to achieve the aspect ratio if it is considered to be important for identification or selection" (RDA 7.19.1.4). Interpreted one way, this seems to misunderstand the nature of aspect itself—for most films the method used to achieve the aspect ratio was the director and cinematographer's original choice of film stock, camera, and editing technique. The text, therefore, must refer to the ways in which the dimensions of the original projection have been accommodated on smaller screens, described above.

If the phrase "Widescreen edition" is printed on the container, record this in a 250 field rather than in a 500 field note. Never represent numerical aspect ratio as an edition statement. Many libraries combine a note recording the aspect ratio with details of additional sound characteristics. However, this has the potential to cause confusion, because aspect ratio and sound characteristics are united only by the fact that the MARC 21 bibliographic standard fails to provide distinct fields for them.

> 500 ## $a Full screen (aspect ratio 1.33:1, i.e. 4:3).
>
> 500 ## $a Wide screen (aspect ratio 2.35:1), letterboxed.
>
> 500 ## $a Original aspect ratio 2.76:1, 'reproduced using pan and scan technique for 16x9 television.'
>
> 500 ## $a Main feature: wide screen (aspect ratio 1.85:1), anamorphic; special features: full screen (aspect ratio 1.33:1).
>
> 500 ## $a Mixed aspect ratios.

SPECIAL FEATURES

Most commercially released films are accompanied by bonus materials. These may include photo galleries, filmographies of cast and crew, audio commentaries, trailers, interviews, and additional documentaries or short films, each of which should be recorded in a 500 note field (RDA 7.6.1.3). If a feature seems significant enough to be recorded more formally—perhaps because it is an important work in its own right—a 505 note (and perhaps a 730 or 740 additional access point) may be more appropriate. Details of special features can normally be found in a text box on the back of the sleeve insert, and transcription of this text will usually suffice. Interactive menus and scene selection are standard features of DVD and Blu-ray Disc technology—they are not "special" features, and should not be recorded:

> 500 ## $a DVD special features include: commentary by Christopher Frayling; "Screening at the Majestic" documentary.

> 500 ## $a Special features include: photo galleries; theatrical trailer; 'making of' documentary.

PRODUCTION/RELEASE HISTORY

A film's production process goes through three phases. During pre-production, filming locations are identified, the script is broken down into individual scenes, sets are constructed, etc. Cameras film actors during principal photography. The film is edited during post-production, when visual and sound effects are added, and the soundtrack recorded. This phase often lasts longer than the actual filming. The three phases vary in length, and the transitions between them are often indeterminate. Their start and end dates are not normally in the public domain, which is why films are referred to by their release date. Some films are notorious for the length of time it took to complete them. *Apocalypse Now* (1979) was filmed over sixteen months; Orson Welles filmed parts of *The Other Side of the Wind* between 1969 and 1976, and continued to edit it until he died in 1985. It remains unfinished, locked in a Paris vault.

Record the year the film was first released or broadcast, or related information about the edition history. The best source will be IMDb, which always includes the year of release next to the film title, and records the date of release in a variety of jurisdictions. The year of general commercial release, which the record should contain, may not be the year the film was first shown in a cinema. Many films are previewed at film festivals, for example, to interest potential distributors. If the release date cannot be determined, but if the production date is known, record it:

> 500 ## $a DVD of the motion picture originally released in 1999.
>
> 500 ## $a Blu-ray Disc of a recording of the play performed in the Gielgud Theatre, October 13, 2003.
>
> 500 ## $a DVD of the television film first broadcast in 2011.

RELATED WORKS

Related works upon which the film is based may be recorded in a 500 note (RDA 24.4.3). This offers an opportunity to expand on the data provided in an added-entry field, because the rigidity of these fields cannot adequately reflect an indirect or complex relationship:

> 500 ## $a Based on the novel of the same name by Jane Austen.
>
> 500 ## $a Based on characters created by Marvel Comics.
>
> 500 ## $a English-language remake of the Spanish film "Abre los ojos" (Open your eyes).
>
> 500 ## $a Based on the short-stories "Rashomon" and "In a grove" by Ryunosuke Akutagawa.
>
> 500 ## $a Loosely based on the play "The tempest" by William Shakespeare.
>
> 500 ## $a Shot-by-shot remake of the 1960 film of the same name directed by Alfred Hitchcock.

OTHER NOTES

The economy of MARC and RDA mean that short, clear statements and data elements must be included in fields where ambiguity would better aid description. 500 fields can be used to acknowledge this ambiguity, permitting catalogers to expand upon, clarify, or explain data recorded in other fields. Elsewhere in this volume there are examples of additional 500 field notes to record when the cataloger wishes to:

- Indicate that the title has been taken from a source other than the title frame (MARC 21 bibliographic field 245).

- Record that the work is accompanied by additional physical material, such as a book or a CD (300).
- Clarify an uncertain series statement (490/830).
- Clarify the information provided about the country of producing entity (257).
- Expand upon information provided about sound characteristics (344).
- Let the user know that playing a disc may not be straightforward, if it has regional coding for a different jurisdiction, or uses a different television broadcast standard, for example (347).

This list is not exhaustive, and catalogers are encouraged to use their own discretion when considering additional 500 notes.

Both indicators in a 500 note are undefined. The field ends with a full stop or other mark of punctuation. A closing full stop should follow any closing bracket or parenthesis. End punctuation should precede subfield $5 if used.

538 System Details Note (R)

538 is a catch-all field for technical information. Before RDA, which triggered the development of the new MARC 33X and 34X fields, it was the only place in a MARC record where many of the important technical details of a film, and many of the additional features present on an optical disc, could be noted. But the new fields are designed to be read by machines, not humans, and many ILSs cannot accommodate their complexity. Field 538 is not (yet) redundant.

It is still an unsatisfyingly vague note, and different libraries choose to enter different types of information here. Unless the cataloger's institution says otherwise, the simplest rule of thumb will be to use the field to record any technical information or system requirements details not included elsewhere in the record in a form that can be understood by humans.

As an indication of what content the field might include, the list that maps MARC 21 to RDA (http://access.rdatoolkit.org/document.php?id=jscmap2) includes special playback characteristic (RDA 3.16.9), video characteristic (RDA 3.18), encoding format (RDA 3.19.3), resolution (RDA 3.19.5), regional encoding (RDA 3.19.6), encoded bitrate (RDA 3.19.7), and equipment or system requirement (RDA 3.20).

Many libraries begin descriptions in this field with the words "DVD" or "Blu-ray Disc." The scope note for the field—"information about the trade name or recording system(s) (e.g., VHS) . . . may be included"—and two of its examples ("$a VHS" and "$a U-Matic") support this practice by analogy.

The 538 field is the only possible place to note the physical details about recordable formats (such as DVD+ and DVD-) if describing non-commercial discs, because RDA lacks instruction on the identification of both the optical disc storage media (i.e., CD, DVD, or Blu-ray Disc) and recording format (e.g., BD-R, DVD+RW, etc.).

The field also allows the cataloger to expand the limited description of sound formats recorded in the 344 field. More complex sound characteristics may be more appropriately included in a 500 note, as when a film contains multiple sound formats, or where a single resource contains multiple works. Some libraries record sound details in the 546 language note—this may be preferable if different language sound tracks use different sound formats. There is no single correct way to describe sound on optical disc; the flexibility of MARC coding, and the established ways it is interpreted, can be useful in recording the differing varieties and complexities of a disc's audio properties.

A 538 field should also provide details of the regional coding (see the earlier discussion of MARC field 347), especially if the institution's ILS does not display the text contained in the 347 field. It should list the television encoding format (see preceding discussion of MARC field 346) if the ILS does not display the text contained in the 346 field. Aspect ratios are both a technical detail and artistic choice, so are better recorded in a generic 500 field note, though some libraries record them here.

Both indicators are undefined, and the field ends with a full stop or other mark of punctuation. A closing full stop should follow any closing bracket or parenthesis. Multiple details may be combined in a single note:

```
538 ##   $a Region 1.

538 ##   $a Blu-ray Disc; 7.1 Dolby TrueHD sound; no regional coding.

538 ##   $a DVD; region 2; PAL.
```

NOTES

1. These figures are sometimes given as 4.37 and 7.95. The discrepancy in data capacities is due to the preference, in computing, for measuring in magnitudes of 1,024 (i.e., 2^{10}), instead of multiples of 10, so that a gigabyte ends up containing 1,073,741,824 bytes. Throughout, this book favors this preference as a basis of measurement, in keeping with most literature on the subject.

2. James Monaco, *How to Read a Film: Movies, Media, Multimedia*, 3rd ed. (New York: Oxford University Press, 2000), 125.

3. For more on the technical and historical details of the varying broadcast standards, see the quirky account provided by Raffael Trappe, Television Standards—Formats and Techniques, 2013, www.paradiso-design.net/videostandards_en.html.

4. A 2012 ALA proposal to the Joint Steering Committee for Development of RDA noted that "Blu-ray" was insufficiently specific, because Blu-ray Discs can hold different types of data. "Blu-ray video" is the correct application format, but at the time of writing, this change had yet to be implemented in RDA. See www.rda-jsc.org/docs/6JSC-ALA-16.pdf.

5. Evan Osnos, "Hollywood and China: Revenue and Responsibility," *The New Yorker*, February 20, 2013, www.newyorker.com/news/evan-osnos/hollywood-and-china-revenue-and-responsibility.

CHAPTER 5

TELEVISION

CATALOG RECORDS FOR TELEVISION SHOWS (AND OTHER recorded versions of dramatic performances) are not very different from records for films. This chapter offers additional advice and guidelines for cataloging discs containing material first broadcast on television. In particular, it highlights the practices that differ from the cataloging of material originally shown, or intended to be shown, on cinematic release.

A History of Television, from Jules Verne to Netflix

Nineteenth-century science-fiction authors imagined machines that could transmit pictures and words over wire. The stories were part projection, part wish-fulfillment, but their theoretical basis was scientifically orthodox. In imagining a "telephonoscope," writers were simply aggrandizing telegraphy, a new technology at the time.

The discovery of radio waves brought a new possibility—the wireless transmission of synchronous sound and vision through the air. The word "television" was first used in the early twentieth century, though the technology was still hypothetical, and then seemed magical—both the Greek "tele" (think "telekinesis" and "telepathy") and the English "vision" hint at wizardry. But inventors soon made it a reality with wooden boxes containing optical, electrical, and (temporarily) mechanical elements. John Logie Baird built his first television in 1923 out of an old tea chest—among other eccentric components it contained a projection lamp housed in a biscuit tin and some darning needles. By 1925, his thirty-line mechanical television could receive recognizable moving images showing gradations of light and shade. The technology advanced rapidly, and by 1936, the BBC was broadcasting using a 405-line electronic system. The first commercial broadcasts in the United States took place in 1941.

The average American now spends over thirty-five hours per week watching television.[1] Ninety-nine percent of American households own one; most have at least two. Television is more prominent, and more popular, than either films or books. Yet it is often dismissed as low-brow, ephemeral, and thoroughly commercial; a device for selling soap, pills, and unrealizable dreams. In 1950, Groucho Marx wrote: "I must say I find television very educational. The minute somebody turns it on, I go into the library and read a good book."[2]

There is something to this charge. When this author types "negative effects of" into Google, the first auto-complete term suggested (above "smoking," "alcohol," "cannabis," and "caffeine") is "television." It has has been blamed for childhood obesity, altering the norms of social propriety, desensitizing viewers to violence, and making them stupid. The popularity of forensic crime shows has measurably affected the practice of criminal law: today's juries pay less attention to eye-witnesses and circumstantial evidence. Thanks to the "*CSI* effect"[3] they expect the presentation of detailed and conclusive forensic evidence against defendants instead. And television may make viewers miserable, too. A recent study has found that although watching television was the happiest daily experience for many people, those who were dissatisfied with life spent, on average, 30 percent more time in front of their TV set than the satisfied. The researchers concluded that television brought "momentary pleasure but long-term misery and regret," as though it were a drug.[4]

But as a report by MediaSmarts (a Canadian not-for-profit organization that campaigns for digital and media literacy) puts it, there are "good things about television" (http://mediasmarts.ca/television/good-things-about-television). Quite apart from the obvious educational benefits, television can expand cultural horizons, help encourage critical thinking about, and engagement with, the world outside our personal experience, and teach us important values and lessons.

Also, consider the genuine popularity of television as a shared social experience. Over 125 million[5] people watched the final episode of *M*A*S*H** (1972–1983) on the night it aired.[6] Only seven films have sold more than 125 million movie theater tickets in the United States (*Snow White and the Seven Dwarfs* [1937], *Gone with the Wind* [1939], *The Ten Commandments* [1956], *The Sound of Music* [1965], *Star Wars* [1977], *ET: The Extra-Terrestrial* [1982], and *Titanic* [1997]).[7] But they've had an average of fifty years to reach these sales. When the finale of *M*A*S*H* aired on February 28, 1983, it was watched by 55 percent of all living Americans.

Consider the economics of contemporary productions. The pilot episode of *Boardwalk Empire* (2010) cost eighteen million dollars to produce. Sixty million dollars was spent on the ten episodes of the first season of the *Game of Thrones* (2011). This is close to the cost of an average Hollywood production. As when the sword-and-sandal epics threatened to bankrupt film studios in the 1950s and early 1960s, so the producers of *Rome* (2005–2007) were forced to cancel the show after only two seasons. The twenty-two episodes had cost them over $200 million. *Friends* (1994–2004) may have been set almost entirely in apartments and cafes, but in its final season, all six members of the billed cast received one million dollars for each of the twenty-two episodes.[8]

Finally, consider the quality of contemporary shows. When HBO began developing high-value original programming in the 1990s, it had a disruptive effect on the once-clear artistic distinction between television and film. The technical and aesthetic divisions between the two formats have become blurred. Today's blockbuster shows have A-list actors, well-bankrolled publicity machines, legions of dedicated fans, and many of the best screenwriters in the industry. Ten years ago shows such as *The West Wing* (1999–2006), *The Sopranos* (1999–2007), *The Wire* (2002–2008), and *Lost* (2004–2010) redefined the medium, and their critical and commercial success has attracted significant investment in high-quality programming unafraid to challenge audiences with complex, long-form storytelling.

The widespread availability of digital cable and high-speed Internet access has altered the economics of broadcasting and distributing television programs. Audiences have fractured, and viewing figures declined, as the marketplace becomes crowded with ever more channels. The ability to watch almost any show at any time results in fewer conversations over the water-cooler, but monetizes programming for longer, and keeps fans in an ever-present state of expectation. As HBO revolutionized television a generation ago, now Netflix (see chapter 9) and Amazon have begun to alter the way producers create, and viewers consume, television programming.

Changes in technology have also led to the quick death of bulky CRT (cathode ray tube) televisions in favor of plasma, LED (light-emitting diode), and LCD (liquid-crystal display) screens. Larger screens make the limitations of standard definition television (SDTV) very apparent. High-definition-compatible sets do not make programming filmed for SDTV look any better—on the contrary, they call attention to cheap sets, heighten the innate absurdity of melodrama, and magnify directorial shortcuts. Most original programming is now filmed in high-definition (HDTV), with an accompanying increase in production quality.

Television on Disc

Television on disc encompasses a variety of different formats. The most popular are described below.

Box- and Multi-Disc Sets

Box-sets of television programs gather an entire series or more of a previously broadcast show. They are usually released about two months after the final episode of a season has aired. The shift toward expensively produced programs with long-running "story arcs" has made these products extremely successful, and helped networks recover the escalating cost of original productions.

In North American usage, a *season* is an episodic or serialized set of programs, which normally runs for ten to thirteen episodes in its first year and, if successful, for twenty to twenty-six in subsequent years. The television calendar for such programming runs from September to May. The entire production is known as a *series*, though in Britain, "series" can also mean what North Americans understand "season" to mean.

A television drama that tells a single story over a number of episodes is known as a *miniseries* in North America. The number of episodes for these dramas is not fixed, but is always less than a typical television season. In

Britain, this format is known as a *serial*, a term that covers a broader range of serialized dramas.

Single Discs

Many types of television production are released on a single disc. Examples include classic episodes, feature-length episodes, Christmas specials, and best-of compilations.

TV Movies

The first *made-for-TV movies* were produced in the mid-1960s. They were commonly broadcast as part of a weekly anthology series, and lasted either 90 or 120 minutes (including commercials). Although there are highly successful examples of the form (such as *Duel* [1971], Steven Spielberg's first mainstream feature film), television films are more usually lower-budget sequels to cinematic releases, or *pilots* (feature-length episodes intended as test productions for new series). The production values of TV movies are similar to *straight-to-video films*. Films produced for television will need to combine descriptive elements of both formats.

Cataloging

The guidelines below note divergences from practices listed in previous chapters. The cataloger may assume that practice is the same as, or analogous to, that for film when specific guidance is not provided for MARC 21 bibliographic fields and subfields.

008/07–14 Fixed-Length Data Elements (Dates)

If the value "p" has been entered in the 008/06 data element, the first date should record the year of publication of the disc(s), and the second the year the program was originally broadcast. Where multiple episodes are included on the disc, the second date should record the year the first episode was aired.

046 Special Coded Dates (R)

If using the 046 field for television productions broadcast over multiple years, record the start date in subfield $k, and the end date in subfield $1.

130 Main Entry—Uniform Title (NR)

The LC-PCC PS for constructing authorized access points for films and television programs refines RDA in one key respect for the latter form. Name authority records for television programs are limited to the work level, excluding the various uses of a 130 field that cover language expressions (such as dubbing, subtitles, and intertitles) (LC-PCC PS 6.27.1.9, Appendix 1). This rule restricts the use of a 130 field for television shows to three situations. In each case, qualify the preferred title of the work with the term "Television program."

1. *Same title, different resources.* Construct a 130 field for a television program that shares its title with another resource in the catalog. If a conflict occurs with another television program, add additional qualifiers in this order: year first broadcast, name of production company or network (in the form given in the authority record), country of production:

    130 0# $a Stingray (Television program : 1960)

2. *Comprehensive title/individual title.* Construct a 130 field for any resource that contains only part of a television series, if the episodes of that series are intended to be viewed consecutively (RDA 6.27.2.2). This requirement, which covers individual episodes, selections, and entire seasons, is likely be applicable to the majority of the television discs in your collection. The entry is constructed by combining the authorized access point representing the work as a whole with the preferred title for the part, described according to the rules at RDA 6.2.1 and RDA 6.2.2.9.1. This entry will usually take the form of a comprehensive title, a numeric designation, and sometimes an individual episode title. Where individual episodes are not meant to be viewed consecutively, a 130 field is not required—the information in the 245 field will suffice.

Use subfields $n and $p, as appropriate, to record the season or episode number in numerical form and the episode title, respectively:

130 0# $a Band of brothers (Television program). $n Episode 2, $p Day of days.

130 0# $a ER (Television program). $n Season 15, $p And in the end.

3. *Compilations.* Most discs of television programs in your collection will also be compilations. They often overlap with the previous category, but the two are not identical. Compilations may include entire seasons, selections from a particular season, or "best of" episodes from different seasons. If the resource includes the entire season, record this in subfield $n, using the word "Season" followed by the season number in numerical form. This may not agree with the form of words used on the resource (see examples below). Follow this with a subfield $k containing the qualifier "Selections" for resources containing a selection of episodes from a single season. Episodes chosen from multiple seasons should not contain subfield $n.

130 0# $a Father Ted (Television program). $n Season 3.
245 10 $a Father Ted : $b the final revelations. $n Series 3.

130 0# $a Breaking bad (Television program : 2008). $n Season 5.
245 10 $a Breaking bad. $n The complete final season.

130 0# $a Glenroe (Television program). $k Selections.
245 14 $a The very best of Glenroe . . .

130 0# $a Dog the Bounty Hunter (Television program). $n Season 2. $k Selections.
245 10 $a Dog the Bounty Hunter. $n The best of season two.

245 Title Statement (NR)

Transcribe stand-alone episodes of television programs in the following order: Series title ($a), series number ($n), episode title ($p) (LC-PCC PS 6.27.1.9 Appendix 1). The series number may be dispensed with if the information is not displayed on the resource, does not exist, or is unlikely to enhance discovery or selection. The name of the episode should always follow the name of the program if both are included on the resource (RDA 2.3.1.7).

The LCRI for AACR2 1.6, taking its cue from the first edition of AMIM, offered an exception for what LC documentation referred to as an "'umbrella-like' television series," that is, programs on different subjects that do not need to be viewed or broadcast consecutively. In these cases, the episode title may be transcribed in the 245 field, and the name of the series recorded in a 730 or 740 field as appropriate. This rule was removed from the second edition of AMIM, but remained as an LCRI until 2005. Nothing similar exists among the LC-PCC PSs, but it seems a sensible guideline, and many AV catalogers still apply it.

If no episode title exists, record the episode number, if known, in subfield $n. If no episode title or number can be determined, record the date the program was first broadcast in this subfield, in square brackets, in the form yyyy-mm-dd. Any parallel title transcribed in subfield $b should follow subfields $n and $p:

>245 00 $a Ulysses 31. $p Kingdom of Hades.
>
>245 00 $a Bosco. $n Episode no. 386.
>
>245 04 $a The late late show. $n [1999-05-21].
>
>245 00 $a Avatar, the last airbender. $p The complete book 3 collection = $b Jiang shi shen tong.

130 fields occur far more often in catalog records for television resources than for films. So if you're used to cataloging the latter, it is easy to forget that if your record has a 130 field, the 245 first indicator must be "1."

246 Varying Form of Title (R)

If the 245 and/or 130 fields record both a comprehensive title (for a series) and an individual title or number (for an episode), create a 246 field to include the episode title where it might be helpful to have additional access in this form (e.g., to provide for a left-anchored title search). The season and episode number may also be recorded here.

>245 00 $a Galactica 1980. $p The return of Starbuck.
>246 30 $a Return of Starbuck
>246 3# $a Galactica 1980. $n Episode 10

380 Form of Work (R)

The 380 field offers a place to explicitly state that television, rather than film, is being cataloged. Use the qualifier "Television program" or "Television series" for any resource originally broadcast on television.

As noted above, films produced for television may have similar production values, budgets, and stylistic features to those of films distributed first on home video (i.e., those which never received a cinematic release, but were released "direct to DVD"). Films produced for television should be qualified in the 380 field (and the 130 field, where applicable) by the term "Television program." When the original distribution mechanism of a film is unknown, or cannot be determined, use the qualifier "Motion picture."

490 Series Statement (R); 830 Series Added Entry—Uniform Title (R)

As with film, the word "series," as used in MARC bibliographic fields 490 and 830, refers only to a group of resources named as such by a publisher; therefore, the names of television series should not be transcribed in either of the series fields.

500 General Note (R)

Film release dates are recorded in a 500 note. Similarly, record the broadcast year or years of television programs in a general note.

505 Formatted Contents Note (R)

For discs containing more than one episode, or sets containing more than one disc, individual episode titles may be listed in a 505 field note. Do not trace with additional 730 or 740 fields. Separate components with a space-dash-space:

> 500 00 $g disc 1, episode 1. $t More with less / $r teleplay by David Simon, story by David Simon and Ed Burns, directed by Joe Chappelle ; $g episode 2. $t Unconfirmed reports / $r teleplay by William F.

Zorzi, story by David Simon and William F. Zorzi, directed by Ernest Dickerson ; $g episode 3. $t Not for attribution / $r teleplay by Chris Collins, story by David Simon and Chris Collins, directed by Joy Kecken and Scott Kecken – $g disc2, episode 4. $t Transitions / $r teleplay by Ed Burns, story by David Simon and Ed Burns, directed by Dan Attias ; $g episode 5. $t React quotes / $r teleplay by David Mills, story by David Simon and David Mills, directed by Agnieszka Holland ; $g episode 6. $t The Dickensian aspect / $r teleplay by Ed Burns, story by David Simon and Ed Burns, directed by Seith Mann – $g disc 3, episode 7. $t Took / $r teleplay by Richard Price, story by David Simon and Richard Price, directed by Dominic West ; $g episode 8. $t Clarifications / $r teleplay by Dennis Lehane, story by David Simon and Dennis Lehane, directed by Anthony Hemingway ; $g episode 9. $t Late editions / $r teleplay by George Pelecanos, story by David Simon and George Pelecanos, directed by Joe Chappelle – $g disc 4, episode 10. $t 30 / $r teleplay by David Simon ; story by David Simon and Ed Burns ; directed by Clark Johnson.

508 Creation/Production Credits Note (R)

Television production crews have less creative influence on a program's intellectual and aesthetic features than their colleagues in the film industry. The look, feel, and style are determined in advance by the production company. Episodes are usually worked on by teams of writers, and directors frequently change from one episode to the next. To reflect this in a catalog record, record only the names of significant crew members if they have worked on all of the episodes contained on the resource.

List the director first for stand-alone programs, or episodes of series not intended to be viewed consecutively. For most multi-episode shows, the executive producer(s) should come first in the listing. In contrast to the holder of this term in film production, the executive producer of a television show is more important than the director and producer. Also known as the *showrunner,* he or she is responsible both for creative direction and day-to-day management. Unfortunately for the cataloger, an executive producer may also be the chief writer, head of the production company, or anyone who has assisted with the production of several individual episodes. Always list a program's showrunner in an additional access point. The showrunner is distinguished from the other executive producers in the credits by the prominence given to his or her name.

The producer, in charge of the organizational elements of filming an individual episode, is prefaced in the credits with the words "produced by." His or her role is similar to, but less powerful than, a film's producer. Many writers of television programs are also credited as producers, but they are credited differently, prefaced only by the word "producer." There are at least a dozen other defined production roles in the television industry.[9]

The credits of television programs distinguish between the names of individuals prefaced by the words "written by" (or "teleplay by"), and "story by." "Story by" usually designates the person who came up with the story concept in general outline. "Written by" refers to the person who turned that concept into a teleplay, the document from which a director and actors work. If listed on the resource, record both sets of writers in your description.

511 Participant or Performer Note (R)

Most television programs have a core set of cast members who appear in every, or nearly every, episode. Record them, even if they do not appear in a few episodes. Determining their significance is usually more straightforward than it is for film: note the cast members who appear in the opening credit sequence. Billing often changes from one season to the next.

520 Summary, etc. (R)

The episodic nature of television means that most resources are likely to contain a number of different stories. As anyone who has tried to explain the complexities of *The Wire* or *Breaking Bad* to the uninitiated will attest, one of the features that make these programs so compelling is their complex characterization and storylines, which can be very difficult to summarize. But nearly all television shows are based on a straightforward premise, because they must also appeal to viewers who have not seen every previous episode. Find a concise statement covering this premise for multi-episode sets, or compose one. Resources comprising single discs should be easier to summarize.

655 Index Term—Genre/Form (R)

Like catalog records for film, those for television programs should contain the term "Fiction television programs" or "Nonfiction television programs," followed by subfield $2 containing the code "lcgft." There is no need to record a form term indicating the running time of the production. Most useful genre and form terms for describing film have television equivalents; they simply replace the word "films" with "television programs" (e.g., "Fantasy films" and "Fantasy television programs"). Television-specific terms cover both genre and form. Examples include "television cop shows," "television game shows," "television mini-series," and "magazine format television programs."

700 Added Entry—Personal Name (R);
710 Added Entry—Corporate Name (R)

Relationship designators specifically applicable to television include "television director," "television producer," and "broadcaster." The designators "commentator," "moderator," "on-screen presenter," and "panelist" are used more frequently in television records than film ones.

See the above entry on MARC bibliographic field 508 for the differences in production roles between films and television shows.

730 Added Entry—Uniform Title (R),
740 Added Entry—Uncontrolled Related/Analytical Title (R)

For works that form part of a television series whose individual programs are unconnected, are not intended to be viewed consecutively, and perhaps have entirely different production crews, create an added entry for the comprehensive title of the television series:

> 730 0# $i Contained in (work): $a Horizon (Television program)

NOTES

1. The Nielsen Company, A Look Across Media: The Cross-Platform Report Q3 2013, 2013, www.nielsen.com/us/en/reports/2013/a-look-across-media-the-cross-platform-report-q3-2013.html.

2. Marx was being facetious—the quote appeared in an article written to promote his new television series. He continued: "That's a pretty cynical attitude for 'the leer'—that's me, Groucho—and now that I'm a part of television, or 'TV' as we say out here on the Coast, I don't mean a word of it. . . . All I can say is this: Walk, don't run, to your nearest television set in October, tune to KNBH, and join us for our first TV session of You Bet Your Life. I think you'll like it." Stefan Kanfer, ed., *The Essential Groucho: Writings by, for, and about Groucho Marx* (New York: Vintage Books, 2000), 207.

3. Nicholas J. Schweitzer, and Michael J. Saks, "The CSI Effect: Popular Fiction About Forensic Science Affects the Public's Expectations About Real Forensic Science," *Jurimetrics* 47, no. 3 (2007): 357–64.

4. John P. Robinson and Steven Martin, "What Do Happy People Do?" *Social Indicators Research* 89, no. 3: 565–71.

5. This figure is not without controversy. See Goodbye, Farewell and Amen Ratings Analysis, 2014, www.mash4077tv.com/articles/gfa_ratings/.

6. Only the Super Bowls of recent years have attracted more viewers, though as the population of the United States has increased, these figures represent a smaller percentage of the American population. The UEFA Champions League final is the most-watched annual sporting event worldwide.

7. Box Office Mojo, All Time Box Office, http://boxofficemojo.com/alltime/adjusted.htm?adjust_yr=1&p=.htm.

8. Bill Carter, "Friends' Deal Will Pay Each Of Its 6 Stars $22 Million," *The New York Times*, February 12, 2002, www.nytimes.com/2002/02/12/business/friends-deal-will-pay-each-of-its-6-stars-22-million.html.

9. For a helpful list, in order of seniority, see Producer's Guild of America, Frequently Asked Questions, www.producersguild.org.

CHAPTER 6

OLDER AND UNUSUAL FORMATS

ON OCCASION, IT MAY BE NECESSARY TO CATALOG FILMS ON old or unusual formats. The principles detailed in the preceding chapters apply almost equally well to these superseded and niche objects, as does the coding and description required in most MARC fields. Bibliographic records for these formats will usually be more straightforward than those for optical discs, because they lack the latter's technical and supplementary features. However, older formats present their own challenges. This chapter offers guidelines on how good RDA cataloging practice might be applied to videocassettes and film stock, the two formats upon which the MARC 21 bibliographic standard and RDA offer the most detail. Other formats are described briefly at the chapter's end. For all fields other than those listed below, cataloging practice will be the same as, or analogous to, standard practice for optical discs.

Videocassette Formats

The VHS videocassette was ubiquitous in the 1980s and 1990s (by 2000, 90 percent of American households owned a VCR),[1] but was only one of many videotape formats. Over sixty different types of videotape were developed between the quadruplex, which transformed the television industry when launched by Ampex in 1956, and the MPEG IMX, the last format to be commercially developed, released by Sony in 2001.[2]

Videotape stores sound and image magnetically (as distinct from film stock, which records images through a photochemical process). The data may be stored in analog or digital form. Videocassettes, first introduced in the early 1970s, house videotape within a robust plastic or metal container, and contain two small tape reels. Unusual formats may be identified using the online Video Format Identification Guide (http://videopreservation.conservation-us.org/vid_id/).

The *U-Matic* was the first videocassette format to be developed with the home video market in mind. It was launched by Sony, JVC, and Matsushita (later Panasonic) in 1971. The earliest U-Matic players were bulky, expensive, and had limited functionality, so the marketing focus was redirected to the broadcasting industry, with some commercial success. U-Matic videotapes are three-quarters of an inch wide, and have a recording time of approximately one hour. The format continued to be refined in the 1970s and 1980s, leading to the development of the U-Matic S, a smaller cassette, which could be played on regular-sized players using an adaptor.

Video Cassette Recording (which, abbreviated "VCR," is not to be confused with "videocassette recorder") was launched by Phillips in 1972. It was the first videocassette format to achieve a degree of success among ordinary consumers. VCRs were square, contained half-inch tape, and were available in three varieties, offering 30, 45, and 60 minutes of video content. The recording quality was high, but the tapes often jammed and tangled in players. VCR was only compatible with the PAL television broadcast standard, and so only distributed in Europe. Plans to develop a United States-compatible version encountered technical difficulties, and were abandoned when VHS was released.

A group of JVC engineers started designing a more versatile, durable, widely compatible, and cheaper videocassette when it became clear that the marketplace for U-Matic was limited. The result was the *Video Home System* (VHS), a half-inch tape that revolutionized television and film. The first VHS players were launched in Japan in 1976, and were an immediate success. VHS was the de facto videotape standard for twenty years, and though extensions of the format were developed, the original design was so robust and simple that consumers had little incentive to upgrade. *Super-VHS* (S-VHS) offered increased resolution, with a shortened recording duration. The compact formats *VHS-C* and *S-VHS-C*, stored in a smaller cassette, were developed for portable VCRs, but achieved more lasting success with camcorder users.

Launched in Japan and the United States in 1975, Sony's *Betamax* (sometimes referred to as Beta), offered superior image resolution and sound quality, and more stable images, than VHS. Much has been written about the "videotape format war" of the late 1970s and early 1980s, but the victory of the VHS was inevitable in hindsight. Sony produced all Beta tapes and players in-house, but JVC licensed VHS technology to other manufacturers, leading to efficiencies of production and a competitive marketplace. The earliest Betamax tapes contained only an hour of content (compared to the two hours of VHS tapes), and the cassettes, being smaller, had more limited capacity. When VHS gained a dominant market share, they undercut the cost of Betamax further and, by 1988, even Sony was making VHS players.

BetaCam and *BetaCam SP* (which uses metal tape) were higher-quality versions of Betamax marketed at the broadcast and film industries. BetaCam tapes typically contain either 30 or 90 minutes of video, and are contained within a 10 x 16 cm, or 14 x 25 cm, cassette. Once established, BetaCam became the standard used by most broadcasters, though a small number, including NBC, favored Panasonic's competing *MII* format.[3]

The *Video8* and *Hi8* formats were both small videocassette formats using eight millimeter videotape, introduced as rivals to VHS and VHS-C for camcorders. Video8 tapes normally stored two hours of content, while Hi8 tapes, a much-improved format with better video quality and high-fidelity stereo sound, were available with 30, 60, and 120 minute durations. The thinner tapes were more delicate than VHS and prone to defects, but their biggest disadvantage was their inability to be played on VCR.

Digital videotape (DV) enables viewing and replication without any loss of information. There are many digital video formats and tapes, but variants of the DV standard (both a storage and physical format) are the most common, used by both broadcast industry professionals and amateur filmmakers. All DV cassettes use one-quarter inch tape, and they come in four different sizes, known as small, medium, large, and extra-large. The most common are the small cassettes, also known as *MiniDV*, available in 30, 60, 63, 80, and 83 minute lengths—the extra three minutes allow for trial recording and camera setup.

Cataloging VHS

Cataloging practices for VHS that differ from optical disc are detailed below. Where distinct advice is not provided, the cataloging of Betamax, U-Matic, etc., may be carried out in an analogous way to VHS videocassettes. Catalogers creating records for video in these formats are advised to read the suggested practices alongside the text of the MARC 21 bibliographic standard.

007 Physical Description Fixed Field (R)

Catalog all videotapes and videocassettes as videorecordings, coded "v" in the 007 field, character position 00 (Category of material).

007/01 VIDEORECORDING (SPECIFIC MATERIAL DESIGNATION)

For VHS and other videocassette formats, code "f - Videocassette." Code "c" for videocartridges and "r" for videoreels. Videotapes in cartridges are held on a single tape hub or reel. Videoreels have no external housing.

007/04 VIDEORECORDING (VIDEORECORDING FORMAT)

Code "b" for VHS. For other formats see the text of the MARC 21 bibliographic standard, which offers a dozen more video format coding options.

007/06 VIDEORECORDING (MEDIUM FOR SOUND)

Always "h - Videotape."

007/07 VIDEORECORDING (DIMENSIONS)

The dimensions coded here relate to the width of the tape, not the size of the cassette. VHS, Betamax, and most other analog videocassette formats contain half-inch tape, coded "o." The earliest videotape formats used one- and two-inch tapes, coded as "p" and "q," respectively. U-Matic, and the first digital videotape formats, were three-quarter inch tapes, coded "r"; 8 mm tapes are coded "a"; MiniDV tapes "m."

028 Publisher Number (R)

Videorecording numbers were often placed in the 037 field prior to its redefinition in 1993. Field 037 has since been redefined as "Source of Acquisition," and its use is now limited to the recording of distributor and vendor stock numbers and codes. Move any videorecording numbers found here to a 028 field.

041 Language Code (R); 546 Language Note (R)

VHS tapes may contain either closed or open captions, or subtitles. Closed captions are embedded in the video signal. A decoder (built into VCRs and televisions manufactured for the American market) is required to display them. Open captions and subtitles are both imprinted on the tape, so cannot be turned off.

300 Physical Description (R)

Record the number, and the total running time, of videocassettes in subfield $a, in the format "1 videocassette (97 min.)." Record the width of VHS and Betamax videocassettes in subfield $c as "13 mm." Other formats should be recorded using the above-indicated sizes. This data must be in agreement with the 007 fixed field, position 07 (Dimensions).

When cataloging non-commercial material on recordable formats, it may be possible to estimate the duration of recorded material by examining the cassette's label. Most VHS tapes are recorded in standard play (SP), but by slowing down the tape speed, some VCRs extend the duration of content by recording and playing at half speed (long play [LP]), or one-third speed (extended play/super long play [EP/SLP]). The extended running time comes at the expense of video and sound quality. A capitalized E, followed by a three-digit number, indicates the playing time in minutes for PAL/SECAM tapes at SP and LP speeds. A capitalized T, followed by a three-digit number, indicates the playing time in minutes for NTSC tapes at SP, LP, and EP/SLP speeds.

338 Carrier Type (R)

Code "videocassette" in subfield $a and/or, if your local policy dictates, "vf" in subfield $b.

340 Physical Medium (R)

This field, which records the details of the physical medium, was expanded to accommodate RDA in 2011. Much of the information duplicates, in natural language, the machine-readable data recorded in the 007 field. It is required for any material that needs "technical equipment for its use or an item that has special conservation or storage needs" (MARC 21 bibliographic field 340). Encode all information in a single field, unless more than one material is specified, in which case the field is repeatable.

The information that may be entered here includes:

- The "material base and configuration," that is, "videotape," in subfield $a.
- The gauge (or width) of the tape in subfield $b (by the rules of RDA 3.5.1.4.3, recorded in millimeters using the symbol "mm").
- The generation of the tape in subfield $j, if your library contains videotape copies. Use a term from the list of options at RDA 3.10.6.3, that is, "first generation," "second generation," "master copy," or another concise term "if none of the terms . . . is appropriate or sufficiently specific."

340 ## $a videotape $j master copy $2 rda

344 Sound Characteristics (R)

See the chapter 4 entry on MARC 21 bibliographic field 344 for general guidelines on the new 34X fields. For VHS, and most other videocassettes, record "analog" in subfield $a, and for all videotape, "magnetic" in subfield $g. VHS can store sound in both mono and stereo formats. A typical videotape would be recorded as:

344 ## $a analog $b magnetic $g mono $2 rda

346 Video Characteristics (R)

See the chapter 4 entry on MARC 21 bibliographic field 344 for general guidelines on the new 34X fields. Record the videocassette format in subfield $a, choosing from among the options provided at RDA 3.18.2.3. This will usually be "VHS," though the list contains many other formats. Record another concise term if none of the options are appropriate or sufficiently specific. Record the broadcast standard (PAL, SECAM, or NTSC) in subfield $b. NTSC, PAL, and SECAM tapes are physically identical—the VCR determines whether they will be recorded and played in a particular format:

    346 ## $a VHS $b NTSC $2 rda

347 Digital File Characteristics (R)

MARC 21 bibliographic field 347 is inapplicable to most videocassettes.

500 General Note (R)

Add a note on the generation (e.g., "master copy," "archival backup") of videotape as recorded in the 340 field, subfield $j, if required for clarity or identification.

Film

Library holdings of film stock are often cataloged as archival objects, and described in standards other than RDA and MARC. However, both RDA and MARC contain detailed guidelines on how to catalog photochemical film. Because the word *film* is used throughout this volume, it would be remiss to overlook the form most appropriate to the vocabulary.

    Both MARC and RDA use the term *motion picture* to refer to reels of photochemical film, though the term is also used with its more general, generic meaning. The phrase "motion picture" is, at the time of writing, found fifty-seven times in the text of RDA (by contrast, "Blu-ray" occurs only twice). Collections of film in libraries are likely to be eclectic and diverse, and no simple description or short set of instructions is likely to be useful to any but a small minority of catalogers. With that caveat, the pages that follow attempt to describe the diversity of physical formats, and the ways these formats are cataloged using RDA.

Film defies simple categorization. Formats, technologies, and techniques have evolved throughout the history of motion picture photography. But the author believes film may be categorized in three main ways: by the stage in the production process at which it is used, by its physical properties, and by its chemical composition.

Categorizing Film: Production Process

Film may be classified according to its users and viewers. *Camera film* is used to capture the original images or performance. There are two main types of camera film. Negative film captures the reverse of color and contrast, and must be printed onto positive film stock before being projected. Reversal film is a positive film on a transparent base, and can be viewed directly after development. *Intermediate* and *laboratory films* are worked on by editors and visual effects technicians during postproduction, where special effects, titles, etc. are applied. *Print film* refers to film upon which no further editing will take place, most familiar as the material which, until recently, was projected to paying audiences in movie theaters.

Categorizing Film: Physical Properties

Film may be described according the physical base on which light-sensitive emulsion sits, its gauge (or width), or the number of perforations along its sides, top, or bottom.

There have been three main types of *film base* in the history of cinema: nitrocellulose (1890s–early 1950s), cellulose acetate (late 1940s–1990s), and polyester (1990s–today). The dangers of nitrocellulose (or nitrate) decomposition cannot be overstated, but acetate is also prone to decomposition. See chapter 8 for preservation and handling guidelines.

Four sizes of *film gauge* are in common use. *8 mm* (not to be confused with 8 mm video), and its successor, *Super 8 mm* (usually just referred to as *Super 8*) was the standard film gauge for amateur filmmakers until the development of digital capture. (Abraham Zapruder recorded the assassination of John F. Kennedy using a camera containing 8 mm film.) Super 8 cartridges replaced standard 8 mm rolls when introduced in the 1960s. It's no accident that J. J. Abrams, a leading contemporary director, named his nostalgic cinematic tribute to his adolescent filmmaking experiments *Super 8* (2011).

In the late twentieth century, *16 mm* and *Super 16 mm films* were used by semiprofessional filmmakers such as ethnographers, scientists, and the makers of educational films and commercials. It was also used for television productions and many European films produced in the 1960s and 1970s. Because of the ease with which it can be digitized, improvements in film stock, and the fact that the native aspect ratio of Super 16 is 1.66:1, close to the ratio of HDTV, this film gauge has had a renaissance in recent years.

35 mm film was the industry standard until as recently as five years ago, and most American feature films and television productions were shot using this film stock.

70 mm film (made with 65 mm camera film) is used for large-format projections such as IMAX.

Film can also be described by the number and position of its perforations. This detail may sound trivial, but is important in postproduction processes such as editing for aspect ratio and sound.

Categorizing Film: Chemical Composition

As with still photography, manufacturers produce distinct types of film, which meet different cinematographic requirements. Black-and-white film has a layer of emulsion consisting of silver halide grains suspended in a type of gelatin. Color film contains three layers of emulsion, along with additional chemicals.

Different films may be characterized by their speed and color balance. The former varies according to a film's sensitivity to light, and controls the granularity and contrast. The latter relates to the film's tendency to exaggerate the color of light. Our eyes adapt the color of light differently than does film, and what appears white to us may look pale blue or orange in a photograph. A skilled cinematographer will select a particular film stock for the natural and artificial lighting conditions under which a scene is filmed, and to influence the texture and mood of the photography.

Cataloging Film Stock

007 Physical Description Fixed Field (R)

Code all film stock, whether on a roll or reel, and contained within a cartridge or cassette, as "m - Motion picture" in the 007 field, character position 00 (Category of material).

The MARC 21 bibliographic standard provides extraordinarily detailed coding for material on film—"motion picture" has more categories than any other format. Field 007 has twenty-three defined character positions, the first eight (007/00–07) of which must always be used (though position 007/02 is undefined, having been made obsolete in 1997). Until 1985, most of the information currently contained in character positions 007/08–22 was recorded in the now obsolete 009 field, a fixed field for coding a physical description of film in archival collections.

Instructions on coding the 007 field for film go beyond the scope of this volume. Readers are advised to consult the full text of the MARC 21 bibliographic standard, which offers commendably clear and concise instruction on the coding of film using this fixed field.

008/33 Fixed-Length Data Elements (Type of Visual Material)

Always use "m - Motion picture." Do not be misled into coding the plausible-sounding "f - Filmstrip," which is used when a series of images on film is intended for viewing frame by frame, not in rapid succession.

300 Physical Description (R)

Record the number of reels, rolls, cassettes, or cartridges in subfield $a, followed by the running time of the film in parentheses, if known. Record the film gauge in subfield $c, in millimeters (e.g., 8 mm, 16 mm, 35 mm, etc.). RDA regards "mm" as a symbol, not an abbreviation, so it should not have a full stop, unless followed by the end punctuation:

> 300 ## $a 1 film reel (16 min.) : $b silent, black-and-white ; $c 16 mm.

336 Content Type (R)

As with the other formats described in this volume, record the RDA content term "two-dimensional moving image" in subfield $a and/or the MARC code "tdi" in subfield $b:

> 336 ## $a two-dimensional moving image $2 rdacontent

337 Media Type (R)

Describe motion pictures on film using the RDA media term "projected," in subfield $a and/or code "g" in subfield $b:

> 337 ## $a projected $2 rdamedia

338 Carrier Type (R)

In subfield $a, chose among the carrier terms "film cartridge," "film cassette," "film reel," or "film roll." The MARC codes for these terms, recorded in subfield $b, are "mc," "mf," "mr," and "mo," respectively. Super 8 film is contained within a cartridge. Nearly all the other major formats were sold on a metal or plastic reel. Film that is wound around itself is referred to as a roll:

> 338 ## $a film reel $2 rdacarrier

340 Physical Medium (R)

As noted in the guidelines on cataloging videocassettes, field 340 enables the cataloger to record detailed information about the physical medium on which a motion picture is stored. For photochemical film this ought to include the "material base and configuration" in subfield $a, according to the instructions at RDA 3.6.2. Chose a term from the authorized list: "acetate," "diacetate," "nitrate," "polyester," "safety base," or "triacetate." A reminder: no one should be getting near enough to nitrate film to be able to catalog it.

RDA instructs the cataloger to record the film gauge numerically, in millimeters, using the symbol "mm" (RDA 3.5.1.4.2, 3.5.1.4.3, 3.5.1.4.9,

3.5.1.4.10). Enter this in subfield $b. When describing 8 mm film, "indicate whether the gauge is single, standard, super, or Maurer." The two most common varieties are Standard 8 and Super 8.

If considered important for identification or selection, record the generation of the film in subfield $j. Use a term from the list of options at RDA 3.10.5.3: "original," "master," "duplicate," "reference print," "viewing copy," or another concise term "if none of the terms . . . is appropriate or sufficiently specific."

Record the polarity ("positive," "negative," or "mixed polarity") in subfield $o (RDA 3.14.1.3). Further details may be provided to assist with identification or selection, but if the text below means nothing to you, don't worry about it! "For motion picture films, record the form of print (e.g., negative, positive, reversal, reversal internegative, internegative, interpositive, colour separation, duplicate, fine grain duplicating positive, fine grain duplicating negative). For master material held in checkerboard cutting form, state if A, B, C, etc., roll" (RDA 3.14.1.4):

> 340 ## $a polyester film $b super 8 mm $j viewing copy $o positive $2 rda
>
> 340 ## $a acetate film $b 16 mm $j reversal master $o positive $2 rda

344 Sound Characteristics (R)

Sound is stored on the edge of film stock, and may be optical or magnetic, analog or digital. Magnetic soundtracks look like thin copper-colored stripes. Optical analog tracks are visible, under magnification, as a monochrome wave. Optical digital shows up as a snowy, static-like pattern similar to a QR code, and is usually stored between film perforations. There is no easy way to determine if an optical digital track is mono, stereo, or surround sound. Films that lack sound may be coded as "silent," though the cataloger may decide that your descriptions of films on standard 8 mm and the early super 8 formats can do without a 344 field.

In subfield $a, record the type of recording, "analog" or "digital."

Enter the recording medium in subfield $b, either "optical" or "magnetic."

Record the playing speed required for the sound to be reproduced as intended by the filmmakers (usually 24 fps), in subfield $c (RDA 3.16.4.3).

Record "edge track" in the track configuration, subfield $e (RDA 3.16.6.3).

OLDER AND UNUSUAL FORMATS | *149*

Where it can be determined, record the configuration of playback channels in subfield $g:

344 ## $a analog $b optical $c 24 fps $e edge track $g mono $2 rda

345 Projection Characteristics of a Moving Image (R)

Field 345 allows for the recording of unusual presentation formats, such as those projected onto curved, multiple, and very wide screens, as well as projections that give the illusion of three-dimensionality. RDA 3.17.2.3 provides an authorized list of these formats; enter as appropriate in subfield $a. The cataloger may also record, in subfield $b, the projection speed, in frames per second, abbreviated as "fps":

345 ## $a 3D $b 24 fps $2 rda

346 Video Characteristics (R)

Reels of film do not have video characteristics so this field will not be required.

347 Digital File Characteristics (R)

Reels of film do not have digital file characteristics, so MARC 21 bibliographic field 347 will not be required.

500 General Note (R)

Add a note on the generation of film recorded in 340, subfield $j, if required for clarification. If important for identification or selection, record the film length, from the first frame to the last. Where possible, record numerically, in meters, to the nearest tenth of a meter, using the symbol "m" (RDA 3.22.4.3). Add details to assist with projection, for example, "For use with a 16 mm projector."

Other Formats

Few catalogers will ever be called upon to describe superseded formats using the RDA standard, and WorldCat contains only a handful of RDA records for LaserDiscs, VCDs, HD DVDs, CEDs (i.e., all types of "videodisc"), et al. In many cases, accessions of these kinds of material will be described according to archival standards, not bibliographic ones. RDA mentions HD DVDs and VCDs just once (as video encoding formats, RDA 3.19.3.3, to be recorded in a 347 subfield $b), and LaserDisc (which retains its own MARC videorecording format code, "g," in the 007/04 position) not at all. Then again, "DVD" is only mentioned nine times. Use common sense, cataloger's judgment, and the instructions provided in this and earlier chapters, if called upon to create records for these formats. See chapter 1 for a definition, history, and summary of their technical features, which should assist with identification and basic description.

Even if uncertain of the terminology, the cataloger should try to provide some description in the 538 field, using common terms or those taken from the resource, which should include details such as the encoding format, and any particular sound or video specifications.

NOTES

1. Marc Graser, "DVD Holiday Sales Hot," *Variety*, January 6, 2000, www.variety.com/2000/film/news/dvd-holiday-sales-hot-1117760567.
2. For a comprehensive listing, see www.tech-notes.tv/Standards-Practices/TVTapeformats.htm.
3. Albert Abrahamson, *The History of Television, 1942 to 2000* (Jefferson, NC: McFarland & Co., 2003), 212.

CHAPTER 7

MARC 21 RECORDS AND AACR2

THE IMPLEMENTATION OF RDA DID NOT MAKE AACR2 RECORDS or practices disappear, and for a long time to come the majority of MARC records for DVDs and Blu-ray Discs will follow AACR2. Copy cataloging of AACR2 records continues among libraries that have implemented RDA. This chapter acknowledges that some libraries may wish to edit these records rather than convert them to RDA, and provides details of input conventions for MARC 21 bibliographic fields where AACR2 practice differs from RDA. It should be read in conjunction with the preceding chapters, which provide background and interpretation on the content of these fields as they relate to DVDs and Blu-ray Discs.

Intellectually, AACR2 reflected the desire to move toward a fully integrated catalog, where different types of resources would be described according to broadly similar rules. The specific application of these rules was outlined in distinct chapters: chapter 7 dealt with "motion pictures and videorecordings," and chapter 9, also relevant to the cataloging of film, addressed electronic resources. In ways both linguistic and structural, the expression of AACR2 rules differs from the more integrated approach of RDA, but in practice most of the instructions amount to the same thing.

151

The guidelines in this chapter only cover the cataloging of films on DVD and Blu-ray Disc; instructions on cataloging other dramatic and physical formats using AACR2 may be extrapolated from these guidelines and the content of previous chapters. AACR2 practices reproduce those of RDA except for the treatment of MARC 21 bibliographic fields below—the instructions offered by the two standards may not match, but the outcome for the cataloger will be the same. A basic familiarity with both standards is assumed, as are their differing practices relating to Latinisms, abbreviation, capitalization, and so forth. Catalogers are advised to read chapter 7 of AACR2 and the associated LCRIs, which are still usefully browsed and, due to the resource-specific design of AACR2, more accessible than equivalent the LC-PCC PS rules for RDA.

008/06 Fixed-Length Data Elements (Type of date/Publication status)

Chapter 4 argued that the FRBR's conceptual model, as imposed upon RDA, made data element 06/p inapplicable to the cataloging of films on optical disc. AACR2 is less bound by questionable philosophy, so catalogers should feel free to code "p" in position 06 if the content of a film on disc is considered to be identical to the theatrical release. If used, positions 07–10 should contain the date recorded in the 260 field, subfield $c; record the date of first theatrical release in positions 11–14.

008/07–10, 11–14 Fixed-Length Data Elements (Date 1, Date 2)

Represent unknown or missing dates by the character "u," for example, "200u."

130 Main Entry—Uniform Title (NR)

Many catalogers are still more familiar and comfortable with AACR2's concept of a uniform title than with RDA's preferred access point, even if the application of this first concept has long been one of the most confusing aspects of cataloging practice. The latter is an RDA core element, but uniform titles are optional in AACR2 records.

Appendix 1 of LCRI 25.5B details LC and PCC practice for assigning uniform titles to films. Its contents are very similar to LC-PCC PS 6.27.1.9, and though differently phrased, application of the instructions will usually result in an identical display.

The only difference of significance occurs in subfield $1. RDA suggests authorized access points (i.e., additional 730 fields) for each language expression contained within the resource, though only one is a core requirement (RDA 7.10), and this would normally be entered in a 130 field. AACR2 allows for more than one language to be recorded in the 130 field. Link two languages with an ampersand. For resources that require a 130 field, and contain three or more languages or language soundtracks, use the term "Polyglot."

245 Title Statement (NR)

AACR2 is less flexible than RDA on the source of a film's title. The title must be taken from the "chief source of information"; for film, the title frames (plural in AACR2, singular in RDA) or, failing that, the surface of the disc (AACR2 7.0B1, 7.0B2). If the title is not available from either of these sources, take it, in order of preference, from accompanying textual material, the disc case, or another source. Enclose title information from these latter sources within square brackets.

A parallel title, most commonly giving the title in the language of original production, may be transcribed only if it appears in the chief source of information (AACR2 7.1D2). Parallel titles appearing elsewhere may be recorded in a note field (AACR2 1.1D4). Subtitles can provide parallel titles and statements of responsibility only if they are not optional.

The rules that apply to the source of the title also apply to the statement of responsibility. Unfortunately, applying AACR2 instead of RDA will not help determine whom, among all the individuals listed in the credits, to transcribe. Record those with "a major role in creating a film (e.g., as producer, director, animator)" (AACR2 7.1F1). Among AACR2's examples are a writer and, somewhat oddly, two editors. LCRI 7.1.F1 provided an instruction to record the producers, directors, and writers, but it was canceled in 2000 when this section of AACR2 was revised, giving catalogers more scope to use their own judgment.

If four or more writers, producers, or other contributors are named in the source for the statement of responsibility, transcribe only the first, followed by "[et al.]." Additional names may be included in a 500 note and/or traced as added entries (AACR2 21.29D). Note that, unlike for monograph cataloging, where the first listed author in the statement of responsibility becomes the main entry, films should still be cataloged under title, apart from under the uncommon circumstances detailed in chapter 2.

The General Material Designation (GMD) is entered in square brackets in subfield $h. GMDs were introduced in the first edition of AACR (1967). Among other reasons, GMDs were implemented to help library users distinguish films from the books of which they were adaptations. More designators were introduced when the revised chapter 12 was issued in 1975. AACR2 (1978) includes two lists of GMDs (AACR2 1.1C)—one for use in Britain, another for North America.

The GMD is optional, and lacks philosophical or practical grounding. Its shortcomings are obvious.[1] The use of "[videorecording]" to describe films on optical disc is misleading and confusing to everyone but librarians. Many libraries use the locally defined GMDs "[videorecording (DVD)]" and "[videorecording (Blu-ray Disc)]." This may be justified on the model of AACR2's: "For materials for the visually impaired, add (large print) or (tactile), when appropriate, to any term in list 2. Add (braille), when appropriate, to any term in list 2 other than braille or text" (AACR2 1.1C1). Some view this as invalid, others accept it as a least-worst, and permissible, bending of the rules. The local use of an alternative GMD that lacks any of the terms within the geographically defined lists (e.g., "[DVD]") is incorrect and invalid. Enter GMDs after subfields $a, $n, and $p, but between subfields $a and $b, though this may cause indexing problems in an ILS.

Inaccuracies are transcribed in AACR2 records, but unlike RDA, which requires an additional 246 field containing a corrected title, they are followed by either "[sic]" or "i.e." and the correction in square brackets. Field 246 may also be used under AACR2 to give access to corrected titles. Supply missing letters in square brackets.

250 Edition Statement (R)

Edition statements should include abbreviations—not transcriptions—and follow AACR2's usual capitalization rules. An edition statement printed on the disc as "Fiftieth Anniversary Edition" would be recorded as "50th anniversary ed."

260 Publication, Distribution, etc. (Imprint) (R)

When a resource has more than one place of publication (which is uncommon for films on disc) list only the first. If this place is in a different country to where the cataloger is working, and is followed by one or more places of publication within the country where the record is being created, record the first of these places additionally. Record a larger jurisdiction, in abbreviated form, where required for clarification or disambiguation. If the place of publication is uncertain but probable, supply the probable place in square brackets, followed by a question mark (AACR2 1.4C2). Use the bracketed abbreviation "[S.1.]" when the place of publication is unknown.

Some older AACR2 records for film included the country of the original production in the publication field. This policy dated from a time before home video was widespread, and international distribution was more unusual. Only a few copied records will contain this oddity.

Use the bracketed abbreviation "[s.n.]" when the publisher is unknown. Recording the distributor, when different from the publisher, is optional (AACR2 7.4D1). Judiciously prune unnecessary words from publisher names.

Most DVDs and Blu-ray Discs will have one or more copyright dates printed on the surface of the disc. The date of publication is rarely, if ever, displayed within the title frame, so the copyright date may stand in its place. When recording a copyright date, preface the year with a lowercase "c," rather than the copyright symbol. Do not record an additional publication date, unless the publication date is known to be different. Separate multiple dates by a comma and space. When discs lack a copyright date, infer a date from information given on the container, and record this in square brackets. Adjacent bracketed elements may be enclosed in a single set of square brackets.

Unpublished items do not require a place of publication or distribution, and should not be recorded "[S.1.]" (AACR2 7.4C2).

264 Production, Publication, Distribution, Manufacture, and Copyright Notice (R)

AACR2 publication statements should be included in a single 260 field.

300 Physical Description (R)

Though AACR2 does not offer the same degree of flexibility as RDA, the 2004 amendment to rule 7.5B1 permits catalogers to use "a term in common usage to record the specific format of the physical carrier." This rule would permit "DVD" in place of "videodisc" in subfield $a, and "DVD-video" [sic] is one of the given examples. Use "ca." in place of RDA's "approximately" when estimating a film's duration.

Abbreviate silent ("si."), sound ("sd."), color ("col."), and black and white ("b&w") in subfield $b. Record toned or tinted films as black and white in subfield $b, with a brief descriptive note in a 500 field (AACR2 7.5C4).

Use abbreviations (e.g., "ill." and "p.") for supplementary printed material recorded in subfield $e. RDA considers "cm" to be a symbol, whereas AACR2 considers it an abbreviation, so use of "cm." is required.

336–338 Content/Media/Carrier Type (R), 344–347 Sound/Projection/Video/Digital File Characteristics (R)

These fields have been designed for use in RDA, and will not be found in legacy records. Though they are standard neutral, opinion is still divided about their use in AACR2 records. Until a consensus develops within the cataloging community (and a consensus is beginning to develop in their favor), addition of the new fields is not advised, unless a matter of local policy.

500 General Note (R)

Record details of sound characteristics in a 500 note (AACR2 7.7B10a). Unlike RDA, AACR2 considers mono and stereo to be abbreviations of monophonic (or monaural/monoaural) and stereophonic—they should be followed by a full stop. Alternately, record information on sound formats parenthetically within a 546 language note.

AACR2 is less prescriptive about aspect ratio than RDA, asking only that the cataloger's description be succinct (AACR2 7.5.C2). Record information on aspect ratio as printed on the container, unless it is in a form that is likely to be unfamiliar to the library user. Some libraries enter aspect ratio in a 538 field.

LCRI 7.7B7 recommends a note to record the original production (or issue) date of films released in different media two or more years earlier than the item being described. The year of production or cinematic release of the original film should therefore be recorded within its own 500 note field.

Related works that are loosely connected to the work being described may be recorded in a general note, because AACR2 cannot accommodate RDA's relationship information (as entered in the 7XX subfield $i).

505 Formatted Contents Note (R)

Separate each item in the contents note by a space-hyphen-hyphen-space.

508 Creation/Production Credits Note (R)

Individuals who have been transcribed in the statement of responsibility should not be recorded in the 508 field (AACR2 7.7B6).

538 Systems Details Note (R)

Record "DVD" or "Blu-ray Disc," to expand upon the unhelpful "videodisc" in the 300 field, subfield $a. This will be unnecessary if the alternative phrasing permitted by AACR2 7.5B1 has been implemented. AACR2 7.7B10 suggests some categories of description that might be recorded here, but as noted in chapter 4, the advice is not helpful or precise enough.

If the 34X fields in AACR2 records are not being used, a 538 note is the most appropriate place to record information about broadcasting format and regional coding. As with standard RDA practice, consider the utility of creating a single field, with each note separated by a semicolon (AACR2 1.7A5).

700 Added Entry—Personal Name (R), 730 Added Entry—Uniform Title (R)

See the preceding entry on 500 field notes for details about what to do with loosely related works.

NOTE

1. Commenting on the publication of AACR2, LC's *Cataloging Service Bulletin* noted that "The Library of Congress is of the opinion that GMDs are less satisfactory than the specific designations that are found in the physical description area." *Library of Congress Cataloging Service Bulletin* 2 (Fall 1978), 5.

CHAPTER 8

MANAGING THE COLLECTION

Collection Development

This book began by asking a straightforward question—why collect film? The entire volume is offered as an extended response. But once it is granted that film is important, and ought to be integrated into library collections, a more problematic question arises: what to collect? This chapter will proffer only a nebulous answer. The film librarian is best-placed to know what to buy, and these decisions will be mediated through his or her institution's collection development policies, and the demands and interests of its users. As with books, there are tensions in film between research or educational collections, and compilations of popular, entertaining titles—these asymmetries are best resolved by libraries on an individual basis.

The cinematic canon is less controversial than the literary one, and it is relatively easy to build a collection of films that have played an important part in social, cultural, and cinematic history. Every decade, *Sight & Sound* magazine asks film critics, academics, and writers to name what they believe to be the best films, in what Roger Ebert termed "by far the most respected of the countless polls of great movies—the only one most serious movie people take seriously."[1] More geographically focused, and in some ways more mainstream, a 1998 poll by the American Film Institute provided a guide to what the American film industry judged to be important landmarks over the first hundred years of cinema. However, these two lists are weighted toward milestones in cinema, rather than films patrons might actually want to watch.

Library organizations are another good source of recommendations. An ALA web page provides a gateway to lists of films suggested for children, young adults, and adults, as well as film collection guidelines for different types of library (www.ala.org/tools/recommended-viewing-movies-and-dvds).[2] The linked websites include those of *Booklist* magazine, the ALA's Video Round Table, and the Association for Library Service to Children. All three of these lists are somewhat didactic.

The number of films produced every year is vastly smaller than the number of books, so comprehensive printed listings are possible. *Bowker's Complete Video Directory* (four volumes) and Gale's *Video Source Book* (nine volumes), both published annually, both very expensive, aim to be complete directories of all films available for purchase. The bimonthly *Video Librarian* magazine reviews about 225 new releases per issue.

Collections of films are different than collections of books, and as with cataloging, so with collection development—quirks and peculiarities need to be considered. Films often exist in multiple formats and editions, so greater care needs to be taken when sourcing material. Most large vendors do not offer comprehensive selections of film, so it may be necessary to rely upon smaller ones. As discs are more fragile than books (for guidelines on care, see below), a higher percentage may need to be replaced.[3]

DVD or Blu-ray Disc?

Blu-ray Discs ought to offer a significant increase in picture and sound quality compared to DVD. They store more informationally complex images and sound, and so come closer to replicating the cinematic experience. New releases should always look better on Blu-ray Disc than on DVD.

But because many people now watch films on the lower-resolution screens of phones and tablets, it is clear that consumers of film do not always want, or even notice, higher picture quality. Some Blu-ray transfers have been carried out so cheaply that they are indistinguishable from the equivalent DVDs. The conversion process is expensive and complex: each frame of an older film must be scanned in high-resolution, pieced back together, and converted to digital form. With sales of optical discs falling, production companies have little incentive to invest in good transfers, even for moderately successful films.

Older films released on Blu-ray Disc often look different than their DVD versions, but they may not look better. An increase in the number of pixels does not necessarily bring an increase in picture quality. Consider the following examples.

Warner Brothers spent over one million dollars on a frame-by-frame restoration of *Ben Hur* (1959), for the film's fiftieth anniversary re-release. The original camera negative was scanned at the highest possible resolution, and so much care was taken that the anniversary was missed: the disc was not released until 2011. *Ben Hur* looks stunning on Blu-ray Disc.

Less convincing is the twenty-fifth anniversary Blu-ray Disc "collector's edition" of *Blade Runner* (1982). Although this five-disc set provided an excuse to remaster a film whose DVD versions had been of variable quality, the new release cynically used the film's notorious history of directorial reworking to its commercial advantage. An "ultimate collector's edition" was released for the thirtieth anniversary in 2012.

Well-meaning directors, rights-holders, and distributors sometimes degrade the aesthetic quality and unity of a film when they reformat it for Blu-ray Disc. The remastering of *The French Connection* (1971), although (or perhaps because) supervised by its director William Friedkin, was condemned by film critics and crew members for undermining the visual style of the original.[4] *The French Connection* helped define the cinematic aesthetic of 1970s New York. But the Blu-ray Disc version looks false: obvious digital filters have been imposed, obliterating the documentary feel of the original.

As films are transferred to Blu-ray Disc, they undergo a process called Digital Noise Reduction (DNR), which smoothes out imperfections. Smoothness is often equated with higher visual quality, but performed too casually, DNR can remove much of the grain from a film. In many cases the film grain *is* the film quality. The overuse of DNR can reduce picture resolution and makes people appear cartoonish. The Blu-ray Disc version of *Predator* (1987) is sharper than the DVD release, but the performers look almost waxy, the textures are dulled, and the colors are so saturated that the actors' clothes appear to glow. As a result, watching the Blu-ray Disc is less satisfying than watching the DVD.

In short, Blu-ray Discs should not always be preferred. Older television shows shot on video or 16 mm film will rarely be improved by transfer to

Blu-ray Disc. If the original production did not use high definition video or quality film stock, its transfer to Blu-ray Disc will not improve the picture. Nearly everyone involved in the creation, distribution, and sale of optical discs gets paid more for the sale of a Blu-ray Disc than a DVD. It is hardly a surprise that the former is presented as the default and authentic edition. Consumers, too, are skeptical—just eleven Blu-ray Disc titles sold more than one million units in the United States in 2013; twenty-eight DVD releases reached this figure.[5]

While some American consumers have complained that extended versions of certain films are now being released only on Blu-ray Disc, European film fans face the opposite problem. Many Blu-ray Disc versions of older films are not made available in Region B versions (nor Region C, for that matter). At the time of writing, forty-one of the hundred greatest films on *Sight & Sound*'s most recent list were unavailable for purchase as Blu-ray Discs in the United Kingdom, where the magazine is published. It may be telling that WorldCat.org offers a search box for DVD, but not for Blu-ray Disc.

Don't Forget VHS!

Just as not every film released on DVD is available on Blu-ray Disc, not all films released on VHS were distributed on DVD. They are rare, but there may be times when it is necessary to purchase a film on videocassette, particularly with genre films, "exploitation" films, and low-budget productions.

Combo Packs

DVD/Blu-ray Disc "combo packs," often called "dual format" editions, include a film in both formats sold within unified packaging. Some have derided these products as a gimmick to generate higher profits, but the market for them is real. Most people who own a Blu-ray Disc player also own at least one DVD player. Viewers may prefer to watch Blu-ray Discs on their main entertainment system, but have a DVD player in their laptop, vehicle, or child's bedroom.

Dual-format products enable economies of scale for film publishers. All new releases by Criterion, a publisher of older, and art-house films, have been issued as dual-format editions since mid-2013. Only large print-runs are economically viable for them, and having to design two separate products containing the same film was challenging the commercial viability of less-popular films.[6]

Collecting and cataloging these sets presents difficulties. If a library uses the prefix "DVD" or "Blu-ray" in call numbers, the cataloger will need to use one of them consistently (or use a hybrid prefix). Many libraries split the packs, and circulate the discs separately. Single bibliographic records are preferable, with individual item records for the different formats. Repeat the 300 field, so as to avoid the confusion otherwise generated from an overly complex subfield $e.

Classification

This section deals with the physical arrangement of films; for information on viewing restrictions based upon age, see the chapter 3 section on MARC 21 bibliographic field 521.

In the second edition of their *Nonbook Materials,* Weihs, Lewis, and Macdonald noted that "the media specialist should choose a classification scheme which is comprehensive, continuously revised, and proven in day-to-day use."[7] Among the non-specialist schemes, only the Library of Congress Classification scheme (LCC) and the Dewey Decimal Classification (DDC) meet these specifications. This does not mean they are suited to the classification of film. There are no good ways of classifying a collection of films, only a variety of bad ways that differ in their level of unhelpfulness.

Librarians must first assess whether films even need to be classified. This decision will depend on the size of the collection, the nature of the organization, and the needs of users.

Alternatives to classification include:

- Ordering by accession number, in a running sequence, as items are purchased. The Library of Congress arranges most of its films in this way. This system will only work when discs are not directly accessible to users, or for very small collections.
- Organizing by title, in a single alphabetical sequence.
- Organizing into a number of broad genres and/or forms—comedy, action, science-fiction, documentary, etc., organized alphabetically, if at all.

Most classifiers interpret DDC as instructing the integration of nonfiction films into the main sequence, while applying classmark 791.4334 to animations, 791.4372 to feature films (including made-for-television films), and 791.4572 to fictional television programs. Call numbers are then subdivided by subject, or sometimes geographically, according to the institution's usual assignment of DDC.

LCC is based on literary warrant, and because LC does not classify its films, LCC does not offer numbers for them. Different libraries approach this problem in different ways. As with libraries using DDC, most shelve documentaries or non-fiction films with books on the same topic—the policy advocated by Weihs, Lewis, and Macdonald. For fictional feature films there are four options:

1. PN1997 and PN1997.2, for films made before 2001 and after 2000, respectively, cuttered by title. These are the LCC numbers for screenplays, but they are widely applied to film. The chronological division is both unhelpful and arbitrary.
2. PN1995.9.A-Z, the LCC number for "Other special topics" in film, cuttering from a defined list of subjects or genres, followed by title.
3. A combination of these two approaches, perhaps classing English-language films at PN1997, but "foreign films" under PN1995.9.F67, and silent films under PN1995.75, the LCC number for books on that topic.
4. Either of the above, with adaptations of preexisting literary works classed next to the original.

Separating a collection can create problems. Through piecemeal accretion and arbitrary application of local policy, collections become disordered. On the other hand, classifying all feature films at PN1997 brings together the film, screenplay, and critical works, but will require longer Cutter numbers.

Handling and Storage

Hugo (2011), Martin Scorsese's love-letter to early cinema, contains a memorable scene of French troops gathering the films of George Méliès in order to destroy them during the First World War. It is a true story, and somewhat ironic, because after extracting the celluloid and silver (from the photographic emulsion), the waste products were remade into shoe heels—Méliès came from a family of shoemakers. Only a minority of Méliès' films survive today, but this is not unusual. An LC study published in 2013 estimated that 70 percent of all the feature films made in America during the silent era have been entirely lost.[8]

When soldiers come to ransack a collection there is little to be done. But throughout history more library material has been damaged through carelessness, poor handling, and poor storage than by warfare, and the ravages of time can be alleviated by good preservation practice.

Optical Discs

DVD cases were meant to approximate the height of a VHS tape and the width of a CD jewel case. Cases for Blu-ray Disc were designed to be distinguishable from DVD cases. Both are made from a single piece of injection-molded polypropylene. The design is extremely simple and effective. First created and patented by Amaray, and still referred to as the Amaray-style case, they are flexible, light, and shatterproof, unlike the brittle polystyrene of CD cases. The containers are also known as keep cases or poly-boxes. DVD and Blu-ray Disc cases usually have an exterior clear plastic sleeve (also polypropylene), and clips on the inside front cover for holding printed inserts. The dimensions of a standard single DVD case are 190 mm x 135 mm x 14 mm. Blu-ray Disc cases are shorter and often thinner, 171.5 mm x 135 mm. European Blu-ray cases are 14 mm thick. Cases made for the American market are either 11 mm or 12.5 mm thick (the difference is a legacy of the format war with HD DVD). DVD cases are usually black, Blu-ray Disc cases translucent blue. Other colors are sometimes used for marketing purposes, as when *The Incredible Hulk* (2008) was released in a green case.

Most cases have a hub at the center to assist disc removal and prevent accidental release. DVDs are made of two pieces of plastic, which remain unbonded at the center of the disc. As a result, the hubs of a DVD are weaker than the rest of the disc. Always remove discs by pushing the center of the hub, and never store DVDs in cases designed for CDs.

Many other storage products exist. Cases designed to hold multiple discs may be thicker, contain hubs on both sides, and single- or double-sided swing trays. Thinner (6 mm or 7 mm) cases allow more discs to be shelved in a given space, but are often of lower quality and will not accommodate the paper inserts of standard-sized cases.

Disc cases tend not to stand well (a major design flaw), slide against one another, and slip skittishly to the end and front of shelves. They should be held in place by book supports every four to six inches.

The surface of the read-side of a Blu-ray Disc is not entirely solid and can, over time, become impressed by anything it touches. The fibers of lightweight Tyvek disc sleeves, which some libraries store in binders, can mark the surface of a disc if in contact for long enough. Discs should never be stored in anything but keep cases or archival storage products designed specifically for optical discs.

DVDs and Blu-ray Discs easily attract dust and fingerprints, which commonly cause films to skip. Optical discs should be held by the central hole and the outer edge, never by their surface. To prevent scratching, avoid placing the data side on a hard surface. Take care when cleaning discs: even gentle surface cleaning may scratch them. Ideally, use canned air and a lint-free cloth. Cleaning movements should be straight and soft, from the center of the disc to the rim—do not rub in a circular motion. If this fails to remove dirt, some libraries have found that briefly soaking the disc in a very light solution of soap and warm water helps free dirt, though one should generally avoid getting any liquid on a disc. LC uses a dilute solution of Tergitol to clean both optical discs and a variety of other objects. Instructions on preparation and use can be found online (www.loc.gov/preservation/care/record.html).

DVDs and Blu-ray Discs have in-built error-correction technology, so minor scratches may not compromise the images. It they do, they can sometimes be repaired using cleaning machines. The RTI DiskChek Eco-Master is a large machine popular with public libraries, which can hold large collections of discs. The smaller VMI 3500 Buffer is often used in libraries with smaller collections.

Discs can be scratched or damaged by writing on, or attaching labels to, their surfaces. When writing on a disc always use a pen designed for the purpose. Only use labels designed for optical discs, preferably circular hub labels. It may be obvious, but remember that some DVDs are double-sided!

For long-term preservation, discs should be kept in stable environments with relatively low temperatures and levels of relative humidity (RH). Store materials of permanent value at between 45 and 50° F (7–10° C), with RH in the range 45 to 50 percent. Store discs upright and in a dark area, away from sources of UV light.

Videotape

Ideal conditions for the storage of videocassettes are similar to those for optical discs. Aim for a temperature range of between 45 and 50° F (7–10° C), and, ideally, low RH—between 20 and 30 percent. High temperatures and high levels of RH will result in an intensification of decomposition; because videocassette tape can begin to separate at 46° F (8° C), avoid temperatures much cooler than this. Store tapes upright, in a dark area, away from sources of UV light. Even in the best storage conditions, VHS tape will start to deteriorate after about fifteen years. Tapes containing unique information should be transferred to disc as soon as possible, or at least duplicated, with a master copy kept for archival purposes. Generally, copying tape to tape is not advised, because VHS suffers picture deterioration with each replication.

Many conservationists are more concerned with the future availability of suitable media players than the condition of tapes. If the library owns a VCR, make sure that it is a good one, and maintain it well. Library machines should be periodically cleaned using a VCR cleaning system, and covered with dust covers when not in use. VCRs are already rare, so it is wise to invest in spare parts now, and obtain a manual if necessary.[9] After deterioration, the biggest danger to VHS tapes is VCR machines.

Other dangers to VHS include condensation, mechanical failure of the tape itself, and damage caused by proximity to magnetic fields. In the past, one of the greatest dangers to videos was inadvertent destruction of data through video re-use, but that is less of a concern now. Ensure that the erase-protection tab is removed to avoid accidental re-recording. As with other media, avoid touching the tape of a videocassette, and handle only by the outer case.

Film Stock

The nature of photochemical film makes deterioration inevitable. Proper storage and conservation can slow the rate of degradation, but transfers to more stable media should be considered, especially in the case of nitrate and acetate film, which are subject to continuous chemical decomposition.

The dangers of nitrate film cannot be overstated. Although nearly all nitrate film has decomposed by now, unless it is marked as safety film or its provenance is clear, treat all film as nitrate film until it has been examined or tested. Consult with an expert (such as a member of the International Federation of Film Archives [www.fiafnet.org]) before handling this type of film, especially before opening film cans that have been closed for some time. Nitrate films can spontaneously combust at temperatures above 120° F (46° C), produce poisonous gases, are extremely flammable, and once they have begun to burn are almost impossible to extinguish. Nitrate film should be transferred to safety film as soon as possible, and then disposed of. In the meantime, it should be stored in an atmospherically controlled vault.

Acetate, polyester, and tricolor films are less dangerous, so the primary concern will be their chemical deterioration. Acetate is most prone to decomposition, which gives off a vinegar smell. Polyester film is more stable, but over time the emulsion layers begin to shrink, and can become detached from the polyester base. Tricolor films are made using a variety of processes, so suffer from different problems, with fading the most obvious.

Different types of film need to be stored in slightly different environments, but the stability of atmospheric conditions is essential. If possible, try to ensure that the temperature does not exceed 50° F (10° C), and keep the RH below 50 percent. Store film flat and evenly wound, with the emulsion side facing outwards.

Staying within the Law

The following sections offer brief coverage of legal considerations as they pertain to the United States. Librarians in other jurisdictions are advised to consult their national library associations or institutional copyright officers.

What follows is a circumspect overview of the law, not definitive advice. Law is inherently complex, variable, and continuously evolving. Many of the legal issues surrounding the management of film collections fall under copyright law, and the thorny concept of fair use. Fair use, as applied to individual cases, can be a matter of interpretation. For legal advice, contact an intellectual property lawyer.

Purchasing

Some specialist vendors of video material offer tiered pricing structures, with prices for institutions significantly higher than those for individual purchasers. Vendors argue that this helps support independent filmmaking by factoring in a supposed additional cost for public performances. And they emphasize that they are different from mass-market vendors, who can expect to sell many more copies, and so offer much greater discounts. Smaller vendors sell fewer copies, so need to sell at higher margins.

Copyright law already contains an exemption for public performance for teaching purposes in educational institutions, so there is no need, and little justification, for paying a higher price. Libraries are legally entitled to purchase DVDs and Blu-ray Discs as cheaply as they wish. So there is nothing to prohibit libraries from purchasing films from Walmart, Amazon, etc., though some librarians have well-founded ethical objections to doing so.

It is quite true, however, that some educational material, and some films sold exclusively by small independent distributors, must be priced high to help recoup the production cost.

Lending

The "first sale exemption" of the United States Copyright Act of 1976 enables libraries to lend films to their users for personal viewing, and to charge a nominal fee for doing so. (This is the same clause that allows bookstores to sell secondhand books without breaking the law.) However, libraries have a duty to avoid lending films for noneducational public performances, and should not lend discs to users who intend to copy them. If library users inquire about copying films on optical disc, they must be advised that only private viewing is lawful. There is no obligation to place warnings on discs advising users of copyright restrictions, but many libraries choose to do so.

Some films on optical disc contain the statement "For Home Use Only" on the disc or disc insert. These statements have no additional legal force, and the first sale exemption (and the copyright exceptions that permit public performance for nonprofit, educational use) is not infringed by the presence of such wording.

Performance

Nonprofit educational institutions are permitted to carry out public performances in face-to-face classroom situations. If the main purpose of the collection, and institution, is to provide researchers and students with materials needed for educational use, then public performance should not be an issue.

The TEACH Act (Technology, Education, and Copyright Harmonization Act, 2002) states that for distance-learning courses, films should not be shown in their entirety, but fair use would seem to justify complete showings. The use of YouTube videos for education and instruction may be in breach of the website's terms of service (https://www.youtube.com/static?gl=GB&template=terms), but no rights holder has yet taken action against an educational institution to prevent this kind of use.

However, a library that shows a mainstream feature film to a public audience for the purposes of entertainment is likely to be breaking the law. Some educational materials are sold with public performance rights, but it is usually necessary to acquire a license from the copyright holder for such performances. The nature of the performance rights will be determined by the terms of the contract.

Copying

In nearly every case, copying the content of optical discs is illegal. Discs can be reproduced only by the holder of a rights license. Libraries may not make additional copies, or transfer films from one format to another, if copies of these films are commercially available. In addition, reproducing a film that has copy-protection technology (as most DVDs and Blu-ray Discs do), will put the library in breach of the Digital Millennium Copyright Act (see www.copyright.gov/legislation/dmca.pdf). Films may be reproduced if the institution is the copyright owner, if the film is not commercially available, or if it exists only in an obsolete format. However, copying short clips for teaching purposes is considered fair use.

The Copyright Code also prohibits the conversion of VHS collections to DVD or digital files in most situations.[10] In cases where it is legal to copy material, storage in digital file format, on a secure server, is recommended. Data burned onto DVD-R and DVD+R discs degrades more quickly than data stored on commercially pressed discs.

Recordings Made from Television

Educators in the United States have limited fair use rights to record, and later show, television programs. Known as the Kastenmeier Guidelines, these rights were entered into the Congressional Record in 1984. They do not have the force of law, but have been cited in copyright cases.

Television programs broadcast by both network television and cable stations may be recorded by nonprofit educational institutions and kept for forty-five calendar days, at which time the recording must be erased or destroyed. Educators may show these recordings to their students within the first ten school days following the broadcast, and no more than twice (the second viewing only to reinforce previous instruction). After the ten-day period has elapsed, educators can view the recording, but only to evaluate whether it should be included in the curriculum. The institution must then obtain permission from the copyright holder if they wish to use the program for such purposes. Educators must request that off-air recordings be made in advance of broadcast—programs may not be recorded in anticipation of potential requests. Off-air recordings may not be altered in any way, but do not need to be shown in their entirety. All copies of a recording must include the copyright notice on the broadcast program as recorded.

Librarians considering the use of off-air recordings are advised to seek advice from their copyright officer or professional body. The United States Copyright Office has compiled an excellent circular, titled "Reproduction of Copyrighted Works by Educators and Librarians," freely available online (www.copyright.gov/circs/circ21.pdf).

NOTES

1. Roger Ebert, "'Citizen Kane' Fave Film of Movie Elite," *Chicago Sun Times,* August 11, 2002, www.rogerebert.com/rogers-journal/citizen-kane-fave-film-of-movie-elite.
2. The web page also contains links to related resources for librarians and educators.
3. This can be difficult: DVDs and Blu-ray Discs tend to go out of print quickly. Replacing individual damaged discs within a set may prove impossible. Midwest Tape (www.midwesttapes.com/home) is a vendor who will, almost uniquely, sell the individual discs of some sets.
4. For a comparison, see "The French Connection DVD versus Blu-ray versus Blu-ray Signature Series," YouTube video, 1:15, posted by "XylonHD," October 9, 2012, www.youtube.com/watch?v=1ZcxdmCreWY.

5. Film buffs seem genuinely to prefer Blu-ray Discs. In mid-2013, Criterion, an arthouse film publisher, revealed that 60 percent of its sales are of Blu-ray Discs, and 40 percent DVDs. See Peter Becker, "Why Dual Format?," August 20, 2013, www.criterion.com/current/posts/2873-why-dual-format.
6. Ibid.
7. Jean Weihs, Shirley Lewis, and Janet Macdonald, *Nonbook Materials: The Organization of Integrated Collections,* 2nd ed., (Ottawa: Canadian Library Association, 1979), 7.
8. See David Pierce, *The Survival of American Silent Feature Films, 1912–1929* (Washington, DC: Council on Library and Information Resources and The Library of Congress, 2013), www.clir.org/pubs/reports/pub158/pub158.pdf.
9. Manuals for many VCRs are available for download at www.manualsonline.com.
10. For further details, see American Library Association, VHS to DVD?, www.ala.org/tools/vhs-dvd.

CHAPTER 9

STREAMING VIDEO AND THE FUTURE OF THE OPTICAL DISC

ALL IS NOT WELL IN HOLLYWOOD. REVENUE IS DRIVEN BY frequent moviegoers, defined by the Motion Picture Association of America as the eleven percent of Americans who go to the cinema at least once a month. But this demographic is declining and aging.[1] The move from analog to digital was meant to cut costs, but the budgets of big Hollywood productions keep rising. Technology has made films, in the author's opinion, less engaging: some blockbusters are now little more than special effects sequences tied together by off-the-shelf set pieces. Technology has also overturned the means of distributing films to theaters and home-video viewers alike, and enabled the zero-cost pirating of new releases. The big studios are making fewer films, more expensive films, and less risky films.

Yet the desire for Tinseltown's products (not to mention those of Bollywood, Nollywood, and the $8.2 billion "Movie Metropolis" being built by China's wealthiest man)[2] is unchecked. In fact, it has become ever greater, as people share clips and trailers on their social networks, and watch segments of films on tablets and phones. Emerging markets continue to expand. Consumption patterns have changed radically, but Hollywood is still a money-making machine—the six major studios made a combined profit of $4.3 billion in 2013.[3]

The Future of DVD and Blu-ray Disc

For a technology in its relative infancy, the future does not look bright for Blu-ray Discs. 124 million Blu-ray Discs were sold in the United States in 2013, an increase of only 4.2 percent on the previous year's figures. Sales may begin to decline in 2014. Blu-ray Discs are well-established in North America, but for most of the rest of the world DVD is still the default medium, and Blu-ray Discs may always be an oddity.

With more consumers accessing digital content online using smartphones, tablets, and cheap laptops (none of which come with optical disc players), DVDs and Blu-ray Discs are increasingly seen as yesterday's technology. Sales of DVDs peaked as long ago as 2004. That year, speaking to the German newspaper *Bild-Zeitung*, Bill Gates said that "The entertainment of the future will definitely not be on a DVD player, that technology will be completely gone within ten years at the most."[4] Gates was wrong, but how wrong? What does the future hold for optical discs?

Future-gazers fall into two camps. Most argue that as the MP3 (and more recently services like Spotify, Pandora, Google Play, etc.) displaced the CD, cloud-based digital film subscriptions and purchases will displace the DVD and Blu-ray Disc. Others suggest that there are greater similarities with the world of publishing, where nostalgia, usability, a cutthroat secondhand marketplace, and attempts to repackage physical books as differentiated products has brought about an ecosystem where both the physical and digital can both thrive. On the surface, the first scenario seems most likely. The experience of watching a film (legally) online is almost exactly the same as watching it on a disc, so the disc offers no additional benefits beyond the "special features."

However, films are less of a commodity than songs. People are likely to want to maintain physical collections, partly from nostalgia, and partly because of the anthropology of materialism. As we're learning from the debate regarding books and ebooks, the dichotomy between virtual and physical is a false one in any case. CDs still actually form the majority of music sales, and the resurgence in vinyl (with sales up 33 percent in the United States in 2013) offers a counterexample to any perceived truisms about technological convergence.[5] But this is just speculation—if the author has learned anything from watching films, it's that predicting the future is a very bad idea.

Streaming Media

The importance of streaming media, and their sudden and transformative effects on the ways people now consume film, cannot be downplayed. In October 2013, the number of subscribers to Netflix, the largest on-demand Internet video-streaming service, overtook the number of subscribers to HBO, the most successful satellite and cable-television service in the United States. The commercial application of video streaming is almost entirely the work of the first company. Netflix's video streaming service was not announced until a month before it shipped its billionth DVD, early in 2007. The number of hours that could be viewed was restricted for the first year, but since this was removed, growth has been explosive. By mid-2014, Netflix streaming accounted for 34.2 percent of all downstream internet traffic in North America during peak hours.[6]

Simply put, streaming media is a process by which the transfer of data and its display to the user are nearly simultaneous. It is the same technology that allows the consumer to listen to or watch live events in real time. Streaming servers send packets of data to a user's computer, which are stored temporarily, and deleted as soon as they are accessed. Films that must be fully downloaded before they play do not count as streaming media. Internet distribution of high-definition video is normally broadcast at a resolution of 1280 x 720 pixels, that most easily accommodated by computer monitors.

There is no universal format for streaming media. The three primary methods of delivering video through a web browser are Adobe Flash Player, Microsoft Silverlight, and HTML5. The majority of videos online are in Adobe's Flash Video file format, viewable by means of Flash Player, a browser plug-in. Flash Video has been the default online video format for some time—it is used, for example, by YouTube. But as a proprietary format built for the PC era it has its critics—Apple's Steve Jobs disliked it so much that he refused to use it on the iPhone or iPad. Silverlight has additional features, such as search-engine optimization, and is used by Amazon's Prime service and Netflix. HTML5 is an open standard that embeds video in web pages. It has not yet been widely adopted, but has active champions in the tech community.

Most of the leading media players, such as Windows Media Player, iTunes, and RealPlayer, can also play streaming media files. Although most players can be downloaded at no cost, they need to be updated on occasion—a technical difficulty if users are streaming media within libraries. Make sure that the necessary technical infrastructure is in place before offering any streaming services.

How Might Libraries Offer a Streaming Service?

The potential benefits of streaming video as part of a library service are great. With the right partners, libraries could offer users remote access to films using a straightforward, user-friendly, always-available service. Streaming files do not get stolen, lost, or damaged.

But Netflix has no partnerships with libraries. Neither does Amazon, whose UltraViolet streaming service is a relatively new entry to the market. Moreover, Amazon is in many ways a direct competitor to libraries, and so unlikely to develop partnerships or services with them. Most of the other major distributors of online film and television have imposed restrictions that prevent libraries from distributing streamable and downloadable materials to multiple users.

This leaves a number of smaller specialist companies offering their services. These include Alexander Street Press's VAST service (http://alexander street.com/products/vast-academic-video-online), Midwest Tape's Hoopla (https://www.hoopladigital.com), Library Ideas' Freegal (www.libraryideas .com/movies.html), and Films Media Group's Films on Demand (www.films .com/ecHome.aspx). Most suppliers offer subscription services with additional features such as MARC records, playlists, bookmarks, etc.

There are also many freely available entertainment and educational titles available online, such as those hosted by the Internet Archive (www.archive .org) and YouTube. Mosfilm, the largest film producer in the Soviet Union (and, at one time, in all of Europe) has, since 2011, made hundreds of its films (with optional subtitles in English and Russian) available for free. Working with YouTube, its stated intention is to prevent pirating and provide users with high-quality versions of its productions.

Other films have been uploaded to the Internet because they are now out of copyright. Any film first shown to an audience before 1923 is in the public domain in the United States. Though the Copyright Term Extension Act of 1998 (www.copyright.gov/legislation/s505.pdf) added twenty years to the previous maximum copyright term of seventy-five years, it did not revive any expired copyrights. After 1923, the copyright status is unclear, and there is no official list of films in the public domain. Because films usually contain different types of elements (e,g., music, text, and photography), which may be covered by different types of copyright law, parts of a film might fall into the public domain while others remain protected by copyright law. However, many post-1923 films are almost certainly in the public domain. In the past, it was easy to fall foul of copyright law, and owners lost their copyright when they failed to include a copyright notice with their film, or deposit a copy or renew registration with the United States Copyright Office. Works created by employees of the United States federal government as part of their contracted duties are not entitled to domestic copyright protection.

Cataloging

The following MARC 21 bibliographic coding refers specifically to streaming video. It follows that for DVD and Blu-ray Disc outlined in the previous chapters where MARC fields are not listed.

Leader (NR)

Streaming video files should, like physical film resources, be coded "g - Projected medium" in Leader position 06 (Type of record).

006 Fixed-Length Data Elements—Additional Material Characteristics (R)

Position 00 (Form of material): Always "m - Computer file/Electronic resource."

Position 09 (Type of computer file): Always "c - Representational."

007 Fixed-Length Description Fixed Field (R)

MARC records for streaming video require two 007 fields, because they consist of two different categories of material—videorecordings and electronic resources.

In the field recording the category of material as a videorecording, code positions 00, 02, 03, 05, and 08 as for a DVD or Blu-ray Disc. For positions 01, 04, and 06, code "z - Other." Make no attempt to code position 007/07 (Dimensions).

In the field recording the category of material as an electronic resource, code in the following way:

- 007/00 (Category of material): Always "c - Electronic resource."
- 007/01 (Specific material designation): Always "r - Remote."
- 007/02 (Undefined): Always "# - Undefined."
- 007/03 (Color): Code "b" for black and white, "c" for color, "m" for films with both black and white and color sequences.
- 007/04 (Dimensions): Always "n - Not applicable."
- 007/05 (Sound): Usually "a - Sound."

The other character positions are usually either inapplicable or useless. But the cataloger may wish to record whether the resource contains a single file format (coded "a"), or multiple file formats (coded "m") in position 09, and/or the level of compression in position 12 (see the text of the MARC 21 bibliographic standard for details).

008/29 Fixed-Length Data Elements (Form of Item)

Record "o" for online. Prior to 2010, the value "s" was used for this format. Streaming media should be coded as videorecordings, not computer files.

024 Other Standard Identifier (R)

Online electronic documents often have digital object identifiers (DOIs), unique and permanent sets of characters linking to a registry containing metadata about the object. This metadata may include a URL location for the object. URLs can change over time, but the DOI remains fixed—the registry is simply updated to link to the new URL. DOIs are a core RDA element if present (RDA 2.15.1.4), and should be recorded in a 024 subfield $a, with a first indicator 7, and the second indicator blank. A subfield $2 should list the source of the code:

    024 7# $a 10.1080/01639374.2012.658989 $2 doi

245 Title Statement (NR)

The content of the 245 should be taken from the title screen. If an online resource has no title screen, take it, in order of preference, from another on-screen textual source, embedded metadata in textual form, or another part of the resource in which the information is formally presented (RDA 2.2.2.3.2).

300 Physical Description (R)

Record "1 online resource" in subfield $a, followed by the duration in minutes and seconds in parentheses. The file type may optionally be included among the pieces of information recorded in subfield $b. Subfield $c is inapplicable to streaming video files.

AACR2 is less prescriptive about the contents of subfield $a, and permits descriptions of the form "1 streaming video file":

> 300 ## $a 1 online resource (94 min., 12 sec.) : $b sound, color, Flash Video file

336 Content Type (R)

Record "two-dimensional moving image" in subfield $a, and/or use the code "tdi" in subfield $b.

337 Media Type (R)

Include two 337 fields. One should record "computer" in subfield $a, and/or use the code "c" in subfield $b. The other should record "video" in subfield $a, and/or use the code "v" in subfield $b.

338 Carrier Type (R)

Record "online resource" in subfield $a, though this is problematic because it is not strictly a "carrier" as defined in RDA 3.0.

347 Digital File Characteristics (R)

Record the file type "streaming video file" in subfield $a (RDA 3.19.2.4).

Choose among the video encoding formats listed at 3.19.3.3 (MPEG-4, QuickTime, RealVideo, and Windows Media). This list is insufficient to describe many types of streamed content. For example, when cataloging a film encoded in the Flash Video format, a "$2 rda" subfield cannot be added, because Flash is not on the approved list. A 2012 ALA proposal to the Joint Steering Committee for Development of RDA proposed the addition of "Flash Video" to the list of video encoding formats (www.rda-jsc.org/docs/6JSC-ALA-16.pdf), but at the time of writing, this change had yet to be implemented in RDA.

Record the bitrate (i.e., the speed of data transfer) in subfield $f, using metric symbols, if it can be determined (RDA 3.19.7.2). RDA's examples are "32 kbps, 7.17 Mbps, 12.52 Mbit/s." Record this information additionally in the 538 field:

>347 ## $a streaming video file $b QuickTime $f 800 kbit/s $2 rda

500 General Note (R)

Record the original production and/or release dates if the film has previously been released in another format, and this information is easily ascertained:

>500 ## $a Originally released as a motion picture in 2011.

>500 ## $a Released as an online video file on August 12, 2013.

Websites containing streaming video will sometimes provide an option to download a copy of the file. Record this in a general note:

>500 ## $a Multimedia file available in downloadable (MP4 file) and streaming (SWF file) formats.

505 Formatted Contents Note (R)

A formatted contents note may be used to record when different bandwidth versions of a resource are available. For example, the BBC's iPlayer service offers many films in both standard and high-definition, and IMDb trailers are generally viewable in three formats. Alternately, this information may be recorded in a 500 general note field. Films available in different resolutions or file formats may need multiple links in field 856 (as discussed below).

506 Restrictions on Access Note (R)

Note any restrictions on access, such as those requiring physical presence or password authentication:

> 506 ## $a Access restricted to those within the University of Cambridge IP domain, or remotely through Raven authentication.

530 Additional Physical Form available Note (R)

Include a note if the resource is also available in the collection in a DVD or Blu-ray Disc version. This field may also be included in records for films on optical disc additionally available as streamed video.

538 System Details Note (R)

Generic system requirements may be added to this note field, in addition to expanded details of information previously entered in the 347 field. Detailing system requirements for access (e.g., "Adobe Flash plug-in required for playback in browser" or "Windows Media Player required for downloadable files") may assist the user, but given the pace of technological change, may also date records quickly.

588 Source of Description Note (R)

If the source of a description, in particular the title recorded in the 245 field, comes from a source other than the title screen, provide details in this field (RDA 2.3.2.2). Record the date on which the resource was viewed for description (RDA 2.17.13.5):

> 500 ## $a Title from HTML title metatag (viewed August 8, 2013).

655 Index Term—Genre/Form

LCGFT offers two categories more applicable to streaming video files than to optical discs: "internet videos" and "webisodes."

856 Electronic Location and Access (R)

Provide a link to the resource using subfield $u. Related resources may also be recorded in a separate 856 field. Both the resource itself and any related resource should be qualified by subfield $3. If more than one URL needs to be recorded, the 856 field should be repeated.

The first indicator should be "4." When providing a direct link to the resource, the second indicator should be "0." When linking to a related resource, the second indicator should be "2." The field contains no internal or end punctuation:

> 856 40 $3 1 streaming video file $u https://archive.org/details/VoyagetothePlanetofPrehistoricWomen
>
> 856 42 $3 Film trailer $u www.youtube.com/watch?v=PdVZ10trxsU

NOTES

1. See Motion Picture Association of America, Theatrical Market Statistics 2013, www.mpaa.org/wp-content/uploads/2014/03/MPAA-Theatrical-Market-Statistics-2013_032514-v2.pdf.
2. See Laurie Burkitt, "Wang Jianlin Aims to Create Hollywood, China," *The Wall Street Journal*, September 22, 2013, www.wsj.com/news/articles/SB10001424052702304213904579090803470556012.
3. Georg Szalai and Paul Bond, "Studio Profit Report: Who's Up and Who's Down," *The Hollywood Reporter*, February 21, 2014, www.hollywoodreporter.com/gallery/movie-tv-studio-profit-report-681784.
4. "TV of the Future Will Be the End of DVD, Claims Microsoft Founder," *The Scotsman*, July 18, 2004, www.scotsman.com/what-s-on/film/tv-of-the-future-will-be-the-end-of-dvd-claims-microsoft-founder-1-1396101.

5. In 2013 CDs made up 60 percent of music sales. Though sales fell year-on-year, so did sales of digital tracks. The Nielsen Company, U.S. Music Industry Year End Review 2013, www.nielsen.com/content/dam/corporate/us/en/reports-downloads/2014%20Reports/nielsen-us-music-year-end-report-2013.pdf.
6. Todd Spangler, "Netflix Remains King of Bandwidth Usage, While YouTube Declines," *Variety,* May 14, 2014, www.variety.com/2014/digital/news/netflix-youtube-bandwidth-usage-1201179643.

FURTHER RESOURCES

KEEPING UP WITH FILMS ISN'T DIFFICULT—THE PUBLIC IS bombarded with the latest releases, which stare from billboards, rain down in sound-bite reviews on television and radio, and flash up as unsolicited advertisements in online social networks. Actors and actresses appear on morning talk shows, daytime talk shows, and late-night talk shows.

Actors are contractually obliged to praise their latest film, even if they think it's a turkey. To learn about the latest trends in film it is necessary to dig a little deeper, and to learn about changes and challenges to cataloging practice, deeper still. The resources below expand upon, and provide context for, much of what appears in this volume.

Introductions to Film

Bordwell, David, and Kristin Thompson. Observations on Film Art. www.davidbordwell.net/blog.

> Bordwell is a legendary figure in film studies and criticism, who published one of the first textbooks in the field. His approach is idiosyncratic and highly formal. His provocative website is maintained with his long-time collaborator.

Corrigan, Timothy, and Patricia White. *The Film Experience: An Introduction,* 3rd ed. Boston: Bedford/St. Martin's, 2012.

An introductory textbook for students of film studies. It is heavy on the formal aspects of film, but brims with enthusiasm. A serious guide, and very useful.

Lim, Dennis, ed. *The Village Voice Film Guide: 50 Years of Movies from Classics to Cult Hits.* Hoboken, NJ: J. Wiley and Sons, 2007.

There are many published listings of films, from the encyclopedic (such as those previously maintained by Leslie Halliwell in the United Kingdom, and by *Variety* in the US) to the personal (critic Roger Ebert's many books). Before the internet, these were essential; now they seem quaint. The *Village Voice* has always been strong on film: this guide contains 150 pieces of the best film writing to appear in the newspaper.

Monaco, James. *How to Read a Film: Movies, Media, and Beyond,* 4th ed. Oxford: Oxford University Press, 2009.

The best introduction to film for novices, and an essential handbook for those who consider themselves experts, Monaco's book explains the history, mechanics, politics, economics, and possible future of the film industry. If only one book about film can be purchased, make it this one.

Scorsese, Martin. *A Personal Journey with Martin Scorsese through American Movies.* Produced by the British Film Institute, released 1995. DVD version available from the BFI and Lionsgate.

America's greatest living filmmaker is also one of its finest film historians. This four-hour documentary covers American cinema from its birth to 1969, the year Scorsese began his professional career.

Taylor, Jim, Mark R. Johnson, and Charles G. Crawford, *DVD Demystified,* 3rd ed. New York: McGraw Hill, 2006.

The best single-volume introduction to the history and technology of the DVD. Highly technical, but authoritative.

Taylor, Jim, Charles G. Crawford, Christen M. Armburst, and Michael Zink, *Blu-ray Disc Demystified.* New York: McGraw-Hill, 2009.

Although Taylor's book on DVDs also covers Blu-ray Discs, he has also published this expanded stand-alone volume.

Cataloging Resources

Bothmann, Robert L., Jessica J. Schomberg, and Nancy Olson. *Cataloging of Audiovisual Materials and Other Special Materials: A Manual Based on AACR2 and MARC 21.* 5th ed. Westport, CT: Libraries Unlimited, 2008.

Dutkiewicz, Scott M., ed. Library of Congress Genre/Form Terms for Library and Archival Materials: Moving Image Genre-Form Terms. 2013. www.olacinc.org/drupal/capc_files/GenreFormHeadingsList.pdf.

Hsieh-Yee, Ingrid. *Organizing Audiovisual and Electronic Resources for Access: A Cataloging Guide,* 2nd ed. Englewood, CO: Libraries Unlimited, 2006.

Library of Congress, AMIM Revision Committee, Motion Picture, Broadcasting, and Recorded Sound Division. *Archival Moving Image Materials: A Cataloging Manual,* 2nd ed. Washington, DC: Library of Congress, Cataloging Distribution Service, 2000.

> LC's in-house cataloging rules for moving images, based on AACR2, chapter 7. The print publication has been discontinued, but is available from Cataloger's Desktop.

Library of Congress, Acquisitions and Bibliographic Access Directorate. Genre/Form Headings at the Library of Congress. 2014. www.loc.gov/catdir/cpso/genreformgeneral.html.

Martin, Abigail Leab. *AMIA Compendium of Moving Image Cataloging Practice.* Beverly Hills, CA: Association of Moving Image Archivists, 2001.

> A snapshot of the cataloging practices of twenty-seven different institutional archives, who catalog film using both MARC 21 and other descriptive standards.

Maxwell, Robert L. *Maxwell's Handbook for RDA: Explaining and Illustrating RDA: Resource Description and Access Using MARC 21.* Chicago: ALA Editions, 2014.

OLAC Cataloging Policy Committee, DVD Cataloging Guide Update Task Force. Guide to Cataloging DVD and Blu-ray Discs Using AACR2r and MARC 21. 2008. www.olacinc.org/drupal/capc_files/DVD_guide_final.pdf.

> This document is likely to remain the definitive text on cataloging optical discs using AACR2. The long-delayed update for RDA is still in preparation at the time of writing.

OLAC Cataloging Policy Committee, Streaming Media Best Practices Task Force. Best Practices for Cataloging Streaming Media. 2008. www.olacinc.org/drupal/capc_files/streamingmedia.pdf.

An introductory guide to streaming media, with instructions on cataloging online audiovisual resources using AACR2 and the MARC 21 bibliographic standard. Evolving technology, not to mention the implementation of RDA, have dated the guide somewhat, but the clear definitions and helpful examples still provide an excellent overview of the subject. Once again, at the time of writing, an OLAC task force is updating the guide for RDA.

OLAC Cataloging Policy Committee, Video Language Coding Best Practices Task Force. Video Language Coding Best Practices. 2012. http://olacinc.org/drupal/capc_files/VideoLangCoding2012-09.pdf.

An update to OLAC's 2007 document, which clarifies and interprets MARC 21 fields 008, 041, and 546 fields as applied to audiovisual resources.

OLAC Newsletter. http://olacinc.org/drupal/?q=node/59.

Published quarterly. The entire run is available free online.

Roe, Sandra K. *The Audiovisual Cataloging Current.* New York: Haworth Information Press, 2001.

Scholtz, James C. *Video Acquisitions and Cataloging: A Handbook.* Westport, CT: Greenwood Press, 1995.

Stanford University Libraries, Metadata Department. Videos—Cataloging (RDA). 2014. https://lib.stanford.edu/metadata-department/clone-video-cataloging-guidelines.

Yee, Martha M. *Moving Image Cataloging: How to Create and How to Use a Moving Image Catalog.* Westport, CT: Libraries Unlimited, 2007.

Also worth looking at are the RDA Toolkit video cataloging workflows from the Pan-Canadian Working Group on Cataloging with RDA (http://rdaincanada.wikispaces.comPan-Canadian+modules) and from Stanford University (http://lib.stanford.edu/metadata-department/clone-video-cataloging-guidelines).

Conservation and Care of Materials

Blasko, Edward, Benjamin A. Luccitti, and Susan F. Morris. *The Book of Film Care.* Rochester, NY: Motion Picture and Television Image, Eastman Kodak Co., 1992.

Conservation OnLine. Motion Picture Film Preservation. 2013. http://cool.conservation-us.org/bytopic/motion-pictures/.

A portal that provides access to an extensive range of information resources about photochemical film.

Finch, Loraine, and John Webster. *Caring for CDs and DVDs.* London: National Preservation Office, British Library, 2008. www.bl.uk/aboutus/stratpolprog/collectioncare/faqs/cddvd/caring_for_cds_dvds.pdf.

Library of Congress, Preservation Directorate. Care, Handling and Storage of Motion Picture Film. 2014. www.loc.gov/preservation/care/film.html.

A short guide from the Library of Congress on how to identify, handle, and care for different types of photochemical film.

National Film Preservation Foundation. *Film Preservation Guide: The Basics for Archives, Libraries, and Museums.* San Francisco: National Film Preservation Foundation, 2004.

National Media Museum. Nitrate Film. www.nationalmediamuseum.org.uk/~/media/Files/NMeM/PDF/Collections/Universal/NitrateFilm.pdf.

A brief but excellent two-page guide to the history, decomposition, dangers, and storage of nitrate film.

Van Bogart, John W. C. *Magnetic Tape Storage and Handling: A Guide for Libraries and Archives.* Washington, DC: The Commission on Preservation and Access, 1995.

Other Aspects of Audiovisual Librarianship

Association of College and Research Libraries, Guidelines for Media Resources in Academic Libraries Task Force. Guidelines for Media Resources in Academic Libraries. 2012. www.ala.org/acrl/standards/mediaresources.

Ellison, John William. *Media Librarianship.* New York: Neal-Schuman, 1985.

Handman, Gary, ed. *Video Collection Development in Multi-type Libraries: A Handbook,* 2nd ed. Westport, CT: Greenwood Press, 2002.

Laskowski, Mary S. *Video Acquisitions in Libraries: Issues and Best Practices.* Chicago: ALCTS Publishing, 2011.

Pitman, Randy. *The Video Librarian's Guide to Collection Development and Management.* New York: G. K. Hall, 1992.

Royan, Bruce, and Monika Cremer. *Guidelines for Audiovisual and Multimedia Materials in Libraries and other Institutions.* International Federation of Library Associations and Institutions, 2004. www.ifla.org/files/assets/hq/publications/professional-report/80.pdf.

Russell, Carrie. "The Best of Copyright and VideoLib," *Library Trends* 58, no. 3 (Winter 2010): 349–57.

Shores, Louis. *Audiovisual Librarianship: The Crusade for Media Unity (1946–1969).* Littleton, CO: Libraries Unlimited, 1973.

Slide, Anthony. *Before Video: A History of the Non-Theatrical Film.* New York: Greenwood Press, 1992.

Weihs, Jean, Shirley Lewis, and Janet Macdonald. *Nonbook Materials: The Organization of Integrated Collections,* 2nd ed. Ottawa: Canadian Library Association, 1979.

Current Awareness

Film Critics

Roger Ebert (*Chicago Sun-Times*) and Philip French (*The Observer*) were the author's weekly go-to critics when starting this volume. Ebert died in April 2013, and French retired in August 2013 (and was replaced by another great film critic, Mark Kermode, who brings both academic polish and idiosyncratic passion to mainstream and genre film alike). Their writing was fluid, intelligent, and suffused with the knowledge and appreciation of half a century of writing about film.

Important contemporary critics include Christopher Orr (*The Atlantic*), Kim Newman (*Empire*), David Thomson (*The New Republic*), and Anne

Billson (various publications). Rotten Tomatoes (www.rottentomatoes.com) and MetaCritic (www.metacritic.com) collate reviews from a variety of critics, both amateur and professional.

Film Magazines

Empire is the biggest-selling populist British film magazine published monthly and distributed internationally. In addition to news and reviews, the magazine contains many regular features, including classic scenes, "masterpieces," and top tens.

Sight & Sound is the monthly magazine of the British Film Institute, published since 1932. It is the magazine of film critics and film obsessives, notable for its attempt to provide reviews and detailed credits of every national release. *Sight & Sound* is perhaps best known for its decennial poll, which consults a huge number of critics, academics, and film professionals to compile a list of the ten greatest films of all time. These lists tend to be eclectic, and only one film, *La règle du jeu* (1939), has appeared in all seven lists.

Little White Lies is a quirky bimonthly magazine published in the United Kingdom. The typographical and design qualities, as well as the content, are influenced by the film featured on its cover.

The Hollywood Reporter was first published in 1930. It was Hollywood's first daily trade newspaper, and has undergone many redesigns, rebrandings, and changes of ownership. It was most recently relaunched in 2010 as a glossy weekly magazine focused on all aspects of the entertainment industry. The *New York Times* has recently noted that, for Tinseltown's aristocracy, it has become "the new Vanity Fair."[1] It has a significant web presence.

Film Comment, the American equivalent to Britain's *Sight & Sound*, is published bimonthly by the Film Society of Lincoln Centre in New York City. Sophisticated but very readable, the magazine covers both mainstream and art-house film, and provides a forum for lengthy feature pieces on contemporary film and film criticism.

Variety is the definitive trade magazine for the entertainment industry, and is now published as a weekly glossy magazine. Its influence exceeds its small circulation, and it has been credited, among other things, with coining the terms "sitcom," "sex appeal," "cliff-hanger," and "biopic." In recent years, it has struggled to compete with glossier and more web-savvy rivals. Its daily edition, published in Los Angeles and New York, ceased publication in 2013.

Mailing Lists for Audiovisual Cataloguers

RDA-L (www.rda-jsc.org/rdadiscuss.html) is an electronic discussion list maintained by the Joint Steering Committee for Development of RDA to help facilitate informal discussion about RDA.

OLAC-L is maintained by the Online Audiovisual Catalogers, Inc. (http://olacinc.org/drupal/?q=node/51).

AUTOCAT is a long-established list for catalogers (and classifiers) (https://listserv.syr.edu/scripts/wa.exe?A0=AUTOCAT). Its archive is an important source of information in its own right.

Glossaries

AACR2 and RDA both contain glossaries, which can be helpful for understanding terms used by the standards when they differ from everyday use.

Though PCC libraries do not use the AMIM cataloging guidelines, its glossary (accessible through Cataloger's Desktop) is an excellent source of authoritative definitions.

The comprehensive Multilingual Glossary of Filmographic Terms (www.fiafnet.org/uk/publications/fep_Glossaryoffilmographicterms.html), maintained by the International Federation of Film Archives (FIAF), is particularly useful for understanding terms used in foreign language material. It includes parallel explanations of terms in English, French, Spanish, Chinese, Italian, and Portuguese, with additional stand-alone terms in German, Lithuanian, Finnish, Danish, Hungarian, and Dutch. The Online Film Dictionary is also a useful guide to foreign terms (http://home.snafu.de/ohei/ofd/md_terms_e.html).

OLAC's AV and Nonprint Glossary (http://olacinc.org/avglossary/) and the IMDb Movie Terminology Glossary (www.imdb.com/glossary/) also provide helpful guidance to the film cataloger.

For a more lighthearted look at the language of film, see Roger Ebert's tongue-in-cheek glossaries of film clichés, first published in 1994."[2]

NOTES

1. Brooks Barnes, "From Has-Been to Life of the Party," *The New York Times*, February 15, 2013, www.nytimes.com/2013/02/17/fashion/the-hollywood-reporter-dusts-off-its-party-clothes.html.

2. Roger Ebert, *Ebert's Little Movie Glossary: A Compendium of Movie Clichés, Stereotypes, Obligatory Scenes, Hackneyed Formulas, Shopworn Conventions, and Outdated Archetypes* (Kansas City: Andrews and McMeel, 1994).

APPENDIX A

SAMPLE RECORDS

THE FOLLOWING EXAMPLES OFFER RECORDS FOR FOUR TYPICAL types of objects: a film on DVD, a film on Blu-ray Disc, a stand-alone television episode on Blu-ray Disc, and a boxed-set of a television series on DVD. Two records describe releases from the United States and two from the United Kingdom. They are internally consistent, but do not attempt to be consistent with each other. There is no single way of cataloging film on optical disc, and with the implementation of RDA the options have grown from many to myriad.

The records are extensive, for the purposes of demonstrating the full range of content that may be included. Most libraries will likely choose to create shorter records. For guidance on which information RDA considers core, and which optional, please refer to the descriptions of individual MARC fields.

TYPICAL DVD RELEASED IN THE UNITED STATES: THRONE OF BLOOD

007	vd#bvaizm
008	100101s2003####nyu109#|#########vljpn||
020 ##	$a 9780780026445
020 ##	$a 0780026446
024 1#	$a 037429175828
028 42	$a THR130 $b Criterion Collection
041 1#	$a jpn $j eng
043 ##	$a a-ja---
050 04	$a PN1997 $b .K86
082 04	$a 791.43/72 $2 22
245 00	$a Kumonosu-jō = $b Throne of blood / $c Tōhō Kabushiki Kaisha ; scenario by Hideo Oguni, Shinobu Hashimoto, Ryûzô Kikushima and Akira Kurosawa, based on Macbeth ; directed by Akira Kurosawa.
246 3#	$a Akira Kurosawa's Throne of blood
246 31	$a Throne of blood
264 #1	$a [Irvington, N.Y.] : $b The Criterion Collection, $c [2003]
264 #4	$a ©2003
300 ##	$a 1 videodisc (109 min.) : $ b sound, black-and-white ; $c 4 3/4 in. + $e 1 booklet (20 pages : illustrated ; 19 cm).
336 ##	$a two-dimensional moving image $2 rdacontent
337 ##	$a video $2 rdamedia
338 ##	$a videodisc $2 rdacarrier
344 ##	$a digital $b optical $g stereo $h Dolby $2 rda
346 ##	$b NTSC $2 rda
347 ##	$a video file $b DVD video $2 rda
347 ##	$e region 1
490 1#	$a The Criterion collection ; $v 130
500 0#	Special features include: audio commentary featuring Japanese-film expert Michael Jeck; documentary on the making of the film, created as part of the Toho Masterworks series 'Akira Kurosawa: It Is Wonderful to Create'; two alternate subtitle translations, by Japanese-film translator Linda Hoaglund and Kurosawa expert Donald Richie.
500 ##	$a DVD version of the motion picture originally released in 1957.
500 ##	$a Wide screen (aspect ratio 2.35:1), letterboxed.

508 ## $a Director, Akira Kurosawa; producers, Akira Kurosawa, Sôjirô Motoki; screenplay by Hideo Oguni, Shinobu Hashimoto, Ryûzô Kikushima, Akira Kurosawa; cinematographer, Asakazu Nakai; original music, Masaru Satô.
511 1# $a Toshirô Mifune, Isuzu Yamada, Takashi Shimura.
520 ## $a "In feudal Japan, a war-hardened general, egged on by his ambitious wife, works to fulfill a prophecy that he would become lord of Spider's Web Castle." Edited summary from the Internet Movie Database.
538 ## $a Blu-ray Disc; Region A; Dolby Digital monoaural sound.
546 ## $a In Japanese, with optional English subtitles.
600 10 $a Shakespeare, William, $d 1564-1616. $t Macbeth $v Film adaptations.
650 #0 $a Samurai $z Japan $v Drama.
655 #7 $a Fiction films. $2 lcgft
655 #7 $a Feature films. $2 lcgft
655 #7 $a Film adaptations. $2 lcgft
655 #7 $a Samurai films. $2 lcgft
655 #7 $a Action and adventure films. $2 lcgft
700 1# $i Motion picture adaptation of (work): $a Shakespeare, William, $d 1564-1616. $t Macbeth.
700 1# $a Kurosawa, Akira, $d 1910-1998, $e screenwriter, $e film director, $e film producer.
700 1# $a Motoki, Sojiro, $e film producer.
700 1# $a Oguni, Hideo, $d 1904-1996, $e screenwriter.
700 1# $a Hashimoto, Shinobu, $d 1918-, $e screenwriter.
700 1# $a Kikushima, Ryūzō, $d 1914-1989, $e screenwriter.
700 1# $a Mifune, Toshirō, $d 1920-1997, $e actor.
700 1# $a Yamada, Isuzu, $d 1917-2012, $e actor.
700 1# $a Shimura, Takashi, $d 1905-1982, $e actor.
710 2# $a Tōhō Kabushiki Kaisha, $e production company.
710 2# $a Criterion Collection (Firm), $e film distributor.
740 02 $a Spider's web castle.
830 #0 $a Criterion collection (DVD videodiscs) ; $v 190.

TYPICAL BLU-RAY DISC RELEASED IN THE UNITED KINGDOM: THE MAN WHO SHOT LIBERTY VALENCE

007		vd#bsaizk
008		131001s2013####enk123#|#########vleng||
024	3#	$a 5051368245638
028	42	$a BSP 2456 $b Paramount Home Entertainment
041	1#	$a eng $a fre $a ger $a ita $a spa $j eng $j ger $j fre $j dut $j ita $j spa $j dan $j fin $j swe $j nor
043	##	$a n-usp--
050	04	$a PN1995.9 $b .W4
082	04	$a 791.43/72 $2 22
245	04	$a The man who shot Liberty Valance / $c Paramount Pictures ; screenplay by James Warner Bellah and Willis Goldbeck ; produced by Willis Goldbeck ; directed by John Ford.
264	#1	$a [London] : $b Paramount Home Entertainment, $c [2013]
264	#4	$a ©2013
300	##	$a 1 videodisc (123 min.) : $ b sound, black-and-white ; $c 4 3/4 in.
336	##	$a two-dimensional moving image $2 rdacontent
337	##	$a video $2 rdamedia
338	##	$a videodisc $2 rdacarrier
344	##	$a digital $b optical $g surround $h Dolby $2 rda
344	##	$a digital $b optical $g mono $h Dolby $2 rda
347	##	$a video file $b DVD video $e all regions $2 rda
500	##	$a Blu-ray Disc version of the motion picture originally released in 1962.
508	##	$a Director, John Ford; producers, Willis Goldbeck, John Ford; screenplay by James Warner Bellah, Willis Goldbeck; cinematographer, William H. Clothier; editor, Otho Lovering; original music, Cyril J. Mockridge, Alfred Newman.
511	1#	$a John Wayne, James Stewart, Vera Miles, Lee Marvin, Edmond O'Brien, Woody Strode, Andy Devine, John Carradine, Lee Van Cleef.
520	##	$a A western portraying the struggle between cattlemen and homesteaders in the town of Shinbone, telling about the encounter of a young eastern lawyer with the notorious gunman Liberty Valance.
538	##	$a Blu-ray Disc; all regions.

546 ##	$a In English (5.1 Dolby TrueHD, and restored mono sound), with optional dubbed mono soundtracks in French, German, Italian and Spanish; optional English, German, French, Spanish, Dutch, Italian, Danish, Finnish, Swedish and Norwegian subtitles.
650 #0	$a West (U.S.) $v Drama.
655 #7	$a Fiction films. $2 lcgft
655 #7	$a Feature films. $2 lcgft
655 #7	$a Film adaptations. $2 lcgft
655 #7	$a Western films. $2 lcgft
700 1#	$i Motion picture adaptation of (work): $a Johnson, Dorothy M. $t Man who shot Liberty Valence.
700 1#	$a Ford, John, $d 1894-1973, $e film director, $e film producer.
700 1#	$a Goldbeck, Willis, $e film producer, $e screenwriter.
700 1#	$a Bellah, James Warner, $d 1899-1976, $e screenwriter.
700 1#	$a Wayne, John, $d 1907-1979, $e actor.
700 1#	$a Stewart, James, $d 1908-1997, $e actor.
700 1#	$a Miles, Vera, $e actor.
700 1#	$a Marvin, Lee, $e actor.
700 1#	$a Devine, Andy, $d 1905-1977, $e actor.
700 1#	$a O'Brien, Edmond, $d 1915-1985, $e actor.
710 2#	$a Paramount Pictures Corporation, $e production company.

TYPICAL BLU-RAY DISC TELEVISION STAND-ALONE EPISODES RELEASED IN THE UNITED STATES: STAR TREK, THE NEXT GENERATION, THE BEST OF BOTH WORLDS

007		vd#csaizk
008		140101s2013####cau085#|#########vleng||
024	1#	$a 032429128478
028	42	$a 7912847 $b CBS Home Entertainment
041	1#	$a eng $a ger $a ita $a spa $a jap $a fre $j eng $j ger $j fre $j dut $j ita $j spa $j dan $j swe $j nor $j jap
043	##	$a zo-----
050	04	$a PN1992.77 $b .S73 2013
082	04	$a 791.45/75 $2 23
130	0#	$a Star trek, the next generation (Television program). $p Best of both worlds.
245	10	$a Star Trek, the next generation. $p the best of both worlds / $c producer, David Livingston, Lee Sheldon ; executive producer Michael Piller, Rick Berman, Gene Roddenberry ; written by Michael Piller ; directed by Cliff Bole.
264	#1	$a [California] : $b CBS Home Entertainment, $c [2013]
264	#4	$a ©2013
300	##	$a 1 videodisc (85 min.) : $ b sound, color ; $c 4 3/4 in.
336	##	$a two-dimensional moving image $2 rdacontent
337	##	$a video $2 rdamedia
338	##	$a videodisc $2 rdacarrier
344	##	$a digital $b optical $g surround $2 rda
344	##	$h DTS-HD Master Audio
344	##	$a digital $b optical $g stereo $h Dolby $2 rda
344	##	$h Dolby Digital
346	##	$b NTSC $2 rda
347	##	$a video file $b Blu-ray $2 rda
347	##	$e region A
380	##	$a Television program
500	##	$a Blu-ray Disc version of the television episodes first broadcast in 1990.
500	##	$a Full screen (aspect ratio 1.33:1, i.e. 4:3).

500 ## $a Special features include: audio commentary by director Cliff Bole, actress Elizabeth Dennehy, visual effects supervisor Mike Okuda and scenic artist Denise Okuda; 'Regeneration: engaging the Borg' documentary; gag reel; episodic promos.

508 ## $a Director, Cliff Bole; executive producer, Rick Berman; teleplay writer, Michael Piller; editing, J.P. Farrell; producer, Ira Steven Behr.

511 1# $a Patrick Stewart, Jonathan Frakes, LeVar Burton, Gates McFadden, Brent Spiner, Michael Dorn, Marina Sirtis, Elizabeth Dennehy, George Murdock, Whoopi Goldberg.

520 ## $a 'The Enterprise team discovers the devastated remains of a Federation colony as an ambitious young officer joins the crew to confirm the presence of the deadly Borg. Soon after, Borg drones abduct Captain Picard, mutilating him horribly as they assimilate him into their collective. Commander Riker must take over as Enterprise captain as Starfleet braces for an all-out battle to defend Earth. But the Borg's power proves overwhelming, and resistance is futile. Will Riker be forced to destroy his former captain to save Earth and the Federation?' Unedited summary from container.

538 ## $a Blu-ray; 1080p High Definition 4:3 presentation; 7.1 DTS-HD Master Audio surround sound (English), Dolby Digital stereo sound (German, French, Italian, Japanese).

546 ## $a In English, German, French, Italian, Japanese or Spanish, with optional subtitles in French, Spanish, Japanese, German, Italian, Danish, Dutch, Finnish, Norwegian or Swedish; English subtitles for the deaf and hard of hearing.

650 #0 $a Picard, Jean Luc (Fictitious character) $v Drama.

650 #0 $a Interplanetary voyages $v Drama.

650 #0 $a Space warfare $v Drama.

655 #7 $a Television programs. $2 lcgft

655 #7 $a Fiction television programs. $2 lcgft

655 #7 $a Science fiction television programs. $2 lcgft

700 1# $a Stewart, Patrick, $d 1940-, $e actor.

700 1# $a Frakes, Jonathan, $e actor.

700 1# $a Burton, LeVar, $e actor.

700 1# $a McFadden, Gates, $e actor.

700 1# $a Spiner, Brent, $e actor.
700 1# $a Dorn Michael, $e actor.
700 1# $a Sirtis Marina, $e actor.
700 1# $a Dennehy, Elizabeth, $e actor.
700 1# $a Murdock, George, $e actor.
700 1# $a Goldberg, Whoopi, $d 1955-, $e actor.
700 1# $a Berman, Rick, $e television producer.
700 1# $a Piller, Michael, $d 1948-2005, $e screenwriter.
700 1# $a Bole, Cliff, $e television director.
710 2# $a CBS Studios Inc., $e film distributor.
710 2# $a Paramount Pictures Corporation, $e production company, $e film distributor.

TYPICAL DVD TELEVISION BOXED-SET RELEASED IN THE UNITED KINGDOM: BLAKES 7, SERIES 1

007		vd#cvaizm
008		100101s2004####enk663#|#########vleng||
024 3#		$a 5014503117627
028 42		$a BBCDVD 1176 $b BBC Worldwide
041 1#		$a eng $j eng
082 04		$a 791.45/72 $2 23
130 0#		$a Blake's 7 (Television program). $n Season 1.
245 10		$a Blakes 7. $n the complete series one / $c written and created by Terry Nation.
246 3#		$a Blake's 7
264 #1		$a [London] : $b BBC Worldwide, $c [2004]
264 #4		$a ©2004
300 ##		$a 5 videodiscs (663 min.) : $b sound, color ; $c 4 3/4 in.
336 ##		$a two-dimensional moving image $2 rdacontent
337 ##		$a video $2 rdamedia
338 ##		$a videodisc $2 rdacarrier
344 ##		$a digital $b optical $g mono $h Dolby $2 rda
346 ##		$b PAL $2 rda
347 ##		$a video file $b DVD video $2 rda
347 ##		$e regions 2 and 4
380 ##		$a Television series
500 ##		$a DVD version of the television series first broadcast on BBC1 in 1978.
500 ##		$a Special features include: '2 out-takes, a missing scene, 1 robot, 2 flat feet and a blooper'; Blue Peter feature: Lesley Judd makes a Liberator teleport bracelet; commentary tracks for 'Space fall' (Michael Keating, Sally Knyvette and David Maloney), 'Seek-locate-destroy' (Stephen Greif, Michael Keating and Jacqueline Pearce), 'Project Avalon' (Stephen Greif, Sally Knyvette and Jacqueline Pearce); trailer for series 2; character introductions; episode synopses.
508 ##		$a Writer and creator, Terry Nation; directors, Michael E. Briant, Douglas Camfield, Vere Lorimer, David Maloney, Pennant Roberts; producer, David Maloney; incidental music, Dudley Simpson.

511 1#	$a Gareth Thomas, Sally Knyvette, Paul Darrow, Michael Keating, David Jackson, Jan Chappell.
520 ##	$a 'In the third century of the second calendar, after the chaos of the intergalactic wars, a powerful dictatorship has risen to dynamic proportions and engulfed most of the populated worlds. Liberty has become a crime punishable by death, and the majority of the population lives in a drug-induced state of docility. This tyrannical authority fulfils George Orwell's prophecy of 1984 to its most terrifying extremes. This government is known as the Federation. Each world has its share of rebels who either turned to crime or the Resistance. This is the story of one such group of rebels, led by a man named Blake. His group is largely composed of escaped convicts, thieves and smugglers, who are thrown together by chance. With even the good guys being criminals, including murderers, this was a galaxy far, far away from previous screen space opera.' Publisher description.
538 ##	$a DVD; 4:3 presentation; Dolby Digital mono sound.
546 ##	$a In English, with optional English subtitles for the deaf or hard-of-hearing.
650 #0	$a Space warfare $v Drama.
655 #7	$a Television programs. $2 lcgft
655 #7	$a Fiction television programs. $2 lcgft
655 #7	$a Science fiction television programs. $2 lcgft
700 1#	$a Nation, Terry, $e screenwriter.
700 1#	$a Thomas, Gareth, $d 1945-, $e actor.
700 1#	$a Darrow, Paul, $d 1941-, $e actor.
700 1#	$a Knyvette, Sally, $e actor.
700 1#	$a Keating, Michael, $d 1932-, $e actor.
700 1#	$a Jackson, David, $d 1934-2005, $e actor.
700 1#	$a Chapel, Jan, $d 1949-, $e actor.
700 1#	$a Maloney, David, $d 1933-2006, $e television producer.
710 2#	$a British Broadcasting Corporation, $e production company, $e broadcaster, $e film distributor.
710 2#	$a Fabulous Films, $e film distributor.

APPENDIX B

SYMBOLS FOUND ON DVDS, BLU-RAY DISCS, AND THEIR CASES

 Closed Captioning

 International Symbol for Deafness, used to indicate that the disc provides support for the hearing impaired.

 Dolby digital sound. Variations cover HD, surround sound, and other formats.

 HD DVD, the unsuccessful successor to the DVD format that was developed principally by Toshiba, which lost out to Blu-ray Disc.

 DVD region codes

 Blu-ray Disc region codes

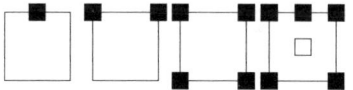 From left to right, mono (1.0) sound, stereo (2.0) sound, quadraphonic (4.0) sound, and (5.1) surround sound.

INDEX

A

AACR2 (Anglo-American Cataloguing Rules, Second Edition)
    comparison with RDA, 151–158
    copyright date, 155
    creation/production credits note, 157
    edition statement, 154–155
    fixed-length data elements, 152
    formatted contents note, 157
    general note, 156–157
    GMD (General Material Designation), 154
    historical background, 24–25
    new fields, divided opinion on, 156
    overview, ix
    physical description, 156
    publication, distribution, etc. (imprint), 155
    publication statement, 156
    systems details note, 157
    title statement, 153–154
    uniform title, 152–153
    use of, 151–158
abbreviations list for this book, ix–xi
Abrams, J. J., 34, 145
Academy of Motion Picture Arts and Sciences, 24
Academy ratio, 16, 17
access points. *See also* variant access points
    additional access points, creating, 89–93
    authorized, 61–62, 128, 153
accompanying material, 72–73
actors, 34
added entries. *See* variant access points
additional material characteristics for streaming media, 177
additional physical form available note for streaming media, 181
Alexander Nevsky, 36
Alexander Street Press, 176
Alien, 90
Alien vs. Predator, 30
Aliens, 90
Allen, Dede, 36
Almodóvar, Pedro, 34
Amazon, 176
American Film Institute, 14, 24, 160
American Library Association (ALA)
    Committee on Relations Between Libraries and Moving Pictures, 23
    Video Round Table, 160
    Visual Methods Committee, 23

207

AMIA Compendium of Moving Image Cataloging Practice (Martin), 187
AMIM (*Archival Moving Image Materials: A Cataloging Manual*), ix, 24, 187, 192
Amistad, 67
analog sound, 148
analytical works, 91–93
anamorphic widescreen, 115
Anderson, Wes, 35
Anglo-American Cataloguing Rules, Second Edition. *See* AACR2
animated films, 49–50
The Apartment, 17
Apocalypse Now, 105, 117
Armburst, Christen M., 186
Arndt, Michael, 35
The Arrival of a Train at Ciotat Station (l'Arrivée d'un Train en Gare de La Ciotat), 1–2
art directors, 37
The Artist, 13, 17
ASIN (Amazon Standard Identification Number), 38–39
aspect ratio, 114–116
assembly edit, 36
Association for Library Service to Children, 160
Association of College and Research Libraries, 189
The Atlantic magazine, 190
Audio-Visual Conservation Center (Library of Congress), 2
audiovisual librarianship
  history of, 23–25
  resources, 189–190
Audiovisual Librarianship: The Crusade for Media Unity (1946-1969) (Shores), 190
The Audiovisual Cataloging Current (Roe), 188
auteur director, 14
authorized access points, 61–62, 128, 153
AUTOCAT, 192

awards
  for cinematography, 17
  notes, 85

B

Bacall, Lauren, 51
Badlands, 14
The Bad and the Beautiful, 13
Baird, John Logie, 124
Baird, Stuart, 36
Batman franchise, 90
Battleship, 15
BBFC (British Board of Film Classification), 39, 82–83
BD-R (Blu-ray Disc, Recordable), 98
BD-RE (Blu-ray Disc, Rewriteable), 99
BD-RE XL and BD-R XL (Blu-ray Disc, Extra Large), 99
BD-ROM (Blu-ray Disc, Read-Only Memory), 99
Before Video: A History of the Non-Theatrical Film (Slide), 190
Ben Hur, 161
Benton, Robert, 35
Berberian Sound Studio, 105
Besson, Luc, 22
best boys, 37
Best of Both Worlds - Star Trek, The Next Generation (sample record), 200–202
Best Practices for Cataloging Streaming Media (OLAC Cataloging Policy Committee, Streaming Media Best Practices Task Force), 188
"The Best of Copyright and VideoLib" (Russell), 190
BetaCam, 139
BetaCam SP, 139
Betamax, 20, 139
"Big Five" (film studios), 33
"Big Six" (film studios), 33
Billson, Anne, 190–191
black-and-white film (photography), 145
black and white films, 72, 100

Blade Runner, 36, 161
Blakes 7 (sample record), 203–204
Blasko, Edward, 189
blockbusters, 14, 15, 30, 173
Blu-ray Disc Demystified (Taylor, Crawford, Armburst, and Zink), 186
Blu-ray Discs
    broadcast standards, 110
    category of material, 100
    collection development, 160–162
    color, 100
    configuration of playback channels, 101
    date fields, 101–102
    digital file characteristics, 111
    dimensions, 101
    fixed-length data elements, 101–104
    form of item, 103
    future issues, 174
    government publications, 103
    handling and storage, 165–166
    language, 104
    leader, 100
    medium of sound, 101
    overview, 22–23, 98–99
    physical description, 71, 100–101
    place of publication, production, or execution, 102
    publication status, 102
    regional coding, 112–113
    running time, 102–103
    sound on medium or separate, 101
    specific material designation, 100
    symbols found on, 205–206
    target audience, 103
    technique, 104
    transfer of film to, 160–162
    type of visual material, 103
    types of, 98–99
    variant access points
        personal name, 89
        uncontrolled related/analytical title, 89
        uniform title, 48, 89
    videorecording format, 100
Boardwalk Empire, 125
Bonnie and Clyde, 14
Booklist magazine, 160
books and films, 2–3
The Book of Film Care (Blasko, Luccitti, and Morris), 189
Boorman, John, 37
Bordwell, David, 185
Borgnine, Ernest, 51
Bothmann, Robert L., 187
Bowker's Complete Video Directory, 160
box sets (television)
    on DVD (sample record), 203–204
    overview, 126–127
Brando, Marlon, 4
Breaking Bad, 133
British Board of Film Classification (BBFC), 39, 82–83
British Film Institute, 191
broadcast standards
    overview, 107–108
    represented on Blu-ray Disc, 110
    represented on DVD, 108–109
Brokeback Mountain, 52
Bruckheimer, Jerry, 33

C

Caine, Michael, 51
camera film, 144
Cameron, James, 35
Canada, rating systems for cinematic releases in, 83–84
Canadian Home Video Rating System (CHVRS), 83–84
Canadian Motion Picture Distributors Association, 83
Cardiff, Jack, 35
Care, Handling and Storage of Motion Picture Film (Library of Congress), 189

Caring for CDs and DVDs (Finch and Webster), 189
carrier type (338 field)
　film stock, 147
　overview, 76
　streaming media, 179
　videocassettes and videotapes, 142
Carruth, Shane, 31, 41
cases for DVDs and Blu-ray, 165–166, 205–206
Cassavetes, John, 34
casting directors, 37
cataloging film and video collections (generally), 3–5
Cataloging of Audiovisual Materials and Other Special Materials: A Manual Based on AACR2 and MARC 21 (Bothmann, Schomberg, and Olson), 25, 187
category of material, 100
CAV (constant angular velocity), 21
CC:DA (Committee on Cataloging: Description and Access), ix
CD (computer disc)
　overview, 96
　as physical description, 71
CD technology, 95–96
CED (Capacitance Electronic Disc), 20, 150
cellulose acetate (celluloid) film, 16, 144, 168
chemical composition used to categorize film, 145
Chicago Sun-Times, 190
children, films for, 160
choreographer, 52
cinema. *See* films
CinemaScope, 17
cinematographers, 35
cinematography, awards for, 17
Cinerama, 17
Citizen Kane, 30, 31–32, 41
classification of film (physical arrangement), 163–164

classification of film (rating systems), 81–85
closed captioning, 59
closing credits, 30–31
cloud-based digital film subscriptions, 174
Cloverfield, 64
CLV (constant linear velocity), 21
Coates, Anne, 36
Coen, Ethan, 34, 36
Coen, Joel, 34, 36
collection development
　Blu-ray Discs, 160–162
　combo packs (dual format editions), 162–163
　DVDs, 160–162
　overview, 159–160
　videocassettes, 162
collections, managing. *See* managing the collection
color film (photography), 145
color in films, 16, 72, 100
combo packs (dual format editions), 162–163
Comcast/General Electric, 33
Committee on Cataloging: Description and Access (CC:DA), ix
compilations (television), 129
composers, 36–37, 52
comprehensive title/individual title (television), 128–129
computer disc. *See* CD
Conan the Barbarian [2011], 90
configuration of playback channels, 101
conservation and care of materials, resources for, 189
Conservation OnLine, 189
constant angular velocity (CAV), 21
content type (336 field)
　film stock, 147
　overview, 74–75
　streaming media, 179
The Conversation, 105
Cop Land, 15

copying video material, legal issues for, 170
Copyright Code, 170
copyright date
    AACR2, 155
    overview, 46–47
copyright notice. *See* 264 field (production, publication, distribution, manufacture, and copyright notice)
copyright restrictions
    legal issues, 169, 170
    streaming media, 176–177
Copyright Term Extension Act, 176
corporate name (television), 134
Corrigan, Timothy, 186
costume designers, 37
country of producing entity (257 field), 42–43
Crawford, Charles G., 186
creation/production credits note (508 field)
    AACR2, 157
    overview, 49–50
    television, 132–133
creators of works, 52–54
Cremer, Monika, 190
crew members, 30–32, 37. *See also specific crew members*
Criterion, 162
The Crying Game, 80
Cuarón, Alfonso, 35
Curtis, Tony, 51
Cutter, Charles Ammi *(Rules for a Printed Dictionary Catalog),* 3

D

date fields
    DVD and Blu-ray, 101–102
    overview, 40–41
    television, 128
date of release differing from date of production, 40
date/time and place of an event note (518 field), 51–52

DDC (Dewey Decimal Classification), 163–164
Deakins, Roger, 35
Dewey, Melvil, 2
diameter of disc, 72
digital cinematography, 18
digital file characteristics (347 field)
    DVD and Blu-ray, 110–113
    streaming media, 180
Digital Millennium Copyright Act, 170
digital sound, 148
digital video disc. *See* DVD
Digital Videotape (DV), 139
dimensions
    DVD and Blu-ray, 101
    videocassettes and videotapes, 140
director of photography, 52
directors, 33–34, 52
director's cut, 36
disc, television on, 126–127
distribution, 44–45
distribution statement. *See* 264 field (production, publication, distribution, manufacture, and copyright notice)
distributor and publisher, distinction between, 45
DNR (Digital Noise Reduction), 161
(DOIs) digital object identifiers, 178
Dolby Digital, 106–107
dolly grip, 37
Don't Look Now, 14
Douglas, Kurt, 51
DTS, 106–107
Duel, 127
duration of film, 71
Dutkiewicz, Scott M., 187
DV (Digital Videotape), 139
DVD-Audio, 97
DVD Demystified (Taylor, Johnson, and Crawford), 186
DVD (Digital Video Disc)
    broadcast standards, 108–109
    category of material, 100

DVD (Digital Video Disc) (cont.)
  collection development, 160–162
  color, 100
  configuration of playback channels, 101
  date fields, 101–102
  digital file characteristics, 111
  dimensions, 101
  fixed-length data elements, 101–104
  form of item, 103
  future issues, 174
  government publications, 103
  handling and storage, 165–166
  language, 104
  leader, 100
  medium of sound, 101
  overview, 21–22, 95–98
  physical description, 71, 100–101
  place of publication, production, or execution, 102
  publication status, 102
  regional coding, 112
  running time, 102–103
  sound on medium or separate, 101
  specific material designation, 100
  symbols found on, 205–206
  target audience, 103
  technique, 104
  type of visual material, 103
  types of, 97–98
  variant access points
    personal name, 89
    uncontrolled related/analytical title, 89
    uniform title, 48, 89
  videorecording format, 100
DVD-R/DVD+R (DVD Recordable), 97
DVD RAM(DVD Rewritable), 97
DVD-ROM (DVD Read Only Memory), 98
DVD-RW/DVD+RW (DVD Re-Recordable), 97
DVD-Video, 97

E

EANs (International Article Numbers), 38
early videocassette tapes, 19
early years of film, 11–13
Eastman Kodak, 17
Eastwood, Clint, 15, 64
Ebert, Roger, 14, 159, 190, 192
Edison, Thomas, 12, 13
edition statement (250 field)
  AACR2, 154–155
  overview, 42
editors, 35–36
editor's cut, 36
Educational Motion Pictures and Libraries (McDonald), 23
8 mm film, 144–145
El Dorado, 90
electronic location and access (streaming media), 182
Ellison, John William, 190
Elswit, Robert, 35
Empire magazine, 190, 191
The Empire Strikes Back, 31
equalization, 106–107
ET: The Extra-Terrestrial, 125
Evans, Robert, 33
examples. *See* sample records
Excalibur, 37
executive producers, 32
The Exorcist, 14
experimentation in filmmaking, 12

F

F for Fake, 32
feature films
  defined, 87–88
  notes, 49
The Fifth Element, 22
film base, 144
film classification, 81–85
Film Comment magazine, 191
film credits, 30–31. *See also* opening credits
film critics, 190–191

INDEX | *213*

film director, 33–34, 52
film formats
    history of, 16–23
    innovations in, 17–18
film gauge, 16, 144–145
film magazines, 191
Film Preservation Guide: The Basics for Archives, Libraries, and Museums (National Film Preservation Foundation), 189
film producer, 33–34, 52
Film Society of Lincoln Centre, 191
film stock
    carrier type, 147
    chemical composition used to categorize, 145
    content type, 147
    fixed-length data elements, 146
    general note, 149
    handling and storage, 167–168
    media type, 147
    overview, 16, 143–144
    physical description, 146
    physical description fixed field (007), 146
    physical medium, 147–148
    physical properties used to categorize, 144–145
    production process used to categorize, 144
    projection characteristics of a moving image, 149
    sound characteristics, 148–149
filmmaker, 41
films. *See also* history of film
    and books, 2–3
    defined, 7–8
    preservation of film, importance of, 2–3
    resources for introductions to film, 185–186
    sample record
        on Blu-ray Disc, 198–199
        on DVD, 196–197

Films Media Group, 176
Films on Demand, 176
The Film Experience: An Introduction (Corrigan and White), 186
Finch, Loraine, 189
Finding Nemo, 49–50
Flash Video format, 175, 180
Flashdance, 14
foley artists, 37
Ford, John, 32, 34
form of item
    DVD and Blu-ray, 103
    streaming media, 178
form of work (380 field)
    overview, 77
    television, 131
formatted contents note (505 field)
    AACR2, 157
    overview, 77–79
    streaming media, 180–181
    television, 131–132
Forrest Gump, 14
4K ultra-high definition resolution, 99
FRBR (Functional Requirements for Bibliographic Records), ix–x
Freegal, 176
French, Philip, 190
The French Connection, 161
Friedkin, William, 161
Friends, 125
future issues for DVDs and Blu-ray Discs, 174

G

Game of Thrones, 125
Gates, Bill, 174
general note (500 field)
    AACR2, 156–157
    aspect ratio, 114–116
    film stock, 149
    other notes, 118–119
    overview, 114
    production/release history, 117–118
    related works, 118

general note (500 field) (cont.)
  special features, 117
  streaming media, 180
  television, 131
  videocassettes and videotapes, 143
genre/form
  overview, 86–88
  streaming media, 182
  television, 134
Genre/Form Headings at the Library of Congress, 187
geographic area code (043 field), 40
glossaries, 192
GMD (General Material Designation), 154
Godard, Jean-Luc, 20, 34
Golden Age of Hollywood, 13–14, 33, 44
Goldman, William, 35
Goldwyn, Sam, 33
Gone with the Wind, 111, 125
government publications, 103
Great Britain, rating system in, 82–83
Guide to Cataloging DVD and Blu-ray Discs Using AACR2 and MARC 21 (OLAC Cataloging Policy Committee, DVD Cataloging Update Task Force), 187
Guidelines for Audiovisual and Multimedia Materials in Libraries and Other Institutions (Royan and Cremer), 190
Guidelines for Media Resources in Academic Libraries (Association of College and Research Libraries), 189
Guidelines for the Usage of Moving Image LC Genre/Form Headings (OLAC), 87

H

Hall, Conrad L., 35
handling and storage
  film stock, 167–168
  optical discs, 165–166
  overview, 164–165
  resources for conservation and care of materials, 189
  videocassettes and videotape, 167
Handman, Gary, 190
Hawks, Howard, 33
HD DVD (high-definition DVD), 22, 150
Heat, 90
Hecht, Ben, 35
Hermann, Bernard, 32
Hi8, 139
history of audiovisual librarianship, 23–25
history of film
  early years, 11–13
  experimentation in filmmaking, 12
  Golden Age of Hollywood, 13–14
  "New Hollywood" movement, 14
  New Wave movement, 14
  1980s, 14
  1990s, 14–15
  overview, 1–2
  sound films, transition to, 13
  2010–present, 15
  2000s, 15
history of film formats
  digital cinematography, 18
  home video, 18–23
  innovations, 17–18
  overview, 16–18
Hitchcock, Alfred, 18, 32, 90
The Hobbit: An Unexpected Journey, 18
Hollywood, California, 13
The Hollywood Reporter magazine, 191
home video
  Betamax, 20
  Blu-ray Discs, 22–23
  CED (Capacitance Electronic Disc), 20
  DVD (Digital Video Disc), 21–22
  early videocassette tapes, 19
  HD DVD (high-definition DVD), 22
  history of, 18–23
  LaserDisc, 20–21
  overview, 18–19
  VCD (Video CD), 21
  VHS (Video Home System), 19–20

Hoopla, 176
How to Read a Film: Movies, Media, and Beyond (Monaco), 186
Hsieh-Yee, Ingrid, 187
HTML5, 175
Hugo, 165

I

If . . ., 72
IMAX (Image Maximum), 17–18
IMDb (Internet Movie Database)
    overview, x
    as source for actors' names, 50
    summaries on, 80
IMDb Movie Terminology Glossary, 192
The Incredible Hulk, 165
Indiana Jones series, 36
Inglourious Basterds, 16
innovations in film formats, 17–18
intermediate film, 144
International Article Numbers (EANs), 38
International Federation of Film Archives, 168, 192
International Serial Book Numbers (ISBN), 38
Internet Archive, 176
intertitles, 58, 59
interviewee, 52
interviewer, 52
Ireland, rating system in, 83
Irish Film Classification Office (IFCO), 83
ISBN (020 field), 38
Ivan the Terrible, Part II, The Boyars' Plot, 100

J

Jackson, Peter, 33
James Bond films, 64
Jaws, 36
Jaws 3D, 14
The Jazz Singer, 13
Jobs, Steve, 175
Johnson, Mark R., 186

Joint Committee on Educational Films, 23–24
Joint Steering Committee for Development of RDA, 192

K

Kahn, Michael, 36
Kalamazoo Public Library (Michigan), 23
Kastenmeier Guidelines, 171
Kaufman, Charlie, 35
Keaton, Michael, 51
Kermode, Mark, 190
Koepp, David, 35
Kubrick, Stanley, 36, 106
Kurosawa, Akira, 36

L

La règle du jea, 191
La Sortie de l'Usine Lumière à Lyon (Workers Leaving the Lumiere Factory), 1, 11
LA Takedown, 90
laboratory film, 144
language
    in 008 field, 58
    in 041 field, 58–60, 141
    closed captioning, 59
    DVD and Blu-ray, 104
    examples, 60–61
    indicators, 59–60
    intertitles, 59
    note, 60, 141
    original language, 58–59
    overview, 57
    punctuation, 60
    spoken language, 58
    subtitles, 59
    of summary, 58
    written form, languages in, 59
l'Arrivée d'un Train en Gare de La Ciotat (The Arrival of a Train at Ciotat Station), 1–2
LaserDisc, 20–21, 150
Laskowski, Mary S., 190

Last Action Hero, 86
LC-PCC PS (Library of Congress-Program for Cooperative Cataloging Policy Statements), x
LCC (Library of Congress Classification scheme), 163–164
LCGFT (Library of Congress Genre/Form Terms), x, 86, 88
LCRI (Library of Congress Rule Interpretations), x
LCSH (Library of Congress Subject Headings), x, 86, 88
Le Voyage dans la Lune (A Trip to the Moon), 12
leader
  DVD and Blu-ray, 100
  streaming media, 177
legal issues
  copying video material, 170
  copyright restrictions, 169, 170
  lending video material, 169
  overview, 168
  public performance, 169–170
  purchasing video material, 168–169
  television, recordings made from, 171
lending video material, legal issues for, 169
letterboxing, 115
Lewis, Shirley, 86, 163, 164, 190
Library Ideas, 176
Library of Congress Genre/Form Terms for Library and Archival Materials: Moving Image Genre-Form Terms, 187
Library of Congress Genre/Form Terms (LCGFT), 86, 88
Library of Congress (LC)
  Acquisitions and Bibliographic Access Directorate, 187
  AMIM Revision Committee, Motion Picture, Broadcasting, and Recorded Sound Division, 187
  Audio-Visual Conservation Center, 2
  audiovisual librarianship, history of, 24–25
  film as term used by, 8
  Moving Image Genre-Form Guide, 86
  Name Authority File (NAF), 41
  Preservation Directorate, 189
  Rules for Descriptive Cataloging in the Library of Congress: Motion Pictures and Film Strips, 24
Library of Congress-Program for Cooperative Cataloging Policy Statements (LC-PCC PS), x
Library of Congress Subject Headings (LCSH), x, 86, 88
library service, streaming media as, 176–177
librettist, 52
Lim, Dennis, 186
line producers, 33
Lionsgate, 33
Little White Lies magazine, 191
Lost, 125
Lubezki, Emmanuel, 35
Lucas, George, 15, 31
Luccitti, Benjamin A., 189
Lumière, Auguste, 1–2, 11–12
Lumière, Louis, 1–2, 11–12
lyricist, 52

M

Macdonald, Janet, 86, 163, 164, 190
made-for-TV movies, 127
magnetic soundtracks, 148
The Magnificent Ambersons, 36
mailing lists for audiovisual cataloguers, 192
Makiewicz, Herman, 31
managing the collection
  classification, 163–164
  collection development
    Blu-ray Discs, 160–162
    combo packs (dual format editions), 162–163
    DVDs, 160–162

INDEX | 217

overview, 159–160
videocassettes, 162
handling and storage
film stock, 167–168
optical discs, 165–166
overview, 164–165
videocassettes and videotape, 167
legal issues
copying video material, 170
copyright restrictions, 169, 170
lending video material, 169
overview, 168
public performance, 169–170
purchasing video material, 168–169
television, recordings made from, 171
Mankiewicz, Joseph L., 35
Mann, Michael, 90
The Man Who Knew Too Much, 90
The Man Who Shot Liberty Valence (sample record), 198–199
manufacture statement. *See* 264 field (production, publication, distribution, manufacture, and copyright notice)
Martin, Abigail Leab, 187
Marx, Groucho, 124
Mary Poppins, 49–50
M*A*S*H, 125
The Master, 18
Maxwell, Robert L., 187
Maxwell's Handbook for RDA: Explaining and Illustrating RDA: Resource Description and Access Using MARC 21 (Maxwell), 187
McDonald, Gerald D., 23
Media Librarianship (Ellison), 190
media type (337 field)
film stock, 147
overview, 75
streaming media, 179

medium for sound
DVD and Blu-ray, 101
videocassettes and videotapes, 140
Méliès, Georges, 12, 165–166
MetaCritic, 191
Metro-Goldwyn-Mayer, 13, 33
Midwest Tape, 176
miniseries, television, 126–127
Monaco, James, 7–8, 104, 186
mono sound, 105–106
Monroe, Marilyn, 51
Morris, Susan F., 189
Mosfilm, 176
Motion Picture Association of America (MPAA), 81–82, 173
Motion Picture Film Preservation (internet portal), 189
motion pictures defined, 144. *See also* films
movies. *See* films
Moving Image Cataloging: How to Create and How to Use a Moving Image Catalog (Yee), 188
Moving Image Genre-Form Guide (LC), 86
MP3, 174
multi-disc sets of television shows, 126–127
Multilingual Glossary of Filmographic Terms, 192
multiple works on disc(s), 68
Murch, Walter, 36
musical films, 49–50

N

NAF (Name Authority File), x, 41
name of person. *See* personal name
National Film Preservation Foundation, 189
National Media Museum, 189
National Television Systems Committee (NTSC), 108, 109, 110
Netflix, 19, 175, 176
Network, 50

new fields in AACR2, divided opinion on, 156
"New Hollywood" movement, 14
New Wave (Nouvelle Vague), 14
Newman, Kim, 190
News Corporation, 33
The New Republic magazine, 190
nickelodeons, 12–13
Night of the Living Dead, 46
1980s, film in the, 14
1990s, film in the, 14–15
Nitrate Film (National Media Museum), 189
nitrocellulose (nitrate) film, 16, 144, 167–168
noise reduction systems, 106–107
Nolan, Christopher, 15, 34, 35, 64
Nonbook Materials: The Organization of Integrated Collections (Weihs, Lewis, and Macdonald), 86, 163, 190
Nosferatu, 30
notes
　awards, 85
　creation/production credits, 49–50
　date/time and place of an event, 51–52
　formatted contents, 77–79
　general, 114–119, 131, 149, 180
　language, 60, 141
　multiple discs, 77–79
　musical films, 49–50
　participant or performer, 50–51, 133
　restrictions on access, 79
　streaming media
　　additional physical form available note, 181
　　formatted contents note, 180–181
　　general note, 180
　　restrictions on access note, 181
　　source of description note, 181
　　system details note, 181
　system details, 119–120
　target audience, 81–85
television
　creation/production credits note, 132–133
　formatted contents note, 131–132
　general note, 131
　participant or performer note, 133
Nouvelle Vague (New Wave), 14
NTSC (National Television Systems Committee), 108, 109, 110
Nykvist, Sven, 35

O

"O Fortuna" (song), 36
Observations on Film Art (website), 185
The Observer, 190
Octopussy, 14
OLAC Cataloging Policy Committee
　DVD Cataloging Guide Update Task Force, 187
　Streaming Media Best Practices Task Force, 188
　Video Language Coding Best Practices Task Force, 188
OLAC-L, 192
OLAC Newsletter, 188
OLAC (Online Audiovisual Catalogers), x, 3, 25, 80, 87, 192
OLAC's AV and Nonprint Glossary, 192
Olson, Nancy, 3, 25, 187
One Flew Over the Cuckoo's Nest, 49
Online Audiovisual Catalogers, 192
Online Film Dictionary, 192
open captions, 59
opening credits
　overview, 30–31
　participants and performers in, 50
　prefatory words, 66, 67
　titles in, 64
optical discs
　future issues, 174
　handling and storage, 165–166
optical soundtracks, 148

INDEX | 219

Organizing Audiovisual and Electronic Resources for Access: A Cataloging Guide (Hsieh-Yee), 187
original language, 58–59
Orr, Christopher, 190
Oruner, 31
O'Steen, Sam, 36
other standard identifier (024 field), 38–39, 178
The Other Side of the Wind, 117

P

Pacino, Al, 90
PAL (Phase Alternate Line), 108, 109, 110
parallel subtitles, 65
parallel titles, 65
Paramount Pictures, 13, 33
Paranormal Activity, 64
participant or performer note (511 field), 50–51, 133
participants and performers in opening credits, 50
PCC (Program for Cooperative Cataloging), x–xi
personal name (100 field)
  overview, 41
  variant access points
    DVD/Blu-ray, 89
    television, 134
A Personal Journey with Martin Scorsese through American Movies (Scorsese), 186
Pfister, Wally, 35
physical description (300 field)
  AACR2, 156
  computer disc as, 71
  diameter of disc, 72
  duration of film, 71
  film stock, 146
  indicators, 73
  overview, 70–71
  punctuation, 73
  sound and vision, 71–72
  streaming media, 179
  supplementary physical material, 72–73
  videocassettes and videotapes, 141
  videodisc as, 70–71
physical description fixed field (007)
  DVD (Digital Video Disc), 100–101
  film stock, 146
  videocassettes and videotapes, 140
physical medium (340 field)
  film stock, 147–148
  overview, 76
  videocassettes and videotapes, 142
physical properties used to categorize film, 144–145
Pierce, David, 13
pillarboxing, 115
pilots, television, 127
Pirates of the Caribbean franchise, 15
Pitman, Randy, 190
place of publication, 45, 102
Platoon, 14
playback characteristics, 106–107
The Player, 34
playing time (306 field), 74
Pleasantville, 72
plot twists, 80
polyester film, 144, 168
Predator, 161
prefatory words in opening credits, 66, 67
prequels, 90
Primer, 31, 41
print film, 144
producers, 32–33, 52
production company, 52
production designers, 37
production process used to categorize film, 144
production/release history in general note (500 field), 117–118
production statement. *See* 264 field (production, publication, distribution, manufacture, and copyright notice)

Program for Cooperative Cataloging (PCC), x–xi
projection characteristics of a moving image, 149
Prokofiev, Sergei, 36
Psycho, 90
public performance and legal issues, 169–170
publication, distribution, etc. (imprint) (260 field), 43, 155
publication date, 46–47
publication statement. *See* 264 field (production, publication, distribution, manufacture, and copyright notice)
publication status for DVD and Blu-ray, 102
publisher, 46
publisher and distributor, distinction between, 45
publisher number (028 field), 39–40, 141
purchasing video material, legal issues for, 168–169

Q

quadraphonic sound, 105, 106

R

Raising Arizona, 64
rating systems, 81–85
ratings symbols, 39
RDA-L, 192
RDA (Resource Description and Access)
  comparison with AACR2, 151–158
  overview, xi
reboots, 90
[Rec], 90
[Rec]², 90
recording medium, 105
recording method, 105
Régie du cinema, 84
regional coding, 111–114
related works, 89–91, 118
relationship designators, 53
remakes, 90

Renoir, Jean, 34
"Reproduction of Copyrighted Works by Educators and Librarians" (United States Copyright Office), 171
resources
  cataloging, 187–188
  conservation and care of materials, 189
  current awareness, 190–192
  film critics, 190–191
  film magazines, 191
  glossaries, 192
  introductions to film, 185–186
  mailing lists for audiovisual cataloguers, 192
  other aspects of audiovisual librarianship, 189–190
restrictions on access note (506 field), 79, 181
Reynolds, William H., 36
Richardson, Robert, 35
Rio Bravo, 90
RKO Pictures, 13, 33, 36
Roe, Sandra K., 188
Rome, 125
Rope, 18
Rossio, Terry, 35
Rosson, Harold, 17
Rotten Tomatoes, 191
rough cut, 36
Royan, Bruce, 190
Rudin, Scott, 33
Rules for a Printed Dictionary Catalog (Cutter), 3
Rules for Descriptive Cataloging in the Library of Congress: Motion Pictures and Film Strips (Library of Congress), 24
running time, DVD and Blu-ray, 102–103
Russell, Carrie, 190
Russian Ark, 18

S

S-VHS-C, 139
safety film, 16

same title, different resources (television), 128
sample records
    for a boxed-set of a television series on DVD, 203–204
    for a film on Blu-ray Disc, 198–199
    for a film on DVD, 196–197
    for language, 60–61
    for a stand-alone television episode on Blu-ray Disc, 200–202
Scalia, Pietro, 36
Scarface, 90
Schaefer, George, 32
Schindler's List, 17, 72
Scholtz, James C., 188
Schomberg, Jessica J., 187
Schoonmaker, Thelma, 36
Schwarzenegger, Arnold, 15, 60
Scorsese, Martin, 34, 165, 186
screenwriters, 34–35, 52, 66
seasons (television), 126
SECAM (Séquentiel Couleur à Mémoire), 108, 109, 110
Selznick, David O., 33
sequels, 14, 15, 90
serials (television), 127
series
    defined, 48, 126
    uniform title, 48–49, 131
series statement (490 field), 48–49, 131
Serpico, 14
70 mm film, 145
7XX added entries for persons, corporate bodies, and related works, 52–54
Shane, 17
Shores, Louis, 190
showrunners, 132–133
Sight & Sound magazine, 159, 191
silent movies, 71–72
Silverlight, 175
Singin' in the Rain, 13, 72
single discs (television), 127
16 mm film, 145
The Sixth Sense, 80

Sleeping Beauty, 67
Sleepless in Seattle, 14
Slide, Anthony, 190
Snow White and the Seven Dwarfs, 125
Solaris, 72
Sony, 33
The Sopranos, 125
sound and vision, 71–72
sound characteristics (344 field)
    equalization, 106–107
    film stock, 148–149
    mono sound, 105–106
    noise reduction systems, 106–107
    overview, 104–105
    playback characteristics, 106–107
    quadraphonic sound, 105, 106
    recording medium, 105
    recording method, 105
    stereo sound, 105–106
    surround sound, 105, 106
    videocassettes and videotapes, 142
sound films, transition to, 13
sound on medium or separate (DVD and Blu-ray), 101
The Sound of Music, 125
soundtracks, 58
source of description note (588 field), 181
source of title, 64–65
special coded dates (046 field), 40–41, 129
special effects supervisors, 37
special features in general note (500 field), 117
specific material designation
    DVD and Blu-ray, 100
    videocassettes and videotapes, 140
Spielberg, Steven, 15, 33, 127
spoilers, 80, 88
spoken language, 58
Stagecoach, 32
Stallone, Sylvester, 15
stand-alone television episode on Blu-ray Disc (sample record), 200–202
Stanford University Libraries, Metadata Department, 188

222 | INDEX

Stanton, Andrew, 35
Star Trek, The Next Generation (sample record), 200–202
Star Trek franchise, 90
Star Wars, 30, 31, 125
statement of responsibility, 65–66
Staying Alive, 14
stereo sound, 105–106
still photography, 145
The Sting, 14
storage. *See* handling and storage
Straight, Beatrice, 50
straight-to-video films, 127
streaming media
    additional material characteristics, 177
    carrier type, 179
    cataloging, 177–182
    content type, 179
    copyright restrictions, 176–177
    digital file characteristics, 180
    electronic location and access, 182
    fixed-length data elements, 177, 178
    fixed-length description fixed field, 177–178
    form of item, 178
    genre/form, 182
    leader, 177
    as library service, 176–177
    media type, 179
    notes
        additional physical form available note, 181
        formatted contents note, 180–181
        general note, 180
        restrictions on access note, 181
        source of description note, 181
        system details note, 181
    other standard identifier, 178
    overview, 175–176
    physical description, 179
    title statement, 179
subject access fields, 85–89
subject headings, 86–88
subtitles, 59
summary, etc. (520 field), 80–81, 86, 133
summary, language of, 58
Summary Notes for Catalog Records (OLAC), 80
Sunset Boulevard, 13, 34
Super 8, 145
Super 8 mm film, 144–145
Super 16 mm film, 145
Super-VHS, 139
Superman 3, 14
superseded formats, 150
supplementary physical material, 72–73
surround sound, 105, 106
symbols found on DVDs, Blu-ray Discs, and their cases, 205–206
system details note (538 field), 119–120, 157, 181

T

target audience note (521 field), 81–85
Taylor, Jim, 186
TEACH (Technology, Education, and Copyright Harmonization Act) Act, 170
technical details of film, note for recording, 119–120
Technicolor, 16–17
technique (DVD and Blu-ray), 104
technological obsolescence, 5
television
    box-sets, 126–127
    dates, 128
    on disc, 126–127
    fixed-length data elements, 128
    form of work, 131
    genre/form, 134
    historical background, 123–126
    made-for-TV movies, 127
    miniseries, 126–127
    multi-disc sets, 126–127
    notes
        creation/production credits note, 132–133

formatted contents note, 131–132
general note, 131
participant or performer note, 133
overview, 128
pilots, 127
recordings made from, legal issues for, 171
seasons, 126
serials, 127
series, 126
series statement, 131
showrunners, 132–133
single discs, 127
special coded dates, 129
summary, etc., 133
title statement, 129–130
uniform title
    compilations, 129
    comprehensive title/individual title, 128–129
    overview, 128
    same title, different resources, 128
variant access points
    corporate name, 134
    personal name, 134
    series - uniform title, 131
    uncontrolled related/analytical title, 134
    uniform title, 134
variant title, 130
The Ten Commandments, 125
Terminator 2: Judgment Day, 15, 60
Terminator franchise, 90
35 mm film, 145
Thompson, Kristin, 185
Thomson, David, 15, 190
3:2 pulldown, 109
Throne of Blood (sample record), 196–197
Tichenor, Dylan, 36
tilt and scan technique, 115
Time Warner, 33

Timecode, 18
tinted films, 72
Titanic, 15, 125
title statement (245 field)
    AACR2, 153–154
    indicators, 68–69
    multiple works on disc(s), 68
    overview, 63–64
    parallel subtitles, 65
    parallel titles, 65
    prefatory words, 66, 67
    punctuation, 68–69
    source of title, 64–65
    statement of responsibility, 65–66
    streaming media, 179
    television, 129–130
titles. *See also* uniform title
    overview, 61–63
    of series, 48–49
    variant titles, 69–70, 130
Toland, Gregg, 31, 35
toned images, 72
Total Recall [2012], 90
Transformers, 80
tricolor film, 168
A Trip to the Moon (Le Voyage dans la Lune), 12
20th Century Fox, 13, 33
2001: A Space Odyssey, 36
264 field (production, publication, distribution, manufacture, and copyright notice)
    capitalization, 47
    indicators, 47
    overview, 44–45
    place of publication, 45
    publication date, 46–47
    publisher, 46
    punctuation, 47
2010–present, film during, 15
2000s, film in the, 15
type of visual material
    DVD and Blu-ray, 103
    film stock, 146

U

U-Matic, 138
UltraViolet, 176
uncontrolled related/analytical title
   DVD/Blu-ray, 89
   television, 134
Unforgiven, 15
uniform title
   AACR2, 152–153
   DVD/Blu-ray, 48
   overview, 61–63
   television, 128–129, 134
United States, rating system in, 81–82
UPCs (Universal Product Codes), 38

V

Van Bogart, John W. C., 189
variant access points
   DVD/Blu-ray
      personal name, 89
      uncontrolled related/analytical title, 89
      uniform title, 89
   television
      corporate name, 134
      personal name, 134
      series - uniform title, 131
      uncontrolled related/analytical title, 134
      uniform title, 134
variant titles (246 field), 69–70, 130
Variety magazine, 191
VAST service, 176
VCD (Video CD), 21, 150
VCR (Video Cassette Recording), 20, 138
VHS-C, 139
VHS (Video Home System), 19–20, 138–139, 167
Viacom, 33
Video8, 139
Video Acquisitions and Cataloging: A Handbook (Scholtz), 188
Video Acquisitions in Libraries: Issues and Best Practices (Laskowski), 190
video characteristics (346 field), 107–110, 143
Video Collection Development in Multi-type Libraries: A Handbook (Handman), 190
Video Format Identification Guide, 138
Video Language Coding Best Practices (OLAC Cataloging Policy Committee, Video Language Coding Best Practices Task Force), 188
Video Librarian magazine, 160
Video Round Table (ALA), 160
Video Source Book (Gale), 160
videocassettes and videotapes
   BetaCam, 139
   BetaCam SP, 139
   Betamax, 139
   carrier type, 142
   collection development, 162
   DV (Digital Videotape), 139
   general note, 143
   handling and storage, 167
   Hi8, 139
   language code, 141
   language note, 141
   overview, 137–138
   physical description, 141
   physical description fixed field (007), 140
   physical medium, 142
   publisher number, 141
   sound characteristics, 142
   U-Matic, 138
   VCR (Video Cassette Recording), 138
   VHS (Video Home System), 138–139
   Video8, 139
   video characteristics, 143
videodisc, 20, 70–71
videorecording format, 100, 140
Videos-Cataloging (RDA) (Stanford University Libraries, Metadata Department), 188

videotapes. *See* videocassettes and videotapes
The Video Librarian's Guide to Collection Development and Management (Pitman), 190
The Village Voice Film Guide: 50 Years of Movies from Classics to Cult Hits (Lim), 186

W

Wales, Jimmy, 39
The Walt Disney Company, 33
Warner, Jack, 33
Warner Brothers, 13, 33
Webster, John, 189
Weihs, Jean, 86, 163, 164, 190
Weinstein, Harvey, 33
Welles, Orson, 31–32, 34, 36, 41, 117
The West Wing, 125
White, Patricia, 186
Who Framed Roger Rabbit, 30
widescreen, 17, 115
Wilder, Billy, 35
Williams, John, 36
Willis, Gordon, 35
The Wire, 125, 133
Wise, Robert, 31
The Wizard of Oz, 16–17, 72, 100
Workers Leaving the Lumiere Factory (La Sortie de l'Usine Lumière à Lyon), 1, 11
Writers Guild of America, East, 34
Writers Guild of America, West, 34
written form, languages in, 59

Y

Yee, Martha M., 88, 188
YouTube, 170, 175, 176

Z

Zapruder, Abraham, 145
Zink, Michael, 186